CLIMATE, COVID AND CONSPIRACY

Peter Taylor

CLAIRVIEW

Clairview Books Ltd.,
Russet, Sandy Lane,
West Hoathly,
W. Sussex RH19 4QQ

www.clairviewbooks.com

Published by Clairview Books 2025

© Peter Taylor 2025

This book is copyright under the Berne Convention. All rights reserved. Apart from any fair dealing for the purpose of private study, research, criticism or review, no part of this publication may be reproduced, stored in a retrieval system, or transmitted in any form or by any means, electronic, electrical, chemical, mechanical, optical, photocopying, recording or otherwise, without the prior written permission of the copyright owner. Inquiries should be addressed to the Publishers

No part of this book may be used or reproduced in any manner for the purpose of training artificial intelligence technologies or systems. In accordance with Article 4(3) of the DSM Directive 2019/790, Clariview Books expresssly reserves this work from the text and data mining exception

The right of Peter Taylor to be identified as the author of this work has been asserted by him in accordance with sections 77 and 78 of the Copyright, Designs and Patents Act, 1988

A CIP catalogue record for this book is available from the British Library

ISBN 978 1 912992 74 4

Cover by Morgan Creative
Typeset by Symbiosys Technologies, Visakhapatnam, India
Printed and bound by 4Edge Ltd, Essex

PETER TAYLOR thinks of himself as 'the cleaner'. He has two Oxford degrees but he left academia in 1978 and—'blessed with companions of a similar mind'—set up operations to clean the oceans and atmosphere. His organisation—the Oxford-based Political Ecology Research Group (1976–1992) worked for citizens' initiatives against very dangerous developments—some were stopped, like the Plutonium Economy, the dumping of nuclear waste at sea and Acid Rain. Other toxic policies were transformed through the instigation of Clean Production Strategies. In 1986, in conversation with his Himalayan teacher when offered a yogic path, he realised even enlightened yogis would need a clean planet—and so that became his yoga. He became an analyst of environmental science, and as an activist got to know the nodal points of influence of what he called 'a long game through many decades'. He is a strong believer in the power of small groups of committed people and is a long-standing member of the California-based Environmental Studies Institute, a founding member of Cambrian Wildwood, a founding member and Associate of the Wildland Research Institute at Leeds University, and founding member of the Institute for Life-based Architecture in Germany. He has children and grandchildren—they are his 'skin in the game'. He is author of *Chill: A Reassessment of Global Warming Theory*, numerous scientific papers on pollution, several books on conservation including *Beyond Conservation* and *The Spirit of Rewilding*, and an autobiography—*Shiva's Rainbow*.

Contents

Preface	1
Acknowledgements	4
Introduction	5
PART 1: *CHILL*	
1.1 *Chill* Revisited	19
1.2 Reviews of *Chill: A Reassessment of Global Warming Theory*	42
PART 2: CLIMATE ALARMISM	
Preface	48
2.1 Weather Chaos	49
2.2 Hothouse Earth	61
2.3 Heatwaves and Wildfires	74
PART 3: SUBTERFUGE	
3.1 Heating Power declines with CO_2 concentration	77
3.2 Clouding the Mind	88
3.3 Encountering the Modelling Mentality	98
3.4 Climate Change: Cloud Cover Evidence Challenges Flawed IPCC Model	110
3.5 Adjustments to Reality	122
3.6 World Climate Declaration	128
PART 4: SCIENCE AND PUBLIC POLICY	
Preface	133
4.1 Science and Changing Climates	133
4.2 Where the Truth Lies	141
4.3 Science and Activism in the 21st Century	147
4.4 Plutonium Man	158
4.5 Net Zero Soul	171
Appendix to 4.5	177
PART 5: COVID, CLIMATE AND CONSPIRACY	
Preface	179
5.1 Covid, Climate and Conspiracy	184
5.2 Masks—What They Show And What They Conceal	199
5.3 Awakening the Dream	217

APPENDICES

1. Responses to Criticism   226
2. Reviews   226
   *State of the Climate Report reviewed, (2018) + Girardet letter.
   * Healthy Planet—global meltdown or global healing book review, (2022)
   *'The Climate Book' by Greta Thunberg—a review (2023) + Barton letter.
3. Are there Gender issues in Climate Science? *Seminar Paper to World Congress on Anthropology of Climate Change* (2016).   228
4. Renewable Energy Strategies—Seminars (2003 & 2016).   228
5. Summary of collaborative work at the Environmental Studies Institute   229
6. Previous critique of UN structures and development of the Precautionary Principle   234

Preface

The idea for this book crystallised during a meeting in the Quantock Hills of Somerset where a small group of ten citizens of Stroud, a 'green' town long known for its strong intellectual, environmental and spiritual base, asked for an update on my book *Chill: A Reassessment of Global Warming Theory*, published in 2009. The group were part of a nationwide network challenging two dominant 'emergency' narratives pervading the mainstream media, political parties, parliaments, governments worldwide and the agencies of the United Nations (UN), relating to the Covid pandemic and Climate Change.

The experience of Covid and the coordinated global response that involved suppression of the virus's laboratory origins, the subsequent fast-tracking of mRNA 'vaccines', lockdowns, flimsy face masks; and neglect of the elderly and most vulnerable, all of which flew in the face of scientific evidence and proven effective responses, led many people to view with some trepidation the consolidation of emergency powers within groups of unelected, quasi-scientific bureaucrats, some of whom have clear conflicts of interest. Adding to this was a complicit mainstream and social media (e.g. Facebook) that would not engage with criticism of the UN's policy.

The final straw for many informed observers followed US Congressional Hearings that showed government scientific advisors colluding with a major science journal to mislead the public as to the origins of the pandemic and the role of scientists in the creation of a dangerous chimeric virus.

Much of this kind of complicity and subterfuge had characterised the climate issue for decades, but this Covid-led awakening has also brought many people formerly accepting of the 'climate consensus' and equally far-reaching global, UN-mediated programmes of response, to question the origins and reality of the climate 'emergency'—hence the delegation of Stroud citizens eager to extend their knowledge. They come from a 'green' town that has openly aligned itself with the 'emergency' of climate. My own Town Council, now led by Green Party councillors likewise voted to acknowledge the 'emergency' of climate and support for government Net Zero policies. A critical debate on these issues at which I spoke in April 2023 filled the Town Hall. I have been approached many times by people formerly accepting of the 'scientific consensus' and role of the UN on climate, only to question this relationship following their experience of Covid policies.

I usually preface my work with a disclaimer—that I have no links to, let alone funding from the fossil fuel industry. The majority of my professional work is as a scientific and political ecologist—not *party* political, but political in the sense of involvement in policy. My expertise is in the analysis of science on issues of environmental pollution, and as an independent advisor and consultant I have worked with a wide range of environmental organisations and citizens' groups from a grass-roots level, through district and regional councils, my own and foreign governments, the European Commission and Parliament, as well as agencies of the United Nations. Working with teams that I have assembled and led we have changed laws and regulations, particularly with regard to marine and atmospheric pollution that have made this world a better place. This remains my motive.

I say this knowing it will make little difference to the left-liberal-green coalition on climate policy—a coalition that involves political parties, environmental NGOs, the mainstream media and even human rights organisations, all of whom have taken on board 'the science' as delivered by the UN's special panel of government-appointed experts. On this issue, my analysis conflicts not only with the fifteen hundred experts convened by that panel, but also currently, every national academy of science. However, I am not alone in my dissent—on the contrary, thousands of scientists, including Nobel laureates, have made their views known in a World Declaration. There are plenty of dissenting books and scientific papers—none of which have made much of a dent in the coalition.

Something other than 'science' is involved. In all the forums of policy that I have previously been involved with, we had a relatively friendly and open mainstream media and the scientific world was open for discussion and change. Not now. For some reason things have changed—environmental groups are closed to discussion, the media impervious, and the science world well-defended against itself. Branding of 'heretics' as 'deniers' is commonplace, and mainstream media such as the BBC have stated they will give no space for discussion with such 'deniers'.

One thing is changing—the Covid Saga has demonstrated the corrupt association of scientific funding, commercial interest (e.g. the vast pharmaceutical industry), the complicity of the media, supine nature of parliaments, captured government and UN agencies, and even the collusion of formerly respected science journals such as *Nature*. The consequences are still reverberating and this book is partly a guide to that process. The fight-back has begun and the aim of this book is to provide scientific ammunition.

The main book is based on published articles from two journals—*Caduceus* and *New View* that have followed my scientific analysis, but whose main focus is the reform of medicine and the broadening of the scientific worldview. Some of the latter emerges in my treatment—however, that treatment is always based upon published and peer-reviewed science. In the world of science itself, I was invited to collaborate with my former colleague in the battle to protect the oceans, Professor Jackson Davis, at the University of California, who founded the International Environmental Policy program at the Monterey Institute of International Studies in 1995, one of the main training grounds for US diplomats. In the past, we worked together to successfully change environmental law and bring in the Precautionary Principle. After working on marine issues, Professor Davis helped found the UN's Framework Convention on Climate Change and as the scientific advisor to Pacific Island states and the Alliance of Small Island States, he authored the AOSIS negotiating brief that shaped the final draft of the Kyoto Protocol.

However, Professor Davis had not thought to question what he thought was 'settled' science, and on receiving the draft of my book, he immediately recognised that my questions required answers. As I document here, we visited research labs and asked direct questions, and realising the issues were not settled, he dedicated several years to the quest.

In our collaboration at the Environmental Studies Institute in California, we re-examined the science of climate cycles of warming and cooling as revealed in the ice-core data, in particular delineating the all-important centennial cycle which we argue drives the global warming and cooling cycle phase of the millennial cycle missing from all computer models of climate change. The appendices provide links to our published papers and to an invited conference presentation.

With regard to motivation—my science work is my *duty* and this partly stems from a sense of obligation. I was educated to the highest standard at Oxford University entirely paid for by the public purse at a time when University education was free and available to persons of humble origins and limited finances. I was schooled to hold a critical edge to my thinking and take nothing on authority alone. My contemporaries in the Honours School of Natural Sciences became professors and even among them a highly respected Major General.

I have other work that is to me equally important considering the issues we face. I work with musicians, dancers, yogis, shamans and magicians—and this has attracted comment from some in the media who have little appreciation of these realms. We work in the shadows with the demons of our rapidly failing democracy and a society on the edge of a precipice. Scientific advances and political inadequacies have brought us to this point. I believe that eventually we will see the restructuring of scientific education, an admission that gender issues are involved and that the origin of our malaise lies within the patriarchal system of thought itself. We have been led astray by powerful but unbalanced minds and we need now something of a rebalancing act!

Peter Taylor
June, 2024.
https://en.wikipedia.org/wiki/Peter_Taylor (environmentalist)

Acknowledgements

I thank Sevak Gulbekian at Clairview Books for agreeing to publish this project and the initiative to publish *Chill* in 2009. The book is still in demand and proving a seminal read on the science and policy issues. I am indebted to Simon Best, editor of *Caduceus*, and Tom Raines, editor of *New View* for their continued interest in my work since 2009 and for permission to compile this volume of articles. Their attention to detail and edits regarding clarity have helped me to make this often-complex material more widely understandable. I thank Professor Jackson Davis for reading the manuscript and for his inspiring work—it has been an honour to collaborate; and I thank Dr Elena Koslova, and Dr Owen Taylor also for their careful reading and comments on the draft, and Dr Richard House for editing the Introduction and his overall encouragement for and indeed inception of, this project.

Caduceus Editor, Simon Best, 14, Wallbridge Gardens, Frome, Somerset BA11 1RJ.
Tel. +44 (0)1373 455260

New View Editor: Tom Raines, 198/15 Lindsay Road, Edinburgh EH6 6ND.
Tel. +44 (0) 20 7317 8302

Introduction

It is now some 15 years, as I write, since my book *Chill: A Reassessment of Global Warming Theory* was published. I observe an overall trend in the dominant narrative of human-induced warming, with the focus having shifted to 'extreme' weather and 'record' temperatures. This focus has drifted far from the science base. Certainly, we are experiencing 'record' daily temperatures—but the 'record' referred to is the last 150 years of instrumental readings. These temperatures are far from unprecedented considering warmer peaks in a past millennial cycle that has been consistent for thousands of years (as determined by proxies for temperature such as the ice-core record, tree-rings and constituents of ocean sediments). The weather does appear chaotic—but this is due to changes in the Jetstream that alter wind patterns and to be expected toward the peak of the cycle.

Even the UN's Intergovernmental Panel on Climate Change (IPCC) in its 6th report finds no long-term trends in droughts, wildfires and floods. The current alarm at 'unprecedented' changes is almost entirely a 'media' creation behind which powerful well-funded 'coalitions' of interest groups operate.

There *is*, however, strong evidence that the world is in a major 'warm' period (see *Chill* Revisited, 1.1). Temperatures of land and ocean have been rising since 1850, along with retreating glaciers and rising sea levels. However, the proxy records do not support any statement that current temperatures and their rates of change, nor the rate of sea-level rise, loss of ice and consequent movements of flora and fauna, are *unprecedented*—as often maintained by the mainstream media, and sadly abetted by some scientific papers upon which there is no consensus.

Proxies are used for past temperature patterns in the pre-instrumental record but they are inexact and caution is needed when they are compared to modern satellite-aided global coverage by advanced instruments. It is *possible* that current northern hemisphere temperatures are now higher than in the previous warm period about one thousand years ago (The Medieval Warm Period) when the Vikings colonised Greenland, but this is by no means an established fact. Whereas we have global coverage of land and ocean temperatures, both surface and atmospheric, from satellites as well as a network of surface stations, the 1,000-year records rely upon 'proxies' in the ice cores, ocean sediments and tree-rings, all of which are localised.

In the case of the Arctic, I reported in *Chill* that many station records up to the year 2000, only just matched the record of the 1940s—an Arctic Oscillation (a regular cycle) was involved (see 2.1, Fig.1). Although some Arctic station temperatures peaked later, the global average showed no trend for the next 15 years—known as the 'hiatus' or 'pause' in surface temperatures. As I predicted in some of the articles—temperature would likely drop *unless* there was a major El Niño. We had two—one in 2016, and one in 2023/24, both riding on top of the longer cycles.

The media and many scientists claimed 'global warming' had resumed—but we need to wait for the expected post-Niño drop, and it is disingenuous of scientists to include these Niño peaks as indicative of accuracy in their modelling, or continuation of a late 20th-century trend.

The pattern is clear—several decadal, centennial and millennial cycles were in their rising phase in the period 1900~2000 at the same time as carbon emissions began in earnest—*but these cycles are neither represented nor predicted in the models that underlie the UN's supposed consensus.*

Since *Chill* (2009), there has been growing interest from the scientific community in my analysis of climate-change cycles. This is the fruit of 12 years of collaborative work with Professor Jackson Davis at the Environmental Studies Institute in California, in the 1980s. Jackson and I worked for 15 years on ocean-pollution issues (1980~1995) when he was an advisor to Pacific Island States at UN conventions. I acted as advocate and chief scientific advisor to Greenpeace International, also at the UN conventions (see Appendix 6). Working closely with a coalition of like-minded parties we successfully curtailed the ocean dumping of toxic and nuclear waste, incineration at sea of dangerous chemicals, and discharges from land-based sources of toxic and radioactive waste streams. This work led to the World Maritime Organisation, which hosted the UN conventions and provided the secretariat, to bring me in as consultant to revise the legal conventions and accommodate the newly drafted Precautionary Principle. I worked on the development of that Principle, engaging a research assistant—Tim Jackson, now Professor of Sustainable Development at Surrey University (see the link in Appendix 6).

It is seldom remarked upon by the media, or indeed by any of the modern-day environmental groups so keen to follow the UN lead on science, that the UN has a long history of being on the wrong side—in particular, a history of its agencies being captured by both commercial and *scientific* 'interests'. At one time, the UN's Scientific Committee on the Effects of Atomic Radiation (UNSCEAR) supported the x-raying of pregnant women despite mounting evidence of harm. This stance was shared by all the major science academies worldwide—with the exception of the US National Academy of Sciences Committee on the Biological Effects of Radiation, under Professor Edward Radford, with whom I also worked.

The fact is, a consensus of world scientists has been *wrong* in the past and gender issues were involved as pregnant women were ignored as a potentially vulnerable subgroup, despite many warnings. Gender issues may also be involved in the modelling of climate where cycles, irregular periods and spiral dynamics, all features of the paleo-climate data records, are missing from the computer models (see Appendix 3). The models are built by male-mind physicists and mathematicians who demand 'exactness' in cycles.

Likewise, the UN's marine-science agency—the Group of Scientific Experts on Marine Pollution (GESAMP)—defended 'dilute and disperse' strategies for toxic-waste disposal despite mounting evidence of harm to marine life and human food chains. In each case, established policies were turned around by concerted, independent 'dissident' scientists having to fight the vested interests not only of industry but also regulators and laboratories specialising in monitoring and surveillance. One key element of our work was the analysis of computer models that created a virtual reality of oceans. Our opponents had a greater belief in their models than in mounting real-world data (see Appendix 6).

In those days, such initiatives were strongly supported by environmental campaigners and the media. Things have changed mightily. Now, environmental campaigners, the media and a large number of collaborators in science have co-created a UN-led 'consensus' to which all governments and their regulatory agencies have signed up. Further, dissident scientific analysis is ignored and marginalised, rather than welcomed as a necessary safeguard against 'captured' agencies. There is also a process of vilification of dissenters—often labelled 'deniers' or 'sceptics' supposedly all funded by fossil-fuel interests and established scientists are not immune to so labelling their critics.

This kind of behaviour was mirrored with 'anti-vaxxer' and 'covidiot' labels from the media and politicians at the outset of the Covid 'emergency'—but in contrast to the climate emergency, dissident scientists gained a presence in alternative media, and in the USA, Congressional Hearings and subpoena of email traffic exposed the level of collusion between pharmaceutical (and broader financial) interests, scientists and government in a), a cover-up of the lab-origin of the virus; and b), the unscientific nature of the governmental response.

There is still much to unfold, for many people there is still a perceived 'consensus' among the world's scientists that climate change is a global emergency demanding a radical restructuring of industrial society (see Net Zero Soul, 4.5). Critics are still labelled 'deniers' or presumed to be in the pay of 'right-wing' free-market forces, or Big Oil interests, and the de-platforming of speakers and personal vilification have been commonplace.

Recently, democratic institutions have awakened to this issue, with US Congressional Hearings (see Preface to Part 5) leading the way and the UK Parliament's House of Commons beginning to question the narrative. Of particular note has been the uncovering of vested interests pervading the medical foundations, academic research institutes and scientific journals, such that regulatory agencies have been 'captured' and dissident views ignored or suppressed. In this, government health agencies as well as the UN's World Health Organisation have been heavily implicated.

At the outset of the Covid epidemic, there were competent scientists arguing that evidence supported a laboratory escape of an engineered virus—in contrast to the favoured political and scientific narrative of a 'zoonotic' source (i.e. contamination of the food chain by a naturally occurring bat respiratory virus). These critics were labelled 'conspiracy theorists', with the term even being used in the top medical and science journals to discredit dissident voices and play to the mainstream media. Ironically, these same actors were themselves conspiring to cover up the lab-origin! (See Preface to Part 5).

Further to the revelations of the laboratory origin of the virus, it has emerged that the 'pandemic response' was carefully planned at the highest level in the year before the pandemic, putting aside tested protocols and instituting 'lockdowns' across the global economy that have had far-reaching economic and social impacts.

If it is not obvious already, it will finally emerge that the Covid pandemic was exaggerated way beyond the reality of a respiratory virus. In the UK at least, the excess deaths were comparable to a 'bad flu' year— which is not to gainsay serious impacts on the elderly and those with comorbidities, as bad flu always has induced. Official data comparisons extended to the previous five-year averages and did not include 'bad flu' years in previous decades.

There are claims that Covid killed tens of millions of people worldwide and that the vaccines also saved millions of lives. Such claims require closer analysis. Firstly, flu registrations all-but disappeared, compounding the attribution data, and secondly the vaccinations came in after the main peaks of a viral epidemic that was losing power naturally and reductions of mortality could not be clearly attributed. In terms of worldwide impacts mortality assumptions are made regarding large relatively unmonitored populations in India, Africa and rural China.

Of particular concern was the way in which older vulnerable people were not adequately protected—almost, as commented by some 'as if killing off the elderly was intentional' (see: https://solitudes.qmul.ac.uk/blog/covid-19-killing-off-older-people/). Many experts were astounded at the abandonment of previous protocols based upon protecting the most vulnerable—as would be normal procedure, rather than a policy of mass vaccination including those least vulnerable. I personally hold that the vaccination of young children and pregnant women (without adequate safety trials) was a crime against humanity. There is recent evidence of serious vaccine damage to women from Japanese scientific reports on increased ovarian cancer (https://pmc.ncbi.nlm.nih.gov/articles/PMC11077472/). The paper was reviewed by John Coleman (https://www.youtube.com/watch?v=onww2X-ecfg), however, despite passing peer review, the editors have retracted the paper claiming correlation studies cannot be performed on the data as presented—the authors disagree with this decision (https://pmc.ncbi.nlm.nih.gov/articles/PMC11204115/).

There is now a growing awakening to the other 'emergency' also driven by UN scientific committees and now morphing into a worldwide, highly profitable financial trade in carbon-credits, new taxation regimes and the furtherance of what may prove to be useless and damaging technologies in the name of 'renewable' energy sources.

However, there is a notable difference: in the UK at least, there are very few dissident climate scientists in comparison to the number of senior virologists and medics, and they are largely ignored. The UK Parliament, in common with many democratic institutions worldwide, voted with hardly any dissent for a Net Zero industrial policy without any strategic environmental or social-impact assessment of its far-reaching implications, let alone any in-depth assessment of the scientific basis of climate change and the role of carbon dioxide.

There is a monolithic consortium of vested interests protecting the climate narrative which is in my view far more pervasive than around the Covid issue. There are a few dissident voices, particularly with regard to Net Zero, where The Global Warming Policy Foundation provides cogent analysis of costs, as well as objective information of what is happening with the climate (I recommend their annual State of the Climate Report by Professor Humlum—see Appendix 2). However, this Foundation could readily be dismissed as right-wing defenders of the free market as well as being anti-environmentalist (for example, avidly pro-nuclear and pro-GMOs), and thus unlikely to be consulted by any 'greens'.

I find it ironic that defenders of personal freedoms as well as resilience to media-driven propaganda are seen more often within the 'conservative' spectrum than the traditional left, to the point where 'left' and 'right' have lost their original meanings. Truth and freedom have become the issues of a new movement beyond the old divisions.

This shift in consciousness presents problems for grass-roots activists who want to support their arguments with science. This is why I have been asked to make a compendium of my ongoing published work on these issues more easily available.

The articles in the compilation that follows are for a general readership, where the editors of the journals have been concerned to provide jargon-free explanations for scientific terms. However, the magazines *Caduceus* and *New View*, which are the original source of the bulk of the articles published here, are far from mainstream. The former specialises in medicine with environmental and spiritual themes, while the latter is strongly influenced by anthroposophical writings; and stylistically, whereas Simon Best at *Caduceus* has preferred detailed scientific references, Tom Raines at *New View* has favoured in-text explanation.

Since the publication of *Chill* (which questions not the reality of global warming, but the percentage influence of humans compared to natural cycles and forces), not a single invitation to talk, meet, discuss or debate has come from any of the 'green' movement—not one in the past 15 years. Not even from Greenpeace, for whom I was for 12 years chief advocate at UN Conventions on ocean pollution.

There is one exception—about ten years ago, the Cornwall chapter of Transition Towns invited me to present on renewable energy sources. I should emphasise that until 2005, when I began my own review of climate science, I was a specialist advisor to the UK government on integrating renewable energy into the landscape, including rural community and biodiversity objectives. I had not thought to review the science, thinking it was 'settled'. I led a small consultancy specialising in 'visualising' change, and we worked with the Countryside Agency to develop a computer virtual reality tool to envision the placement of the wide range of renewable options, each with their respective impacts upon the different English landscapes (see Appendix 4).

I made my presentation in Penzance, and was informed a few weeks later by the organisers that they had been severely upbraided by the founder of Transition Towns, Rob Hopkins—they should not have entertained a *denier*. In the past ten years, this has remained the standard response of all environmental groups, the BBC, *The Guardian*, *The Independent* and *The Observer*, upon which modern 'greens' are so reliant for their news and views.

In stark contrast, in the time since *Chill* and my instigation of a research programme with Jackson Davis, and after publication in climate-science journals, there has been a great deal of interest in our work. Professor Davis endorsed my 2009 book (stating that its many questions must be answered before global-warming theory could be accepted). Since this endorsement, we have jointly published scientific papers focusing upon natural climate cycles and outlining our theory on their causes based upon the marshalling of substantial evidence from the ice-core records.

None of these credentials made any difference to the 'greens'. I rapidly became *persona non grata* with all the campaign organisations with which I had hitherto had good relations, including contracts and consultancies—the World Wild Life Fund, Friends of the Earth and Greenpeace. All of these organisations are part of a 'Climate Coalition' lobbying for mitigation strategies that have morphed over the years into the Net Zero policy. None of them have critically reviewed the science—they follow the UN assessments, and of course, the mainstream media interpretation, and gain thereby much financial support.

In 2010, following the publicity around *Chill*, the director of documentaries at ITN (Independent Television News), a major TV channel in the UK, on the advice of their resident science journalist, wanted to produce a documentary on my work. Being televisual, they asked what could I suggest? 'Fly me to Greenland' I said—and where David Attenborough had looked out on glaciers crumbling into the sea, I would look down at the thawing permafrost and recently uncovered Viking graves, and tell the story of the one-thousand-year *cycle*.

After three meetings, the director called me in to apologise—the programme had been pulled due to pressure from above—'the Gorites', he opined. The science journalist resigned in protest and asked how he could help. I told him that I needed to go to the US, see my colleague

Jackson Davis and visit the top US modelling lab. He paid my air-fare from his own pocket.

We began with a visit to the top US government-sponsored climate modelling laboratory—The National Center for Atmospheric Research (NCAR), where I presented data drawn from my review. The chief modeller, Gerry Meehl, had not seen the data—essentially, evidence that more energy came into the Earth system by a change in the amount of sunlight absorbed by the oceans. This was caused by reduced cloud cover. 'They were worried' opined Jackson Davis, and thus began our collaboration.

On the basis of our joint work over a ten-year period and after the publication of our first paper, I was invited to be keynote speaker at a major global-warming science conference in Prague in the Spring of 2019 (see Appendix 5: *'Causes of Global Warming'*). Our first paper had drawn widespread interest from the climate-science community, and was widely regarded as impressive work (Professor Davis should take maximum credit for that). At the conference, I was able to challenge the model-based predictions of the UN's Intergovernmental Panel on Climate Change (IPCC)—in particular, in discussions with their lead modeller, Professor Ramaswamy Venkatachalam, director of the Geophysical Fluid Dynamics Laboratory at Princeton University. He agreed that they had not handled the issue of climate cycles at all well. I have appended abstracts of these papers and links to the full text: they are not lay-reading, though the Prague presentation is aimed at the general scientist.

I tell this story here because, as with the Covid saga, it has lessons about the nature of what has been called 'noble-cause corruption' in modern science, where scientific rules are bent for the greater good of humanity. I have no doubt that at the outset, a small group of scientists believed that the future of humanity was at stake. Scientists in that position naturally seek to engage in policy-making, and policy makers demand simple answers with no caveats. I saw this process happen with those scientists who developed the 'dilute and disperse' policies for toxic discharges and ocean dumping of toxic waste—that policy involved regulations and relatively cheap costs for industry. When real-world data started to challenge the models that justified the policy, the institutions of science put up great resistance—as a consequence of what I have called 'prior commitment bias'. I have appended links to this work including to papers that still draw citations after 30 years (Appendix 5 and 6).

We can see the same phenomenon in relation to Covid. In order to press forward with a new experimental programme of 'vaccination' which scientists believed would be superior and could be rapidly deployed, safety protocols were compromised. For example, no safety trials could be conducted on pregnant women and only later was it discovered that the 'spike protein' generated by the 'vaccines' genetic code, did not stay in the muscle tissue of the arm but spread and concentrated in the uterus.

When it became apparent that the virus had not morphed naturally from bats but had been the subject of laboratory 'gain of function' (i.e. genetic manipulation), a group of top specialist professors wrote a paper for *Nature*—the top science journal—stating that the virus could not possibly have originated in a laboratory, and that such claims were mere 'conspiracy theory'. That paper, early in 2020, was of course widely publicised in the mainstream media, and critics were immediately branded as conspiracy theorists. If not for the US system of Congressional Hearings and the subpoena of emails regarding that paper, we would not know that several of the co-authors believed it quite possible, even likely, that the virus came from the Wuhan lab. In the email traffic they openly discuss the potential detrimental impact on 'science', and in particular on collaboration with China upon which much pharmaceutical research and investment depend (see links to documentation in Preface to Part 5).

The email 'leaks' from the University of East Anglia Climate Research Unit in 2009 had much the same flavour—ranging from collusion to prevent publication of contrary research, personal denigration of critics, abuse of the peer-review system and the covering up of scientific malpractice (e.g. the 'Hockey Stick' controversy). However, that was not the opinion of three supposedly independent inquiries, including one by the House of Commons Committee on Science and Technology, to which I submitted a memorandum. I recommend the treatment of this scandal by Andrew Montford in two detailed books: *The Hockey Stick Illusion* A.W. Montford, Stacy International, London. 2010; and *Hiding the Decline: a history of the Climategate affair*. A.W. Montford. Anglosphere Books, London. 2012; and in addition *The disclosure of climate data from the Climatic Research Unit at the University of East Anglia,* Eighth Report of Session 2009-10, House of Commons Science and Technology Committee. Memorandum submitted by Peter Taylor Vol. II, pp185~191, Montford's history of the affair includes a detailed critique of how the establishment mobilised to exonerate UEA and the Climate Research

Unit of any wrongdoing. Much the same can be expected of the UK Covid Inquiry.

Thus far, I have heard no 'green' critique of the origins and lab-creation of the virus, nor of the close relationship of the pharmaceutical industry and US government in its creation, and also nothing on the vast profits made from the pandemic by that industry. Similarly, I have heard no 'green' critique of Net Zero and all the UN/Davos/World Economic Forum programmes (with their 'lessons learned from Covid') as now taken up by governments worldwide in order to meet the 'threat' of climate change. Yet these programmes—of wind turbines, global biofuel plantations and hydro-schemes—threaten pristine wildlife habitats, whole landscapes and the rights of indigenous peoples—and not withstanding also the huge cost and diversion of resources from important social and environmental programmes. There are substantial financial interests at stake in carbon credits, taxation and global investment in technology—with much of the latter dominated by Chinese industries. Trillions of dollars are involved.

Net Zero social engineering on a scale now practised by China is openly embraced as the 'Green New Deal'. And the 'greens' seem quite happy that 80~90 per cent of the technological fix for climate comes from Chinese factories which now lead the world in carbon emissions, and whose labour forces live in the social poverty of cell-block high-rise towers and work without proper labour rights or environmental protection (see 5.1, 5.2 and 5.3). It is for me, who was partner to the first shoots of the Green Movement, quite bizarre. I do not recognise modern 'greens' as the same kind of people.

If still at all possible—I would herewith reach out to my former allies—in Greenpeace, the World Wildlife Fund, Friends of the Earth and the Green Party, and ask for a hearing. They can bring as many experts as they wish.

Most of those experts would not know the computed relationship of carbon-dioxide *concentration* to the actual *effect* measured in watts at the Earth's surface, nor would they know *how this compares to the natural flux*. They would be well aware that concentration has increased by 50 per cent—a scary number, but few know that this adds less than 1 per cent to the natural flux at the surface (the only significant source of heat for the planet). Few ecosystem specialists would regard this as an 'emergency' situation, and would immediately ask what was the natural *variability* over time in decades or centuries—because ecologists generally would know that long-term cycles exist.

In my work with Professor Davis, some of it previewed in *Chill* but most in scientific papers, we have argued that natural variability of the global average temperature is about 5 per cent, and that we are now in a warm phase where that 5 per cent increase—of about 1°C, would have been expected. The global warming is *on time*. My colleague would even argue that this points to additional CO_2 having potentially zero impact as a greenhouse gas because the atmosphere is already saturated, and very small increases in natural flux are likely to be compensated by natural feedbacks. I append links to his paper on this issue (Appendix 5).

Professor Davis is far more concerned about the acidification of the sea-surface micro-layer central to almost all marine larval species (zooplankton and fish), and the potential for a marine mass-extinction event within the next century. He has published a recent paper on mass extinction and the potential role of carbon dioxide, and we are in intense scientific discussion over the data—I have appended links in Appendix 5 and added some commentary.

In these realms of science my credentials have never been impugned. Although I am not an academic, I have lectured widely in universities, written scientific papers, helped to develop university courses and oversee Masters and Doctoral theses, though my working life has been more concerned with policy than the actual doing of science. However, there occurs in some of my essays in this book comments on the relationship between the outer scientific perspective and the inner, often referred to as yogic 'science', and in some cases the shamanic dimension of reality as applicable to the ecological and political issues of our day. I have written separately for scientists—many times—but here I will embrace something I consider essential in our future endeavour regarding truth and freedom—the 'outer' scientific realities of the physical world *should not* be separated from the 'inner' realities. Indeed, all of the truly great scientists sought to balance inner and outer work—Newton and Boyle, for example, embraced Alchemy as a process of 'inner work' (its apparent concern with the transformation of base-metals to gold was a 'cover' to protect it from the religious Inquisition, as well as to attract funding from financially challenged monarchs). Newton was also a strong defender of Astrology as a tool for inner work on the nature of consciousness.

All of these perspectives are relevant to the crucial political issue we all face—that of 'control'. Few people today have an entirely free will, where you wake up in the morning and can freely decide to do what is in your heart to do. The rest of us must negotiate a world that has power over us. We are born into a web of power. The philosopher of science, Paul Feyerabend, foretold of the times we now face in his book *The Tyranny of Science*—where 'a view may be false but show a prodigious power of performance'. All political parties are now mesmerised by this power (see 5.1, Covid, Climate and Conspiracy).

In my scientific work, where I focused on combatting pollution and environmental risk, I saw the power structure very clearly—but first, only on a political level. We used to call the organised enemies we faced a 'mafia'. They were scientists who worked for industry, corporations and the State, and believed in their right to make decisions about technology and control on behalf of others—and all according to an econometric cost–benefit analysis. It was only sensible, they argued, that some people must be exposed to some risk for the majority to benefit from technological progress. The problem for science is that its institutions become, over time, so closely enmeshed in the 'interests' of their funders—always government or industry—that their judgement goes awry. This is not to entirely gainsay the role of science in society—in the course of my own work, I have met some extraordinary scientists—people totally dedicated to humanitarian issues and to the truths and role of science and I have done my best to summarise their work.

At the same time as I have worked with individual scientists and was regularly consulted by governmental and non-governmental organisations, I was training in the 'science' of yoga. It was not easy to bridge those two worlds, given the antagonism of the 'enemy' (mostly the media and campaign groups), and how my opponents sought to denigrate and cast doubt upon my competence and analyses. Ironically, no scientist ever publicly did that: rather, it was *political* writers determined to sling mud.

Finally, there is one conclusion above all others with which I will preface this collection of essays. It is that there exists a cadre of souls with strong esoteric training akin to that which yogis and shamans undertake but one particular to the modern 'Western' world, and which has as its work and goal an influence upon the collective mind, and though this cadre is capable of affecting and controlling individuals, its main focus is the 'maintenance' of the Western civil order. There is, of course, a hidden power structure within an overt Masonic Order, but few are aware of its historical roots in the Western 'magical' tradition.

The historian Paul Kléber Monod's *Solomon's Secret Arts: The Occult in the Age of Enlightenment* traces the evolution of modern scientific thought during the 17th century, showing its origins in Alchemy and Astrology with Elias Ashmole and later Isaac Newton. The scientific Royal Society was founded by active 'magii' (see Tobias Churton's *The Magus of Freemasonry*—a biography of Elias Ashmole). Surprisingly, Monod concludes that science publicly divorced itself not through any natural antipathy, but because of a popular fear of occult practice as the work of 'the Devil'. The well-developed esoteric tradition then remained hidden and science divorced from Sophia (wisdom) morphed into the cold rationalism identified by Feyerabend.

Everything we now see present in that civil order—the architecture, the technology, the hierarchy of control and risk and benefit—has to have been dreamed before it could be constructed (see 5.3, Awakening the Dream). Each human being is born with that same power to dream. It is, in my view, the ultimate *creative* power—and, as such, 'divine'. No other creature on Earth, as far as I can tell, has 'evolved' this power.

It is my impression, and I know one shared by many of those around me, that humanity is trapped within a mesmerism of the cold-hearted paradigm of economic values, perpetual growth and material benefit. This paradigm has led us to the brink of annihilation—either by nuclear war and the nuclear 'winter' that follows, or as consequent ecological dangers of stripping the planet of its natural ecosystems. There is an acute lack of *wisdom*. Ironically, those early shoots of science respected *Sophia*—the realm of intuitive wisdom, as it was in the very name of the Royal Society for the promotion of Natural Philosophy. It was a male endeavour, of course, and although science itself opened its doors to women, they had to adopt the rationalist paradigm. The esoteric wing—the 'dreamers', kept women at bay, and in my view, it is this Order that is responsible for bringing us to the brink. If we *can* step back, the future priority must be a deep-rooted educational reform that creates a fundamental equality between the feminine polarity of love and the masculine polarity of thought, an equality of heart and mind.

I have a few close associates and friends who work together in different ways as healers, musicians, dramatists, dancers, drummers, storytellers, shamans and yogis. I will talk about that but briefly here, since we are evolving a network. We are, everyone, committed to the humanitarian task of bringing more love and awareness into this creative world.

PART 1: *CHILL*

This article first appeared in New View *magazine, no. 95, Spring 2020, pp. 59–70. There is some repetition following themes in the Introduction that I have not edited out.*

1.1 *Chill* Revisited

The editor of *New View* magazine has asked me to write an update[1] of my climate book *Chill: A Reassessment of Global Warming Theory*, which was published in 2009. It was reviewed in *New View,* and I have read the original article by Richard Phethean republished in the last issue, as well as Terry Boardman's take on COP25 in Madrid last year,[2] the most recent meeting of the UN Climate Convention (the next is scheduled for Glasgow later this year, as I write). It is clear that readers of *New View* magazine place climate change, the science and the politics, in a certain context, a much wider one than is typical in the circles of environmental science which I have occupied for over 40 years. Climate science does not address the impact of the policies it generates upon the human psyche, or soul. Neither does it examine *itself* as a science generated by its own collective psyche. It could do so—but only if scientists were regularly taught self-examination and humanistic psychology—which, of course they are not. On the contrary, they are taught to actively repress and ridicule astrology, homeopathy and any alternative medicines, without understanding that reality has two dimensions—the seen and measurable, and the unseen and not measurable. In all my scientific and policy work, I made the choice to keep to the dimension science understands— so deeply rooted is the prejudice and fear of the 'unscientific'.

In my book *Chill*, I argued that the science of global warming—both the extent of the warming and its causation—could not be fully established other than in the context of natural cycles. Since its publication in 2009, I have given a seminar to the World Congress of Anthropology (in 2016), organised by the Royal Anthropological Institute, addressing the social and anthropological issues around climate change. I proposed that the masculine mindset of science was prejudiced against 'cyclic' behaviour, especially irregular periods, spiral dynamics and elements of chaos—all of which were in some way 'feminine'. The reason for this was that several well-documented natural warming cycles were peaking together during the main global-warming period, which I take to be 1980–2000. Readers may not be familiar, but the world warmed rapidly from 1920 to 1940, cooled until 1980, and then warmed again; and the curve then flattened out after 2001.

As evidence to support my argument, I showed data on the flux of energy at the Earth's surface—a strangely neglected data-set—because the coalition of scientists at the UN focused their attention upon the energy flux at the top of the atmosphere (TOA). The reason for this focus lies primarily in the nature of modelling and the requirements of the mathematics. The data to which I drew attention showed clearly that over the key warming period of 1980–2001, 3–4 times more energy was reaching the surface from short-wavelength sunlight than from the infrared spectrum associated with carbon dioxide and other greenhouse gases. Further evidence was presented to show that over the same period, cloud cover thinned to allow more sunlight through.

The real-world data was, I thought, incontrovertible. There were also three high-level scientific papers published in 2005 on the surface flux which supported my conclusions drawn from the raw data. In fact, the flux of sunlight (in wattage) was so great that it meant that the carbon-dioxide model that related concentration to effective warming must be seriously wrong. A basic calculation left the carbon-dioxide effect at a maximum of 25 per cent of the driving force. The models had to be overstating the potential of CO_2 to warm the surface layers of the planet by at least a factor of two.

My Motivation in Studying Climate Science
The above conclusions were made after three years of intensive, unfunded, study of climate-science papers and data sources. I had a strong motivation. As a scientific ecologist and conservationist with a series of ongoing cooperative endeavours with major UK landowners such as the Forestry Commission and the National Trust, part of my brief was to keep track of climate change and its implications for countryside policy. Indeed, as long ago as 1996, the then Countryside Commission contracted me to examine advice they'd received from the University of East Anglia on this very issue.

Furthermore, between 2000 and 2003 I sat on a UK government advisory group—the Community Renewables Initiative—during which time I reviewed the Royal Commission Report on Climate Change with its policy recommendations for renewable-energy sources. And then, in collaboration with the Countryside Agency, I developed a visualisation tool—using computer virtual-reality landscapes (at the time, leading-edge work)—to look at the Royal Commission recommendations and their environmental impact up to 2050. I would have given you the link to that work, but my website has been under continual destructive attack.

The consequences of those policies for renewable power were enormous: thousands of giant aerospace turbines on the hills, large acreage of solar panels in the field-scape, and huge demand for biofuels, including wood-burning power stations. It was also obvious that nuclear-power sources would experience a renaissance. I care about wild as well as cultural landscape, tranquillity in the countryside, rural communities, and what is called biodiversity. Much of what we value would be severely compromised, and I wanted to know just how urgent things were. Many people, including environmentalists at Friends of the Earth and Greenpeace—two organisations for which I had often worked as a consultant and advisor—were calling for the sacrifice of these values on behalf, for example, of 'Bangladesh', deemed to be threatened by sea-level rise.

These were, and remain, my motivations, and I state them here because a large part of my update will relate to people questioning my motives and competence, rather than actually looking at my scientific analysis. I will also take a moment at this point to rehearse my scientific qualifications—since they, too, are regularly impugned.

I studied Natural Science at Oxford, gaining a good degree in 1970. In 1976, I returned to study linguistic anthropology and the meaning of symbolic language, and was set for an academic career; but by 1980, I had decided that that world would be too restrictive, and so I left to set up my own research group. I pulled together an inter-disciplinary team of engineers, physicists, biologists and sociologists, and we set our expertise at the service of communities and environmental groups. We ran the group co-operatively for 12 years, and we became experts in the critical review of scientific evidence used to support various policies of government, the European Union and the UN.

We had a broad focus—from oceanic and atmospheric pollution, nuclear risks, whaling, wildlife conservation, organic farming, climate change and carbon sequestration. In that time we developed particular expertise in understanding the role of computer models. We obtained several such models (by subpoena), ran them ourselves and picked apart their assumptions. In addition to community work, we were contracted by governments in Ireland, Sweden, Germany, Spain, among others, and eventually the UK, as well as the European Parliament, the

European Commission and the International Maritime Organisation. I also represented Greenpeace International as advocate at the UN for 12 years until 1993. My own work on pollution control, technology, law and risks has all been published in the scientific literature.

Attacking the Messenger
If you search on the internet for my name and work, you may well come across material from journalist George Monbiot at *The Guardian*, Rob Hopkins at Transition Towns, and Alistair MacIntosh, author of many environmental works—all of whom ignore the science, and instead scurrilously mine an autobiographical account (my book *Shiva's Rainbow*) of the period 1984, when I first began intensive yoga training with the Himalayan master, Herakhan Baba (the Babaji of Yogananda's autobiography). In that rather too honest an account, I talk of my encounters and experience of homeopathy, astrology and astral travel—and all of this those commentators interpret as signs of madness, despite the obvious juxtaposition of my yogic efforts with major international science and policy work. I will not detail here the idiocy of their commentary; I will merely point out that these people are perfectly capable of understanding the science, and yet chose not to. They play to the gallery of public misunderstanding. I readily admit that having one foot in the science world at a high-policy level and one foot in the realms of psyche (at a rather lowly level), maintaining sanity was not always easy!

The Science since *Chill*
It should be a simple task to look at how the science has changed in the last ten years. I could present many graphics—the continued rise of sea level, the loss of summer sea ice in the Arctic, permafrost thawing, ocean heat content increasing, and so on. This is what science focuses upon. But it is what is *not* researched that is harder to see. The increases are not the issue: rather, the issue is how much they are due to human emissions of greenhouse gases and how much is natural, and how this answer affects policy. Climate science is skewed towards modelling that assumes that most of the warming is anthropogenic. There are no cycles in the models, and institutionally—one could say *constitutionally*—climate science exerts a wilful blindness to natural processes that are cyclic in nature.

Thus, as I weave into this chapter the updates of data and published papers, I will comment on the institutional context—in particular, a phenomenon called 'prior commitment', which I first named in a published paper on ocean pollution in 1993. The phenomenon starts with a 'model' of what science thinks is happening—a virtual reality built inside a computer. This is standard scientific practice, from the smallest model of part of an ecosystem to a global-circulation model of atmosphere and oceans, including geochemistry and even solar physics. It is important in science to remain aware that the model is an heuristic device, not an objective reality. Its function is to generate insight and direct further research. The danger—which we encountered time and again in all fields that used complex models (ocean dispersion of toxic substances, nuclear aerial releases, radioactive waste storage, toxicity of low-level radiation, acid rain—amongst others)—is that models were believed over and above conflicting data.

The reasons were obvious; *prior commitment* of industry and major investment based on the conclusions of the early models that governments had used to legitimise strategies of, for example, waste dispersion, or a worldwide industry of x-raying that included pregnant women. Often, huge investments had been made. I rehearsed these examples in my book *Chill*: the disposal of toxics to the coastal regions; the dumping of nuclear waste in the deep ocean; the use of a threshold value for the effect of low-level radiation; the use and release of CFCs[3] in refrigeration, or PCBs[4] in electrical transformers. In all of these policy areas, there was great resistance to acknowledging the validity of new data that might show the model to be wrong. For example, mercury concentration rising in fisheries; leukaemia rates in children born to mothers x-rayed in pregnancy; plutonium showing up on the seashore and being blown into homes; PCBs found, rather late, to be carcinogenic and immune-suppressant, but only after they had been licensed for unregulated landfill from which they volatilised and reached the pristine Arctic food chains; and of course, CFCs, which nearly destroyed the Earth's ozone layer in the 1970s.

Every one of these examples was licensed on the advice of the scientific institutions, and under the advice or guidelines of UN special committees. Every example involved faulty models, great risks, new data, resistance to that data—short-lived in the case of CFCs—often trumpeted as a great success with the Montreal Protocol which banned their use; whereas as persistent organic compounds, they should never have been released in the first place; and then finally either revision of the models, or cessation of the activity. In all my contact with UN science, it has been the worst of culprits. At least the International Maritime Organisation brought me in, on admission that the models were wrong, to help revise the Annexes of their written Convention on ocean pollution. I also worked with the UN to develop the Precautionary Principle and Clean Technology Strategies, where several of my colleagues led the field, and still do.

I say this now because one thing does need to be said: the institutions of science collectively cover their asses. They do not publicise these errors and, in my opinion, have not learned the key lessons. The paper I wrote on this theme in 1993, published in a leading journal, is hardly ever cited.[5] One sociology of science unit in Sussex University is an exception, as well as one marine biology professor in Ecuador!

So, the institutions indulge in self-protection. Critical scientists I knew experienced:

i) difficulty in getting published; if published, few citations; if impossible to ignore, then often scurrilous ad hominem attack;

ii) pressure on funding and money for Ph.D. students; non-renewal of contracts; and antipathy from colleagues.

That is the reason my research group remained outside of academia, always keeping copyright and hardly ever working for industry or government. We were poor as church mice as a result! But our work was acknowledged globally; and when we disbanded, some of my colleagues were head-hunted by prestigious organisations. No such critical science research group exists today—to the best of my knowledge.

Given that experience and background, perhaps the following view could carry a little weight: *I have never seen anything as bad as current climate science, the behaviour of the UN special group on that science, the Intergovernmental Panel on Climate Change (IPCC), and their relations to the media and campaign groups.* The science is full of holes; and the cover-up is massive. The behaviour of key scientists is outrageous. In almost every sphere of data production I see manipulation and adjustment of raw data according to the needs of the model. This is unprecedented. It is not a hoax, nor a scam, as the President of the US once intimated: rather, it is an Emperor of naked self-interest.

Here is a list of data-adjusted fields:

i) sea-level rise—the models predict acceleration, whereas the raw data does not show it, so the satellite data is adjusted accordingly;

ii) global temperature—the past raw data is adjusted downwards, and more recent data upwards, hence creating a greater rate of temperature rise;

iii) as if ii) were not enough, original and highly reliable 'raw' station data from long-term monitoring sites across the world, once freely available, has been adjusted to match the expectation of models—getting the raw data, or even knowing that the published data has been altered, is not easy;

iv) ocean heat content data—when it showed cooling in 2003–2005, the algorithms for analysis were adjusted to align the results with top of the atmosphere (TOA) satellite data on energy flux; but...

v) the margin of error on the TOA flux was ten times the sought-after figure needed to confirm the ocean heat content rise; thus, the chosen 'reality' for the TOA was also calibrated to the ocean heat content—a completely circular argument!

vi) The first published solar data showing a rise since 1850 (from the Little Ice Age) had two components—the magnetic field change and the irradiance: the former rose by 200 per cent during the 20th century; the latter rise had a figure of about two watts/square metre, roughly the same energy as the increase in human sources of greenhouse gases (GHG). Both magnetic and irradiance data were revised downwards in subsequent papers by different authors who were also close to the IPCC.[6]

vii) likewise, the first published data on sunlight hitting the surface of the planet (as opposed to leaving the Sun) showed a large increase over the key global warming period from 1980 to 2000, in the range 4–6 watts/square metre, and were also revised downwards (again, by scientists within the UN network). Note: in comparison the cumulative CO_2 effect was estimated at 1.8 watts, and only in the last few years have direct measurements been published, which by my reading show a 50 per cent over-estimate.[7]

Two data-sets which I cited—the cloud-cover figures from the International Satellite Cloud Climatology Project and the NASA FD-data-set that calculated surface fluxes, both of which contradicted the models—were both deemed 'unreliable' by James Hansen, director of the NASA climate programme, thus disrespecting the work of some very competent and senior people. This data hardly ever gets into the public domain.

That said, I will outline the changes in the climate since I wrote *Chill*.

Global Temperature

I predicted in 2008, based on new work from an oceanographic laboratory in Germany, that temperatures would flatline or even cool for the next decade or two due to declining ocean cycles, unless there was a very big El Niño warming,[8] which would obscure the cooling. This is indeed exactly what has happened. There was no significant surface rise from 2000 to 2015. There are over 40 scientific papers attesting to that fact, all seeking explanations, with about the same number of theories—the main likelihood being that surface heat was transferred to the deeper ocean (where it will not come back for centuries).

If you see a graph of global temperature, look for the period 2017–2020 as it is often missed out—that is, after the peak of 2016 caused by a 'super' El Niño. A big El Niño–Southern Oscillation (ENSO) event occurs roughly once every 12 years—the last was in 1998. You will see temperature first falling down to the pre-Niño peak, but rising and falling a bit since, in what may be a cooling curve. The 2016 peak is marginally higher than the 1998 peak. If you subtract the El Niño peak (0.6 degrees), you get a rise of 0.6 since 1980 and a flat-line on a data graph since the year 2000.

The defenders of the model argue that the oceans have eaten the heat. Never have I seen these defenders talk about how the oceans release heat in cycles, absorbing and releasing, and with each ocean basin having a slightly different period of oscillation. And of course, the media don't talk cycles, either. And nor do Greenpeace et al. Yet every oceanographer and paleo-climate specialist knows that such cycles dominate the climate: the literature is huge, with thousands of high-quality papers looking at ocean sediments, lake varves,[9] peat deposits, tree-rings, stalagmites and ice cores.

Global and regional temperatures are cyclic by nature and not just the ice-age cycle of 100,000 years. There is a key 1,000-year cycle that can be found in both hemispheres, and with lower amplitude in the tropics than in the polar regions. It has a profound effect on rainfall, drought, wind patterns, ocean currents, wildfires and floods. Riding upon that sine-wave (the undulating line you get if you plot this data on a graph) are several centennial cycles and multi-decadal oscillations in each ocean basin, sometimes in-phase and sometimes not. All of these known cycles peaked together in the period 1980 to 2016.

If we compare the current warming with data from these cycle records, there is no difference in amplitude or rate of change in the global warming period compared to the natural cycles; hence, we are not yet in uncharted territory. The rise from the bottom of the current cycle—i.e. from the Little Ice Age (named because glaciers the world-over started to grow after the previous warm period)—is also coincident with the 'pre-industrial' era used as a baseline for 'global warming' (see Figure 1). That rise is one degree (Celsius), and the media use this figure to describe man-made warming, as if *all* of it is man-made. Furthermore, the so-called 'danger level' of 1.5 or 2 degrees above pre-industrial levels was common in previous such cycles (about 6–8 thousand years ago) and there were no 'tipping points' or ecosystem collapses, though

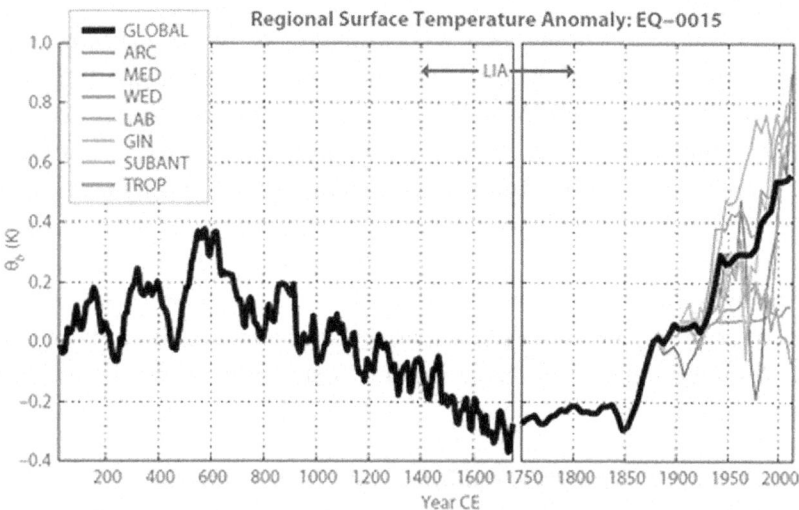

Figure 1. Reconstructed surface temperatures from blended paleo-oceanographic and instrumental data.
Source: G. Gebbie, 'Atlantic warming since the Little Ice Age', Oceanography 32 (1), 2019. pp.220-30; doi:org/10.5670/oceanog.2019.151. https://tinyurl.com/4cxuz684 (accessed 14 May 2024).

Note: In most of the global-warming debate, protagonists only show the right-hand box with the 'alarming rise' from 1850 (from the 'pre-industrial era'), and the media portray all of this rise, of about 1 degree, as human-induced. The black line is the global average (oceans constitute 70 per cent of the globe's surface, meaning that oceanographic data constitutes an important source for gauging temperature changes). In fact, even the IPCC models regard human influence before 1950 as marginal. On the right-hand box, the rise since 1900 is shown to consist of two 'steps' (1920–1940 and 1980–2000). We can readily see the potential human effect as the difference between the two peaks—about 0.20–0.25 degrees, which was also my estimate in my book Chill, made in 2009.

'Anomaly' simply means the deviation from a selected base period, in this case '0' in the graphic is the date 15 ce (Common Era). The selected baseline does not alter the data, but in this case emphasises the peaks and troughs of the long cycle, something few research papers show. The coloured lines (in the original) represent the different regional seas: ARC = Arctic, MED = Mediterranean, WED = Weddell Sea (Antarctica), LAB = Labrador Sea, GIN = Greenland, Iceland and Norwegian Seas, SUBANT = the sub-Antarctic region of the Atlantic, TROP= the remaining subtropical and tropical regions of the Atlantic. The 'LIA' double-headed arrow shows the extent of the Little Ice Age.

there was much change in species abundance and range. For example, 1,000 years ago white storks nested in Scotland, and 8,000 years ago people in Somerset ate pelicans for breakfast.

Climategate
This phenomenon deserves a whole chapter of its own. It concerns leaked emails in late 2009 from the University of East Anglia (UEA), a hub for the 'team' working at the IPCC. In short, those emails demonstrated collusion to hide awkward data and blacken critics, but UEA was absolved by the institutions of any wrongdoing, stating that much of their behaviour was standard practice in science! I don't think the emails were 'hacked' by the Russians—the early claim: rather, they were brought together to be deleted because of pesky Freedom of Information requests, and some conscientious insider leaked the whole lot. But it is a long story, and an internet search will doubtless give you both sides.

Floods, Storms, Droughts, Wildfires and Chaos Climates
Of all the data sources, the only one which shows deviation from relatively recent cycles (i.e. centennial rather than decadal) is the heaviness of local rainstorms. All other indices show a roughly 60-year cycle, with no increase of the second peak over the first, which is usually pre-1950. This is very clear for tornados, hurricane landfalls, drought and flood. Wildfire appears to be an exception, though data is scarce, and follows a 1,000-year pattern in the northern hemisphere and a 750-year pattern in the southern. Past wildfire extent can be seen in charcoal deposits. So again, the phenomenon is cyclical.

That said, one thing has changed above all other factors, and this makes for greater risk—that is, 1,000 years ago there were perhaps 300 million people on the planet, and today as I write there are 7.5 billion, with huge encroachment in natural ecosystems and fragmentation of biodiversity, loss of forests, soil impoverishment and exhaustion of groundwater supplies. Humanity is very vulnerable to floods, droughts, hurricanes and wildfire, as the previous decade amply demonstrates.

Arctic and Antarctic Sea Ice and Ice caps
Arctic summer sea ice has fallen by about 50 per cent since 1996. This has led some to predict ice-free summers within... well, before now—and as far away as 2030. Currently as I write, the fall has halted for about three years. The Arctic was ice-free about six cycles ago, when the planet was about one degree warmer, perhaps two. No species went extinct, and no tipping point was reached.

However, in Antarctica the sea ice did not obey the model; it actually began to grow—until 2016, when it then began to retreat. The two poles have a pattern of doing the opposite. Overall, right now the global sea-ice cover is slightly down—as one might expect for the long-cycle.

Cloud Cover

This data was a key part of my argument. Fortunately, skilled scientists still maintain the database. Cloud cover fell by 4 per cent from 1980 to 2001. As noted above, more sunlight reached the surface and warmed the planet. Land hardly absorbs heat; by morning it cools, whereas oceans store heat as they receive light energy from the sun. In 2001, there was a 'regime shift', as it were, and cloud cover recovered by 2 per cent and has remained stable.

These data-documented changes in cloud cover have led to about three times the amount of energy reaching the Earth's surface than is computed for carbon dioxide over the same period, yet the models do not feature such decadal changes in cloud cover.

In my book *Chill*, I reported a conversation with NASA (National Aeronautics and Space Administration—in America) experts who admitted that two theories were possible: i) the clouds changed naturally and caused warming; or ii) they were caused by 'global warming' and hence feedback from CO_2. In my view, the regime shift in 2001 does not support the feedback theory, because temperature stopped rising and stayed stable, apart from El Niño oscillations, despite the continued rise of CO_2 levels.

A word is appropriate here about Professor Henrik Svensmark's theories, which I also dealt with in *Chill*. A Danish meteorologist, Svensmark built on the work of colleagues looking at the 11-year solar cycle and its variability. They had found that the shorter (longer) the cycle (e.g. 9–10 years, or 11–12 years), the higher (lower) were the global temperatures. There was a big shift towards shorter cycles during the global-warming phases. Svensmark reasoned that as the visible light varied little over the cycle, something else might be causing the observed relationship. He knew that during the height (trough) of the cycle, the magnetic field of the Earth was stronger (weaker), and he reasoned that the resulting higher or lower flux of cosmic rays would ionise the atmosphere more or less, and these ions would act as 'seeds' for cloud formation. He did find a consistent pattern over two cycles prior to 2001; but whether the cycle repeated was disputed by others.

Svensmark suffered a lot of ridicule, and at first could not get funding, but eventually the European Space Agency drew him to the CERN laboratories in Switzerland to research the cloud seeding on a laboratory scale. The latest results from the labs involved (reported in 2017) show only minor effects. Thus, cloud cover may not be a function of solar-induced magnetic variability. But that is just one theory. For sure, cloud cover does vary on relevant timescale and magnitude.

Another theory, which I signposted in *Chill*, is that solar ultraviolet light, which we now know varies very significantly in cycles, has the power to alter stratospheric temperatures and the polar vortex or Jetstream.[10] This was first proposed by a NASA scientist working under James Hansen and published in 2001. I tried to contact him for follow-up research because he had noticed that wind patterns in the Little Ice Age were different and he surmised that the Jetstream had shifted. I had worked out that such a shift would cool the planet by altering cloud cover and heat release from the oceans. I thought his work was outstandingly important. He didn't reply, however, which is rare. Later, I discovered that he had been moved on to more 'relevant' work, and had been promoted to the UN's special panel.

Nevertheless, work continues on Jetstream dynamics. I still think it will provide a mechanism to explain natural climate cycles, solar derived, but not the kind of solar energy the UN has considered in its models. One US laboratory I visited subsequently revised its model to do just that; and when they explored a dip in solar output (which some solar scientists expect in the next decade), the planet then cooled slightly, despite CO_2 levels.

Sea-level Rise
Sea level has been rising steadily since the world began to warm after the last trough of the 1,000-year cycle. The rate has been around 2 mm/year drawn since 1850 with worldwide data from tidal gauges, and 3 mm/year as assessed by satellites using different methodologies. The satellite group is convinced that their adjusted rates show an 'acceleration', but others are not convinced. The higher rate gives 12 inches per century, of which 4 inches could be man-made. Higher values depend on extrapolating the acceleration. Personally, I am not convinced there is acceleration.

Solar Factors and Internal Variability
The cycles of temperature indicated above—in particular, centennial and millennial patterns—are also found in paleo-records for rainfall, drought,

wildfires, floods and storminess. As noted, this could be entirely due to internal variability and patterns that can result even from a constant flow of energy into a complex system. However, we now know that solar output varies, and this variability has been intensely studied by solar scientists such that they can map the rise and fall of the magnetic field, the flux of cosmic rays, and the output of visible and UV light. These solar specialists primarily rely upon two isotopes—carbon-14 and beryllium-10—both produced in the atmosphere according to the amount of cosmic rays, and hence providing a record of strong or weak solar output. These isotopes are measured in all of the sediments, tree-rings, ice cores, etc., and there is good correlation between the cycles recorded for temperature, rainfall, wind speed and direction, using different 'proxies'. In short, the solar cycles match the environmental cycles.[11]

Thus, there are two potential causes of natural cycles, and in my view they doubtless work together. Even if there is a constant energy flow into a system, the system itself can resonate and generate internal cycles—a phenomenon known as 'stochastic resonance'. Many scientists prefer the simplest of models, and believe 'internal variability' to be ample to explain global variability. The problem is that science always finds multi-factor causes difficult to analyse, and it accounts for many of the failures of predictive environmental science which I outlined above.

An example of resonant systems is the water 'Flow-forms'—water-cascading sculptures, often seen in the grounds of Steiner Waldorf Schools. The top basin receives a constant flow, whereas the outflow has a pulse imparted to it by the shape of the basin. Ocean basins may also share this property. My colleague, whom I will talk about next, feels that this is sufficient to explain the cycles. However, as I noted there is abundant evidence of solar periodicity (ebbing and flowing in intensity) in the records of temperature and rainfall. The Sun has cycles of output, less than 1 per cent for visible light, much more for magnetic flux—by a factor of some 200 per cent—and perhaps as much as 26 per cent for ultraviolet (UV) light. Solar scientists map cycles internal to the Sun—11 years, 22 years, 88 years, 220 years, 500 years, 1,000 years, 2,500 years, and many harmonics of these. These periodicities occur in spectral analysis of sediments, ice cores, stalagmites, tree-rings and so on, and even in ocean surface temperatures. However, the mechanics are not understood. Furthermore, the correlations are complicated by the internal variability. Modern climate scientists seem to avoid the word 'cycle', preferring 'variability' or 'oscillation', hence avoiding the linguistic implication of a 'return'.

Some solar scientists are predicting an imminent return of the Maunder Minimum—a persistent drop in magnetic status that some believe caused the Little Ice Age. The science is not sufficiently developed for accurate prediction, however. I do not expect another LIA trough for 300–400 years, but the descent may begin soon.

Basement Man—W. Jackson Davis
During my time working on ocean issues, I collaborated with Professor W. Jackson Davis, a marine biologist at Santa Cruz, University of California. In his battles with the US establishment (they supported ocean dumping and incineration at sea of toxic waste), he was constantly pressured, even to the point of having his external funding cut. Eventually, his adversaries capitulated, and he was asked by the Monterey International Policy Institute to found an environmental programme for US diplomats. After the marine-policy successes, he went on to co-found the UN Framework Convention on Climate Change, represented a coalition of Pacific Island States as a delegate, and was a drafting author of the Kyoto Protocol on emission reductions.[12] When I sent him a draft of *Chill*, he read it carefully and concluded that the questions I raised must be answered before global-warming theory could be accepted. He had never personally checked the science. He endorsed the book on the cover—something that counted for nothing with some of my 'green' critics.

In the year after the publication of *Chill*, ITN television documentaries wanted to cover my work. We planned to visit Greenland, where I would point to the same retreating ice that so mesmerised David Attenborough, but also to the area where Viking graves were being exposed—thus illustrating the 1,000-year cycle which is outlined above in paleo-cycles and solar science. During the last warm period, the Arctic Ocean was ice-free and the Vikings raised cattle in Greenland.

After several planning meetings, the director of documentaries apologised, telling me that the 'Gorites' above him had pulled the programme. Here the term 'Gorites' refers to supporters of Al Gore, whose documentary film *An Inconvenient Truth* brought people's attention to climate issues on its release in 2006. ITN's science advisor resigned in disgust, and asked me if he could help. I told him I needed to visit Jackson Davis; and he gave me the air-fare (I live as a yogi, with rather slender financial resources). Jackson, having retired, lived then in Boulder, Colorado, coincidentally home of the main US climate laboratory.

I arranged that we would visit two labs, one at the University of Colorado, the other a government special computer lab modelling climate change. We were cordially received by the university, spending five hours there discussing oceanic heat release mechanisms. At the government lab, the meeting was curtailed on a pretext when they saw the data I had, demonstrating clearly that their model was wrong. 'They were worried,' said Jackson. From then on, he decided to help, and asked what he could do. I recommended that he look at the ice-core data.

Jackson spent seven years in his basement crunching numbers—old school, no models. Then we wrote some papers together on the cycles in the ice. It is a long story, with refusals by the leading Western journals and antipathy from the ice-core community of scientists who had not found the cycles; but eventually, as I had told him would be the case, we were published in a leading Chinese-owned international journal of climate science. Our work reached a record number of downloads from the journal's website—around 10,000 scientists worldwide were reading our work and are beginning to cite it. On the back of this we receive weekly new requests to write in other journals, present at conferences and sit on editorial boards. I took up one such request, which I crowd- funded[13] to raise the money to attend, in Prague in February of 2019. It is worth noting here that even invited speakers are usually expected to pay conference fees, hotel and flights—in all, over £1,000.

The Response of the Scientific Establishment to My Work
At the Prague conference there were some very senior scientists, one of whom directed the Geophysical Fluid Dynamics Laboratory at Princeton University, the premier modelling laboratory, and he was a lead author of the IPCC scientific reports. My presentation on the cycles, outlined above, was directly challenging his projection, which ignored them. He admitted they did not do a good job on cycles, and invited me for discussion at his lab. In my paper to the conference, I calculated that natural cycles accounted for 75 per cent of the global-warming signal—and no one questioned that figure.

It is an easy calculation to make, and he admitted that all warming prior to 1950 would be almost entirely natural—indeed, their models show that. The globe warmed by half the current one degree by 1950, and at the same rate as post-1950 warming. However, the remaining half-a-degree, so the IPCC surmise, is 'mostly' anthropogenic (human causation). 'Most' is not an accurate assessment—it could mean anywhere from 51 and 99 per cent. They could not get consensus on a more accurate figure precisely because of the peaking natural cycles, or 'variability', as they prefer to call it.

I presented data which showed that North Atlantic and Pacific cycles likely contributed half of that remaining half (it might be a little less or a little more). A handful of scientists are working on quantifying that ocean effect—some of whom readily agree with my figure of 75 per cent natural, including a Professor of Atmospheric Science, custodian of the key satellite records and a (recent) chief advisor to President Donald Trump. If the second half of the centennial rise is 50 per cent natural, as I reckoned, then the total is readily seen as 75 per cent natural.

Thus, despite a few obstacles and a general lack of invitations, science itself has shown a lot of respect, and a willingness to engage. A great deal of that respect is down to the quality of Jackson Davis's work.

The Response of the Green Movement with Its New Deal

In rather stark contrast, I have received not a single invitation from any environmental campaign organisation, despite my 30-odd years of collaboration with them. Instead, I have been the subject of vilification, slander and libel, the likes of which would have shocked the nuclear and chemical industries of yore, who always treated me with respect and were willing to debate. The left-liberal-green press refused to review my book *Chill*. I have been branded a 'denier', and this has strongly affected other areas of my work as people do not wish to be associated with 'deniers'. Such is the power of labels.[14]

Alert now to the depth of this 'green' antipathy and lack of scientific expertise and understanding, I have monitored the activities of their campaigners. They receive hundreds of millions of dollars to campaign on climate issues, from foundations, governments, the European Union and the UN. They only publicise the things that fit the narrative. And of course, they never mention the 'cycle' word.

The Green New Deal, based entirely on carbon accounting and taxes, is a major movement to establish a global carbon banking system. None of the 'renewable' energy schemes are properly costed, none would be viable without carbon credits,[15] and there is no environmental impact assessment. At the Prague conference, I met a Brazilian professor whose job it was to try and save the Matto Grosso (Serengeti of South America) from the sugar-ethanol industry bent on exporting biofuels to Europe. That is just one example. There are thousands of hydro-projects, biofuel plantations and turbine arrays planned for areas of wilderness, high biodiversity and indigenous communities throughout Africa, SE Asia, SE Europe and South America. It appears that the Greens do not want to know about the impact on people and wildlife.

The Lessons—Science, Media and Control
One of the most salutary lessons for me has been the collusion of science, media and environmental campaigns. Vast funds are available. Scientists, via press release specialists in the Institutes, feed the media, which now includes all environmental groups also with their media specialists, always emphasising 'threat'—and governments respond by increasing science funds. The UK government has announced a grant of £1.2 billion for one new climate computer that will rival any in the world. Globally, I estimate that at least $5 billion is spent annually on climate science.

The lesson of past environmental science was always clear: prediction is a waste of resources—the environment is too complex. There is always a simple calculation of the 'envelope' for change—in any direction—and thus resources should be focused on clean production technologies and resilience to change. Unfortunately, there is not much profit, nor computer science, in sustainable, ecologically robust systems, and much, much more in the technology to mitigate the predicted changes. And, of course, that supports a global technocracy as well as attendant bankers, brokers and investment managers. With carbon taxes in the pipeline, together with credits and derivatives, there are trillions of dollars on the table.

That is one very big 'prior commitment' to a complex global ecosystem model, and no one is enthusiastic about changing it. But science does move on. Without fanfare, the goal posts have been moved. No one now talks about 3 degrees—the danger level is now 1.5 degrees. Behind the scenes, the crucial parameter for the heating power of CO_2 has been halved. I mooted this in my book *Chill*, based on specialist advice to the UN in 2004 which they were then ignoring. It has been generally recognised within the science community that the models overstate the expected warming by a factor of two. Of course, this is not given much publicity; and all this is totally ignored by the left-liberal-green coalition, which continues to promulgate the fiction that all of the one-degree warming since pre-industrial times is man-made.

'Warming' is not the issue. In all prehistory, warming has been ecologically beneficial, and it is cooling that is dangerous because it is accompanied by mega-drought. This has turned many a civilisation to dust. The natural 1,000-year cycle is small in temperature—just one degree globally, and three degrees in the polar regions—but key areas suffer drought, caused by Jetstream changes: China, the northern plains of the USA, Argentina and Australia. These are all areas that produce the global food surplus that feeds 67 countries that cannot feed themselves.

In our work on Antarctic cycles, we proposed a 'mother cycle' that generates the other global cycles. It is regular as clockwork, and though not exact, its variance is calculable. We expect natural cooling over the next two decades, followed by a plateau of warmth with a few decades-long dips for perhaps 100 years, and then a descent into the next Little Ice Age in about 300 years' time. My concern is that with no warming, the bottom will fall out of the environmental cause, and then right-wing forces will dismiss all of the environmental concerns as a fear-mongering attempt by socialist greens to command and control the global economy.

Many 'greens' think that 'capitalism' is the cause of the global crisis; however, capital can only follow the demands of consumers. The 'demand' side of the equation, not the 'control' side, is where consciousness needs to be changed, but it requires a rather different set of 'campaigners'. It is just possible that the corona virus pandemic will put consumers in touch with other values, and the system will change to become community- and planet-friendly. Or otherwise, where the command-and-controllers try to manage the crisis such that the 'normal' global economy is re-instated, with all its planet-destroying consumerism.

I doubt the world can return to normal—many people may experience economic as well as mortal fears, but they cannot fail to notice cleaner air, the birdsong and the quiet.

Notes

1. Following the article by Richard Phethean in issue 94 of *New View* magazine (Winter 2019), where he drew upon my work, a number of the magazine's readers pointed to the fact that my book *Chill* was, at that time, some 11 years old, and so perhaps 'out of date'. Of course *Chill* was also an historical document, showing how the science and politics had become enmeshed, eventually driving the lack of debate on climate issues. So I agreed to write an 'update' for *New View* readers—an article on which the current chapter is based.

2. Richard Phethean, 'What is the truth about Global Warming?', and Terry Boardman, 'NATO's 70th birthday and the UN COP 25 Climate Conference in Madrid'—both published in *New View* magazine, issue 94, Winter 2019–2020 (see www.newview.org.uk/issues.php).

3. CFCs are a class of volatile organic substances—chlorinated fluorine-carbon compounds, at first classified as so inert that it was 'the least toxic substance known to man'—such that computer technicians who used it as a cleaning fluid were reputed to also wash their dishes with it. However, once it volatilised, it ascended to the upper atmosphere where it met heavy-duty radiation which liberated the chlorine atoms, and they then stripped the ozone layer. This reaction was predicted by a few scientists, but their minority warning was ignored and it went into mass production and uncontrolled release. One assumption of the 'dilute and disperse' policy was that the tap could be turned off if data showed an impact. In fact, the first data from the UK Antarctic science team was disbelieved because it clashed with computer models. Once realised, the international community did act quickly to ban and substitute the use of this substance.

4. PCBs are poly-chlorinated hydrocarbons and were used extensively throughout the world as insulation fluid for electrical transformers. Their disposal to landfill was initially unregulated: they volatilise, and can be found throughout the oceans and, most especially, in the Arctic food chains upon which indigenous people depended. Only later was it discovered that the compound is carcinogenic, immune-suppressant and gender-bending. Production was banned, but it can be found in the fatty tissue of all marine mammals, and many Arctic communities can no longer hunt traditional prey such as seals and whales.

5. See Peter Taylor, 'The state of the marine environment: a critique of the work and role of the joint Group of Experts on Scientific Aspects of Marine Pollution (GESAMP)', *Marine Pollution Bulletin*, 26 (3), March 1993, pp. 120–7; DOI: 10.1016/0025-326X(93)90120-9, available at https://tinyurl.com/2j35f5rx (accessed 14 May 2024). This analysis reviews the failure of the UN system of pollution control based upon 'dilute and disperse' policies for toxic substances—in particular, the treatment of dissenting voices in the scientific community. Other relevant work can be accessed at: https://www.researchgate.net/profile/Peter-Taylor-5/research.

6. This is a complex field. The Sun emits a constant stream of radiation (rays) such as sunlight, as well as 'particles' or ions known as the 'solar wind'. The latter carries with it a magnetic field, which both augments the Earth's magnetic field (geomagnetism) and protects the Earth from heavy-duty cosmic 'rays'—actually, also regarded as 'particles' that travel at high speed and come from outside the solar system (also known as Galactic

Cosmic Rays). Until the satellite era, it was assumed that solar output was a 'constant'. In fact, visible light varies by only 0.1 per cent over the short-term 'sunspot cycle' of 11 years, enough at 1.36 watts/square metre to cause slight changes in ocean surface temperature (between 0.1 and 0.2 degrees Celsius). It was assumed that such changes cancelled out over the rising and falling of the cycle. However, late in the satellite era two discoveries emerged: i) there were long-term fluctuations over centuries, which accumulated from about 1650, the low point in a cycle of 1,000 years (and these were significant, with estimates varying from 1.5 to 2.5 watts/square metre—note that the cumulative CO_2 effect is calculated at 1.8 watts); papers began to appear from 1999 showing a long-term rise in the magnetic flux over the same long-cycle of about 200 per cent. Almost immediately, scientists, some well connected to the IPCC, began publishing critiques of the methodology, and with lower estimates that would not challenge the attribution figures for CO_2 in their models. Furthermore, in the last decade, data has emerged that ultraviolet (UV) wavelengths vary much more, at about 26 per cent. Again, the models assume no tangible effect on surface temperatures, but this ignores papers from as early as 2001 that pointed to wind-pattern changes, hence ocean-current changes, cloudiness, rainfall, storminess and heat transfer. There is now a flurry of papers looking at the UV link to changes in the Jetstream—the high-atmospheric winds that drive storm-tracks (see below for other effects). The literature is large and complex, but a very good summary exists in Jasper Kirkby, 'Cosmic rays and climate', *Surveys in Geophysics*, 28, 2007, pp. 333–75, doi: 10.1007/s10712-008-9030-6; some details available at https://tinyurl.com/28er655e.

7. The flux of CO_2 infrared radiation at the surface is what accounts for 75 per cent of the computed anthropogenic GHG effect (other GHG molecules from industry add to this). However, clouds and water vapour emit the same kind of radiation—known as long-wave or infrared—and until recently there were no deployed instruments that could resolve the slightly different wavelengths. To my knowledge, only one science team has been working on this (Daniel Feldman & 5 others, 'Observational determination of surface radiative forcing by CO_2 from 2000–2010', *Nature*, 519, March 2015, pp. 339–43; doi: 1038/nature/14240, available at https://tinyurl.com/4ctfvejx, accessed 14 May 2024); and although they conclude their paper with 'these results confirm theoretical predictions of the atmospheric greenhouse effect due to anthropogenic emissions', my reading is that they show an almost 50 per cent less effect, and I am in communication with the researchers in an attempt to resolve this question.

8. El Niño was named after a rhythmic collapse of the anchovy fisheries off the coast of Peru, because it often occurred at the Christmas celebration of 'the Christ child'. In fact, it is an oscillation of wind patterns. Niño years are those

when the 'normal' easterly offshore winds die down, with the result that wind-forced upwelling of the cold nutrient-rich waters which sustain the fisheries begin to fail. This happens roughly every three years, but 'super El Niños' occur approximately every 12 years. The effects are not limited to Peru, but are felt throughout the tropical belt, bringing heavy rainfall, flooding and landslides in some regions, and drought in others. The phenomenon is a 'charge–recharge' oscillator involving the top 300 metres of the central Pacific, and known as ENSO—or El Niño Southern Oscillation. There was a super Niño in 2016 and it raised global temperatures by 0.6 degrees. They have fallen back over the last three years, but without the dip expected from 'La Niña', when the winds start up again, and which cools the planet.

9. Varves are lines of dark and light sediment associated with deposition in lakes. The darker layers have more organic matter. In many cases they provide an annual record, rather like tree-rings. Each layer can be analysed for pollen, charcoal, blown sand, and other indicators of a variety of environmental conditions surrounding the lake. This is the primary source of data on the cyclic nature of wildfires, which are primarily a function of drought and changes in wind patterns. Statistical analyses reveal long-term cycles, two of which, the 100-year and 750-year cycles, occur in the southern South American continent, concurrent with northern hemisphere cycles of 60–100 years, and 800–1,100 years.

10. Each polar region is surrounded by an atmospheric vortex of high-level wind known as the Jetstream, where westerly winds of 200 km/hour are common. The jets are driven by the temperature difference between polar and sub-tropical masses of air. Early work (in 2001) showed that the vortex contracts and moves polewards during times of high solar output, and vice versa. When contracted, speeds are higher and the winds more 'zonal' (i.e. horizontally flatter), and when expanded, speed is slower and the pattern more meridional (i.e. longitudinal) and 'loopy'. This is readily seen to affect 'weather' across the globe: when expanded and loopy, Arctic or Antarctic air masses are drawn further south in the down-loop, and warm air drawn north in the up-loop. When contracted and zonal, more warmth is generally drawn up from the tropics. The key piece of new research showed that during the Little Ice Age (part of the 1,000-year cycle), the winds were stronger but also less zonal, perhaps also loopy. A pattern such as this can also be seen in the 11-year cycle. These patterns strongly affect the weather and in cycles, also therefore, the climate. Yet research is perfunctory. In 2008, I visited the UK's main climate-computer team at the Hadley Centre near Exeter, and asked to see their Jetstream specialists. Not only did they not have any, but they didn't even know where to find the best data (from services to airlines which used the Jetstream to save fuel!). Now, it is a

key area of frontier research and, so far, is all-but ignored by the IPCC reports. According to my simple analytical perspective, 'loopy-ness' means a cooling planet and is a consequence of reduced solar output in the UV spectrum. We will eventually hear more of this.

11. Carbon-14 is an isotope created when high-energy cosmic 'rays' hit and transform nitrogen atoms in the upper atmosphere, from whence it pervades all levels. The isotope can be tracked when it is absorbed in terrestrial carbon, such as sub-fossil organic material, and thus found in tree-rings etc. It is therefore a 'proxy' for the strength of the solar 'wind' and the shielding effect that has on cosmic rays entering the Earth's atmosphere. Similarly, Beryllium-10 is created by the collision of cosmic rays with oxygen atoms, but falls as a metallic dust and can be measured in ice cores.

12. The Kyoto Protocol was drafted in 1995 and signed in 1997 in Kyoto, Japan, by the majority of nations, with the key exception of Russia, China and the USA. After about ten years, Russia and China joined the mechanisms relating to carbon credits—where other countries could purchase their forgone emissions. Essentially, the Protocol set targets for global emission reductions from a baseline of 1990. However, the treaty acknowledged that economic growth was still dependent upon fossil fuel consumption, and thus 'developing countries', including China, were given generous allowances for continued growth, whilst the 'Western' economies, including Japan, agreed to reduce their emissions to compensate and slow the growth of global carbon-dioxide levels. Cynics would say it was a way to appease environmental campaigners, whilst not compromising global economic growth, as a large amount of Western industrial production relocated to China (and Indonesia, Brazil and India). Of course, the industrialists benefited hugely from lower wages and less environmental and safety regulation. In effect, Western emissions were exported, and global emissions continued to rise at the same rate. Meanwhile, the Western economies invested heavily in 'renewable energy' supply. Thus, this two-pronged programme reduced Western emissions and met the Protocol targets. Kyoto was replaced by the Paris Agreement in 2015, with significant dissent only from the USA.

13. Usually, scientists belong to an institution which pays such fees—publication, travel, conference fee, accommodation etc. It is in the interests of the Institute to promote their science. Publication fees for journals range from $4,000 for the top journals like *Nature* or *Science*, to a few hundred dollars for Chinese, Russian or Indian journals. Exceptions are usually only made for scientists from the developing world. In our work, some friends who follow my work at a German institute of landscape architecture offered at the outset to cover such fees. They contributed half of the Prague costs.

14. The 'denial' label is largely used by the media and environmental campaigners to justify excluding critics, or as in the case of the BBC, not giving unjustified airtime to dissenting views which apparently conflict with 'settled' science. It is never defined. Most critics do not deny the globe has warmed or that carbon dioxide and human emissions have a part to play; but they disagree with either the percentage contribution, the final outcome, or the consequences and the cost.

15. Carbon credits are varied, but essentially carbon emissions are costed and then factored in to economic decisions. For example, the UK's latest nuclear-power project, at an estimated £24 billion, would never be funded (even by the Chinese state, which is the main contributor) without guarantees of a premium price for its carbon-free electricity. That premium is recovered from an effective carbon tax on consumers. Wind farms and solar arrays are similarly funded. There is also an international trade in 'carbon derivatives'—too complex to go into here!

1.2 Reviews of *Chill: A Reassessment of Global Warming Theory* in the Scientific Journal *The Holocene* (2009) and in *Caduceus*, 78 (2009)

Review by Professor Frank Chambers, University of Gloucester, in *The Holocene* (2009) of both Global warming—the complete briefing (4th edition), John Houghton, Cambridge: Cambridge University Press, 2009, 438 pp. £24.99, paperback. ISBN 978-0-521-70916-3, and *Chill: A Reassessment of Global Warming Theory* Peter Taylor, Forest Row: Clairview Books, 2009, 416 pp., £14.99, paperback. ISBN 978-1905570-19-5

> Just as the Arctic and Antarctic have in the past exhibited opposite climatic tendencies, so too are these volumes poles apart in their portrayal and assessment of scientific views on climate change. Houghton's new edition of *Global warming—the complete briefing* is a third re-write (and hence fourth edition) of a volume that first appeared in 1994. Earlier editions have been widely praised as succinct and accessible accounts of the findings of successive deliberations of the Intergovernmental Panel on Climate Change (the four Assessment Reports); Houghton, of course, was chair or co-chair of the IPCC from 1988 to 2002. This fourth edition is very well illustrated with coloured graphs, photographs and diagrams, which add to its attractiveness. As an accessible summary of the Fourth Assessment Report (FAR), it cannot be beaten. As well as setting out the scientific case for 'Global Warming', albeit with only a brief look at past climates (pp. 69–92), Houghton looks to the twenty-first century and beyond (pp. 137–71), the impacts of climate change, why we [*sic*] should be concerned, weighs the scientific uncertainty, considers climate-change mitigation, looks at energy and transport (this latter aspect omits discussion of shipping and rail, referring mainly to (road) motor vehicles, and a paragraph on aviation), and reviews technologies 'of the future' (photovoltaics, fuel-cells). The final chapter on the 'Global Village', in exhorting environmental stewardship, shows the influence on Houghton's thinking of the John Ray Initiative and his deeply held Christian faith. *Chill* has a very different take on the veracity of the IPCC's findings. Its author, Peter Taylor, takes a personal journey through some of the published literature on climate change. In the ten chapters of Part One, Taylor examines the case for human-induced Global

Warming, focusing his attention on research that seems to refute the hypothesis. However, he ranges more widely than this, and from mainstream climate science he decodes the cryptic messages in scientific papers containing data that also appear to contradict parts of the IPCC thesis, but which the authors failed to point out. He finds the evidence for carbon dioxide as a major driver of climate change to be weak; the climate models used to project future climate scenarios to be deficient to the point of uselessness; and the part of the IPCC thesis that relies on carbon dioxide as the principal driver of recent climate change to be not just dubious but discredited. Interestingly, Taylor is much less dismissive of the possible roles of atmospheric methane, nitrous oxide and CFCs in effecting changes in climate, but focuses his attention on CO_2.

He believes 'the carbon dioxide forcing effect has been overstated by at least a factor of three, and as much as four or five' (p. 185) in computer simulations used by IPCC. Having found the IPCC guilty of 'prior commitment' to the influence of CO_2, Taylor constructs an alternative theory to explain most of the 'Global Warming' of the late twentieth century, based largely on the combined natural forcing factors of solar forcing (visible light, UV, and electromagnetic pulses), ocean cycles and cloud thinning. Taylor is an avowed environmentalist, so it is not possible to dismiss his volume as the ranting of an unreconstructed fossil-fuel combusting industrialist—far from it. Though not a climate modeller, climatologist or a paleo-climatologist, in Part Two of the volume he establishes his environmental, scientific and policy reviewing credentials, and as a consequence he becomes the most cited author in the reference list. Nevertheless, Taylor writes well and persuasively. Those who think the IPCC's case is watertight would do well to read *Chill*: it risks turning the claimed watertight 'consensus' scientific case into a colander. In the six chapters of Part Two, Taylor discusses the politics of climate change, with a focus in the later chapters on the UK. His polemical commentary on politicisation of the science is perspicacious, illuminating, and—dare I say it—chilling. He contends that environmental groups have colluded with governments to promulgate a dangerously simplified message about climate change in which—he argues—the current remedies are more damaging than the purported ailments. In his deconstruction of the IPCC case he contends: 'Man-made global warming ... is an illusion borne of a particular way of looking at the world ... a mass delusion coupled to massive collusion of interests' (p. 360). Whether or not one concurs with his earlier reassessment of the climate science, which is based on selected reading of the scientific literature, field-based readers of *The Holocene* may well find themselves agreeing with his complaint that huge sums are spent on climate modelling of a virtual world, but far less money goes into extracting data from the real world –; yet it is the real world that we (and our ancestors and descendants) inhabit. He finishes with an anthropological reflection on 'Global Warming' and the reasons for disagreements (cf. Hulme, 2009) over both the science and mitigation policies, advocating instead a focus on adaptation and resilience. Undergraduates can use Houghton's volume as an entree to the IPCC Assessment Report(s); for detail, they are guided to the IPCC assessment reports, and to some other supportive literature. If a university education is to mean anything, however, it is to the peer-reviewed literature that they should be guided—but to which, and to whose papers? Interestingly, of 230 citations by Taylor to other authors, Houghton cites fewer than ten of these. While 'Global Warming' features in the titles of both volumes, it is as if their authors are reviewing completely different scientific fields. In Part Two of Taylor's volume the reasons for this become apparent.

The most valuable aspects of Taylor's volume are less his reassessment of climate change, with which many readers of this journal may take issue, and which contains some errors and inconsistencies (not least the assertion that the 'Little Ice Age' is the largest amplitude climate change in the past 20,000 years (p. 126), overlooking the rather stronger fluctuation of the Younger Dryas); rather, the strength is his perspicacious commentary on the way the real scientific uncertainties, indeterminants and nuances concerning climate change are ignored and the case simplified, distorted and misrepresented in the environmental campaigning, political and policy-making arenas, not to mention in some scientific circles. For example, Taylor comments that the contribution of the sun in recent climate change is acknowledged by the IPCC in FAR (albeit in his view downplayed), but in the Summary for Policymakers, it is ignored. Indeed, it is only mentioned briefly in Houghton's volume (p. 81) and is later dismissed as insignificant (p. 166), yet the sun's role and percentage contribution to recorded climate change is far from resolved (cf. Scafetta, 2009).

In this respect, one could argue that an unsatisfactory aspect of Houghton's volume is the failure to discuss more fully the criticisms and evident (or not-so-evident) shortcomings of the IPCC work; but that is not the purpose of the book. Taylor's volume more than compensates for this. Indeed, reading the two may leave students puzzled as to whether the authors inhabit the same 'Global Village' (or planet); both have strong ethical beliefs and environmental credentials, yet are worlds apart in their views both as to the cause(s) of recent climate change, and the direction of current (Houghton's continued warming; Taylor's flat-lining, with a recent fall) and future climate change (respectively: strong warming; chilling) in the twenty-first century. Time will tell who was more wrong. While Houghton's volume is intended as an undergraduate text and has the weight of the IPCC FAR and the earlier Assessment Reports behind it, Taylor's volume (particularly Part Two) is the more challenging read, for all—irrespective of one's views on the primary causes of recent climate change.

References

Hulme, M. 2009: *Why we disagree about climate change*. Cambridge University Press.

Scafetta, N. 2009: Empirical analysis of the solar contribution to global mean surface air temperature. *Journal of Atmospheric and Solar-Terrestrial Physics*, in press.

Chill reviewed by Professor David Bellamy in *Caduceus*, 78 (2009)

> The truth is out—as I have always suspected, carbon-induced global warming is a scam. My congratulations to Peter Taylor for spilling the beans so elegantly. This meticulously researched book comes from decades of his involvement in pollution research and his critique of mathematical modelling in that field. This alone gives him much authority to criticise the modellers who have deliberately or accidentally projected their output as 'predictions' rather than 'scenarios' or 'story lines', for that is all they are.
>
> His very strong presentation of the role of cyclic changes (and their drivers) as the underlying factors in climate change is exemplary. One can only enquire why these factors are almost entirely missing from the UN committee's projections, despite the fact that climate has changed repeatedly and regularly in sync with those cycles. Taylor outlines the pressures and prejudices, prior commitments and the need for simplistic messages to policy-makers that have so misled the UN's panel.
>
> His detailed coverage of the impact of heat storage and transport in the oceans is first-rate; again, leaving us to wonder why this is more or less ignored in much of the conventional, 'global warming' approach.

This book details how what he believes may prove to be the world's biggest scientific error gained impetus thanks to the fact that the media thrives on bad news and many of the perpetrators fell for their own dogma.

Taylor outlines matters in a polite but devastating critique of the UN system—where it is obvious to me, in blunter language, that a research gravy-train developed, backed by jet-set travel to conferences in choice locations around the globe, each well laced with cordon bleu cuisine for the top tables and adulation from a regular caravanserai of hangers-on, swelling a spurious and unscientific consensus, based upon 'garbage in garbage out', and backed by an inner clique of peer-reviewers who push the party line. In my view, this makes a mockery of the scientific process of rigorous debate, relegating it to the level of McCarthyism.

It is clear from Taylor's more measured tone that as soon as real-time data from ice cores and satellites challenged the cherry-picker's shapely models paraded on the catwalks of media hype, things began to get a little fraught. Cries of 'deniers' and worse were slung at any scientist who spoke against the Armageddon cries of doom and gloom.

Those with most to lose began to quaver, dropping the term 'global warming' and replacing it with 'climate change', thus extending the time-scale of their fears, while continuing with alarm calls about unproven tipping points just around the corner.

As this timely book was approaching publication, 'Aunty BeeB', lauded for her impartiality and in cahoots with the Met Office, warned we were heading for three of the driest, hottest summers on record. They got them all wrong, including this year, tipped as 'summer of the barbecue'.

Mr Fish, famous for his gaff about the 1987 hurricane that actually did happen with catastrophic results, brought things back into focus. A colleague from the Met Office, who had openly castigated him for his 1987 'one that got away', was the same person now warning us about the pending barbecue.

They still can't even get their short-term forecasts right, so what hope for their long-distance fantasies? In fact, the BBC has just had to announce that the globe has been cooling for the past 10 years and that the cycles Taylor warns about are turning the ocean so cool that global warming will be put on hold for another decade.

As he points out, you can't have it both ways—if natural cycles can now dampen down warming, they could also have amplified it in the first place—and he gives a figure of 80% for natural drivers and a maximum of 20% for greenhouse gases. He goes on to argue that cutting emissions by half will then only affect 10% of the driving force and have no discernible effect on what the climate does next.

Lest we forget, back in the swinging seventies we were being warned of an impending, catastrophic ice age. Then climate change notched up a rise of around 0.6—or was it 0.7—of one degree Celsius and the gravy-train set off. Now the real, chilling truth is that over the past decade, despite the fact that more and more carbon dioxide has been pouring into the atmosphere, much of the rise that the global 'warmers' have done their best to scare the world with, has been wiped out. The glib response from the warmers is that, if this recent cycle of global cooling had not started, the temperatures would already be climbing higher. None of their models revealed such a trend or, if they did, they were not placed in the public domain.

Please read this book and chill out about carbon-induced, global warming.

Professor David J Bellamy, OBE, FLS.

PART 2: CLIMATE ALARMISM

Preface

I use here the term 'alarmism' as it points to the well-funded alliance between climate scientists as an institution—particularly at the UN, the mainstream media and campaigning organisations supported by billionaire philanthropists. This is openly advertised as a Climate Coalition and it clearly promotes *fear* that is particularly aimed at young people. I recommend a timely new book by Mike Hulme, at one-time director of the Tyndall Centre for Climate Research at the Manchester—*Climate Change is(n't) Everything* (Polity Press, London, 2024), in which he uses the term 'climatism' to describe the way climate alarmism has trumped all other issues. Hulme is now Professor of Geography at Cambridge University. Note: despite his detailed critique of the way science has been affected by the political realm, he is still convinced human-sources of emission are the dominant driving force of global warming.

Part 2. 1 Weather Chaos

This article first appeared in Caduceus No.88, (2014) *'As Current Weather Chaos: IPCC models fail'.*

Five years have passed since my original article in *Caduceus*—*Cool inconvenient truths expose flawed CO_2 model*. The alarmist position of the UN's climate panel still holds sway over governments, academies and environmental groups, but there has been no further surface warming, as I expected. Much new science and data supports my position as outlined in my 2009 book, *Chill: A Reassessment of Global Warming Theory*.[1]

In this short time there have been some discernible shifts in regional climate patterns—for example, in 2007 the UK had its first torrential summer flooding and in 2008 the first of five colder winters, with some severe weather in the North. On a global level, there have been five more years with no further warming, with some databases now registering 17 years without warming, some showing a slight cooling but all showing what is termed a 'pause' in temperature rise that has confounded the predictions of climate models (computer simulations of the global dynamic).

My original predictions

In the autumn of 2008, after a summer of torrential rain and floods, I visited the Hadley Centre, the UK Meteorological Office's research headquarters, near Exeter, for discussions on natural cycles and solar activity. I was cordially received, spending several hours with their leading scientists. I followed up the meeting with a detailed briefing note to their chief scientist, Vicky Pope, outlining what I believed were major omissions in their computer programming (the absence of ocean cycles and any link to solar magnetic activity and the Jetstream). Based on my reading of the marginalised science of ocean cycles and solar activity, I made the following predictions:

- Global temperatures would fall, *unless* a major El Niño event intervened toward the end of the decade, in which case a global cooling would be delayed. (As I expected, there was a strong El Niño in 2010, temperatures have not risen and without that event, cooling would be more evident—most data-sets now show a slight cooling since 2003.).
- In the North East Atlantic region, severe winter weather would return (it is on a 60-year oceanic cycle), whereas the Met Office simulations wrongly assumed the carbon dioxide effect was more powerful than these natural cycles.
- Summers would become wetter—and the torrential rains and floods, first evident in 2007, would be repeated (the flooding has become stronger and extended also into this last, milder winter).
- The Sun's magnetic field would continue to flatline, despite the expected peak of sunspots in 2012/13 (NASA predicted an early onset and record maximum for this 24th cycle in 2006; some of its critics predicted a late onset and low peak, which proved to be correct). I predicted this would eventually lead to the first public discussions of a possible new Little Ice Age where food supplies would become a key issue and even the BBC covered this topic toward the end of 2013.[2]

I also thought that Arctic summer sea ice would return to normal—and certainly would not disappear by 2013 as predicted by a tranche of US and UK experts. In fact, the sea ice rebounded by 20% in 2008/9, but fell to a modern record low in 2012, only to recover to within normal bounds in 2013.[3]

At the other end of the globe, Antarctic sea ice *exceeded* modern records and more than compensated the Arctic variability, leaving the global average slightly raised over the past 30 years [4]. Arctic warming is understood by all the real Arctic specialists to be due to the transfer of heat from the Pacific and Atlantic Oceans and subject to a long cycle of 70-80 years (see Figure 1), as well as a very long cycle of 800-1,000 years, where the last peak saw Vikings growing crops and raising cattle on the coast of Greenland (until about 1350 AD when they were forced to abandon the settlements as the sea ice and deep cold returned). All these predictions were based upon a reading of peer-reviewed science literature, which had been systematically marginalised by the Met Office, NASA and the UN Panel. [5]

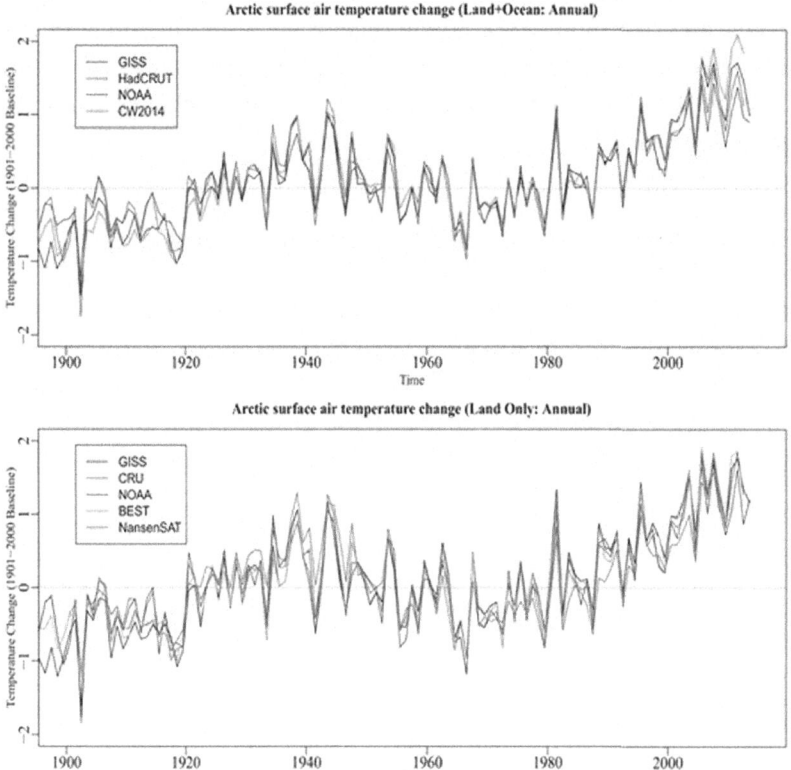

Figure 1. Arctic Surface Air Temperature—land only, over the last century. Note the 70-80 year cycle peaks. There is a long-term (the last 100 years) warming trend in the Arctic of approximately 0.2 C per decade, which is twice the global rate over the same period, but the first degree is clearly of natural origin and the second phase will have some natural component too. {2024 Note: GISS, CRU, HadCRUT, NOAA, BEST and NansenSAT are different compilations from the US, UK and Norway of Arctic station data}.

Control of global temperatures

Global temperatures are controlled by sea-surface temperature—roughly 70% of the planet is ocean. Only the oceans can *store* significant amounts of heat (from solar rays) and 80% of land-surface warmth is derived from the oceans. The balance of warmth on the planet varies as the seas store or release heat in cycles of warming and cooling in the different ocean basins—sometimes in phase and sometimes counteracting each other.

The mechanisms are not well understood. During the global warming peak period (1980-2005), no less than *five* shorter-term cycles (from 10 to 100 years) peaked together and on top of one longer-term cycle peak (800-1,400 years)—responsible for the Little Ice Age (a trough) and Medieval Warm Period, The Dark Ages (trough), Roman Warm Period and Minoan Warm Period. Currently, sea surface and land temperatures have flatlined (Figure 3, 4, 5) at the top of this global warm cycle. So—yes, all ecosystems are changing along with the climate, and will continually do so, and all of the concerns expressed by, for example, the IPCC's most recent report on the 'impacts' of climate change would be with us anyway.

Extreme weather not caused by 'accelerated' warming

This ten-year hiatus needs to be borne in mind when claims are made that 'extreme weather' events are caused by 'accelerated' warming; first, there is no evidence that extreme events are more common (accepted by the IPCC working group of scientists), merely that they are 'expected' to increase according to computer models; nor is warming accelerating.

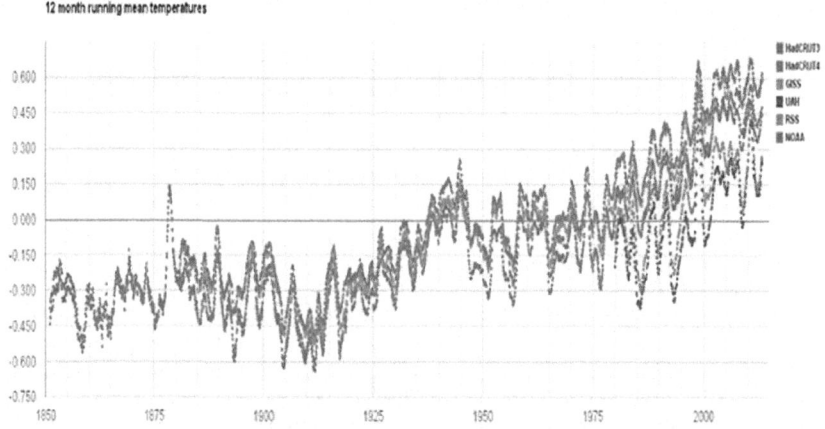

Figure 2. Long-term temperature changes in the instrumental record from six sources (including satellite data from 1979).

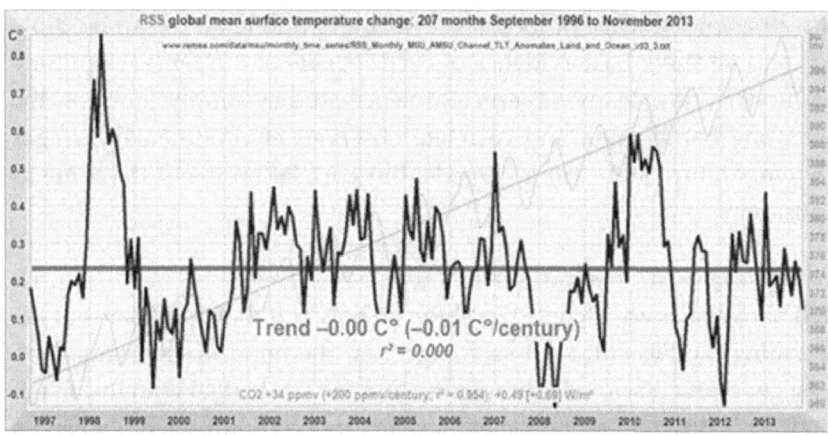

Figure 3. Global mean surface temperature change derived from satellite measurements showing the longest period of zero trend (from Remote Sensing Systems on contract to the US Government). Note: other data-sets vary from 10-17 years with zero trend). 2000-2010 is the warmest decade in the short 150 year instrumental record, but 2003-13 is slightly cooler than the previous 10 years.

Figure 5 shows the accumulated cyclone energy for *all* global storms (source: University of Florida); despite media hysteria *all* data, including the number of tornadoes and cyclones, show recent falls in storm intensity and frequency.

The ongoing 'melting' of the Greenland ice cap and Arctic sea ice, Himalayan glaciers, Arctic permafrost and calving of Antarctic ice-shelves, with consequent minor rises in sea level (totalling 2mm/year),

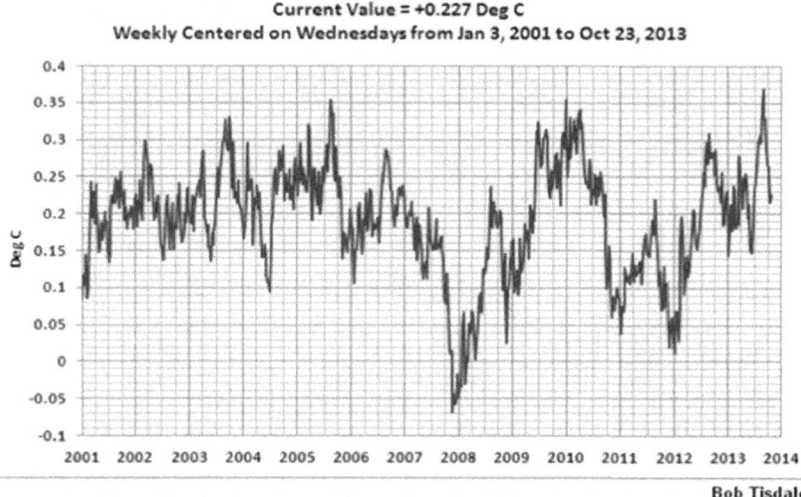

Figure 4. Global mean sea-surface temperature change (SST) since 2001 (from Bob Tisdale's specialist blog).

are all a consequence of long-term warming unrelated to carbon dioxide and all show past evidence of cyclic events of the same magnitude as modern day. Many superficial science studies simply jump on the warming bandwagon and correlate observed environmental changes to temperature and carbon dioxide, but correlation is not the same as causation.

Defending a 'prior commitment' model

The above facts are incontrovertible—so how is it that defendants of the alarming models still hold such a grip on the mind of environmentalists, governments, science academies and the UN? I deal with this in my book: it is down to a phenomenon called 'prior commitment', when an apparently scientific model of a potential problem is first accepted and then followed by massive investments of finance, technological solutions and, of course, political *face*. Critics have pointed out the huge mismatch of model predictions and actual data (Figure 6)—most particularly over the past two decades—but such critics are marginalised by the scientific and political establishment. There is nothing new in that, of course, but the self-insulated science community are now joined by all *environmental* groups in a broad coalition of perpetual alarm.

It is possible, given how little we know, for the world to warm further by natural means. We are at the peak of a natural long-cycle that could

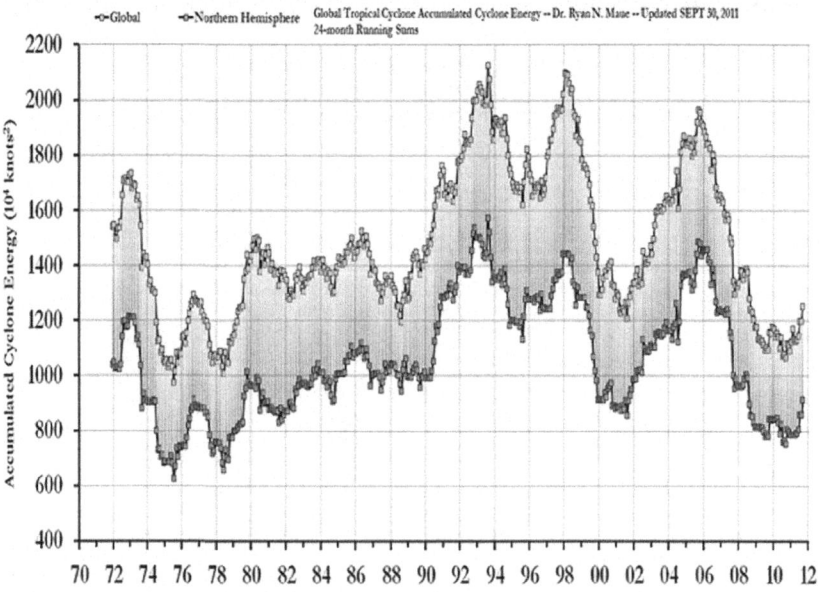

Figure 5. *Accumulated cyclone energy for all global storms*

have several peaks before the next fall. Defenders of the suite of models are now claiming that 'natural variability' (they studiously avoid using the term *cycle*) has only temporarily overridden the global warming effect of carbon dioxide. In this they are admitting that right now natural forces are more powerful than anthropogenic influences—but then completely fail to acknowledge that these same forces could have amplified the past warming signal, thus falsely confirming the more extreme carbon-dioxide calculations—which range from a relatively harmless 1.5 C rise by 2100, through to a dangerous 4.5 C. [6]

One explanation for the slowdown claimed by the modellers is that the 'missing' heat has been transferred from the surface (0-700m) to the deeper ocean (700-2000m). If this is indeed the cause of the hiatus, then that heat is well-dissipated and demonstrates the ability of the natural system to balance itself, but there is no good evidence to support this new assertion—the data is simply not detailed enough at the depths involved.[7] There is a current alarm ringing with regard to heat build-up in the Pacific that could herald the strongest El Niño yet. We will know later this year—but whatever the records it sets, the main force is natural, on top of a much smaller greenhouse-gas effect. The planet will start to cool when La Niña years outnumber El Niño events and that is what I think will kick in over the next decade. Either way, 'extreme' events, even cooling, will all be laid at the door of carbon emissions—too much has been invested for anyone to say, 'we got the science wrong'.

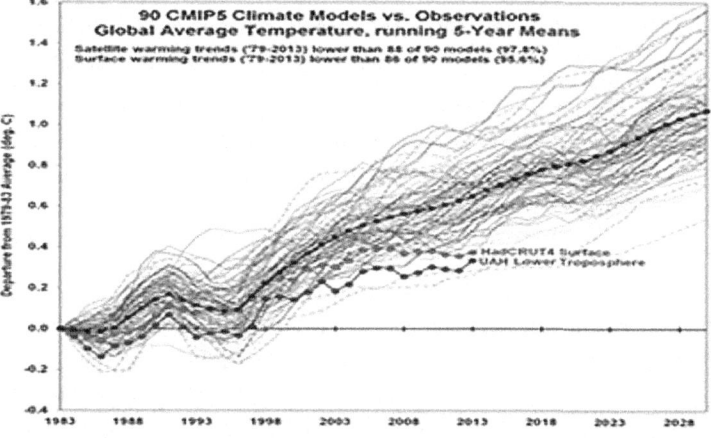

Figure 6. Showing 90 different model projections, only two of which track observations. The black line is the average of all models and the standard adopted by the UN's IPCC (courtesy: Roy Spencer, UAH, USA).

Sun's magnetic and other cycles

In my view, the current rise, the pause and a potential future cooling are all driven by whatever under-researched and poorly understood mechanisms *have driven these cycles in the past*. Some scientists working on the causes of these natural cycles *do* expect a fall. This is because there is evidence that these peaks and troughs are driven by changes in the non-visible radiation and magnetic fields of the Sun—which, as I pointed out in my previous article, produce long cycles of magnetic variability that coincide with warm and cool periods. Such mechanisms are now under intensive research precisely because there *have* been major changes in the Sun's behaviour in the last five years that coincide with the lack of temperature rise. Scientists have matched cyclic changes in ocean currents, in particular the Gulf Stream, with changes in solar activity (see Figure 7).

The current 11-year cycle (Figure 8) had a delayed start in 2009, by almost two years (which NASA's expensive predictive computer models completely failed to predict). During such delays the magnetic field drops, more cosmic radiation enters the atmosphere (some scientists think this seeds cloud cover) and, whereas visible radiation, the wavelengths responsible for heating the oceans, only falls by 0.1%, radiation in the far-UV spectrum plummets by a factor of 10. My own reading of the science (outlined in *Chill*), points to this far-UV as the causal factor of ocean cycle.

The low magnetic field level is a *correlate* and thus a potential 'proxy' in the record obtainable from ice cores. There may be a number of factors at play, including cosmic rays, but the UV variability affects the stratospheric transfer of heat to the lower atmosphere, most particularly in the northern hemisphere, and low periods of UV are associated with a southerly shift of the Jetstream and 'break-outs' of the polar vortex—exactly as has been observed in the past five years.

If this situation continues, we will soon know whether major cooling is on the cards. The Sun's past is known reasonably well from the ice-cores proxies and several low periods have occurred, ranging from one to five solar cycles (10-50 years). At present, nobody knows the mechanism, but some calculations based on correlation of the Solar Inertial Momentum (in cycles determined by the giant planets) predict a prolonged shutdown. This is why the BBC has aired the views of solar scientists, including a chief advisor to the Met Office, that a new 'Maunder Minimum' of solar activity is probable and could herald another Little Ice Age.[9]

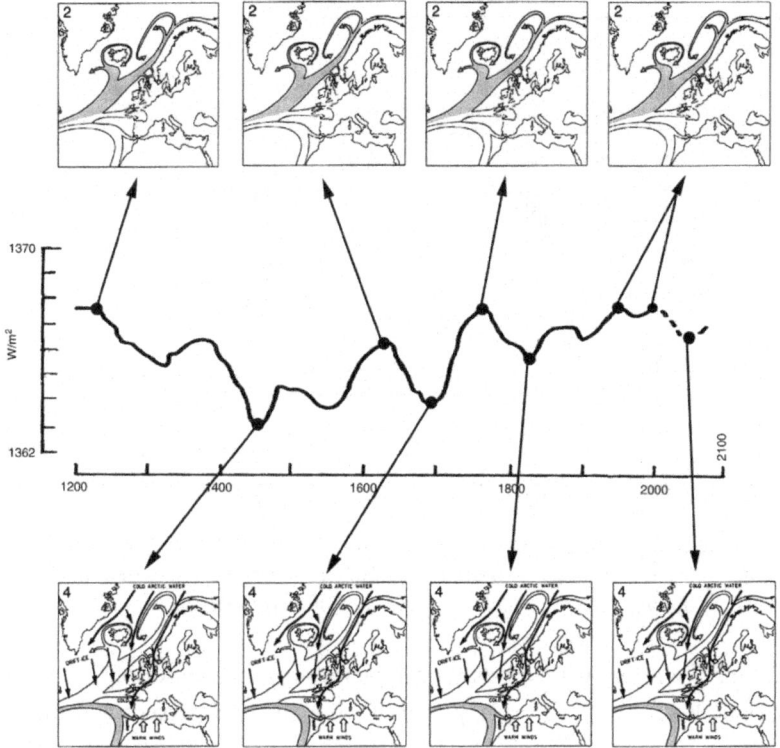

Figure 7. Phases of the westerly movement of warm Atlantic water (grey shade) toward Europe (from sediment data) are correlated with solar variability: the low points in activity match a southward shift in ocean currents.[8] The drivers of these surface currents are wind patterns which are themselves determined by the variable course of the Jetstream[9] (from Mörner, Global Planetary Change, 2010).

More accurate, revised model

Early in 2010, determined to get some answers to the questions raised in *Chill* and accompanied by my long-term colleague, Professor Jackson Davis (drafting author of the Kyoto Protocol, who also endorsed *Chill*), I visited the main US government climate research centre (National Center for Atmospheric Research) in Boulder, Colorado. We discussed modelling, the past cycles, the role of solar UV, future solar cycles and deficiencies in the way the models treated aerosols.

Three years later, the NCAR team produced a revised model incorporating these factors, including the potential longer-term drop in solar magnetic activity.[10] This model—the most advanced of its kind, in my opinion—though I am no fan of modelling, predicts no further warming and some cooling between now and 2050, and thereafter a return of the warming (Figure 9).

58 | CLIMATE, COVID AND CONSPIRACY

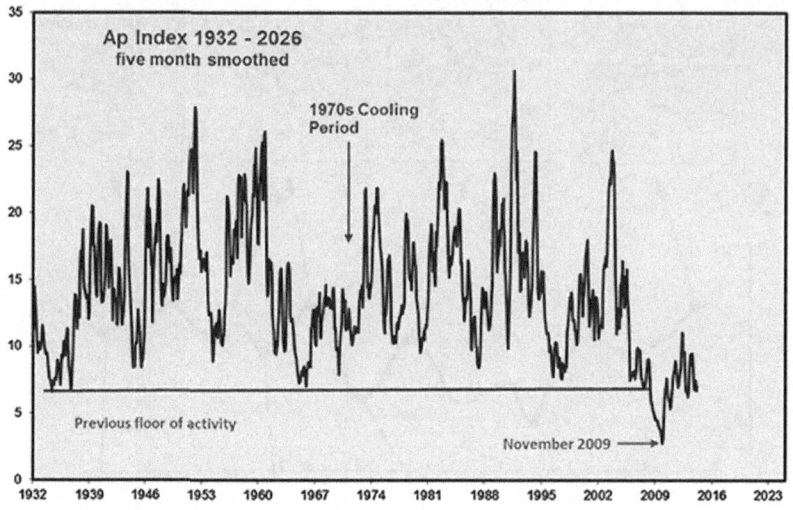

Figure 8. Recent fall in the solar magnetic field (Ap Index). {2024 Commentary: curiously this abrupt fall coincides with a steep fall in global temperatures of 0.6°C—see Figs 3 & 4) during 2008 for which there is no obvious explanation}

The NCAR team still prefer some factors for the power of CO_2 which I would hold are no longer justified—hence they project a return of warming. If the CO_2 effect has been over-estimated, then there will be cooling and the eventual return of warming is unlikely before the end of this century—and then not by 2.5 degrees since 1950, as shown in Figure 9, but more likely 1.5 degrees and hence below the supposed 'danger' threshold of 2 degrees promulgated by the IPCC. One can understand the reluctance of the IPCC bureaucrats to publicise these shifts in the science in their recent 2013 Summary (of the science) for Policy Makers.

However, this is *not* to say there is no danger, as some 'sceptics' claim—I have argued that we are *already* at the danger threshold for climate change as far as the most vulnerable human populations are concerned.

NGOs' remedy betrays the world's poor

The apparently green remedy for international climate aid and sustainable development relies upon carbon trading and global taxes, which will mobilise *trillions* of dollars. But these funds will be channelled through an unreformed IMF and directed toward very expensive renewable energy paths—turbines, hydro-schemes, solar PV and biofuels, all industrial technologies provided by multinational corporations.

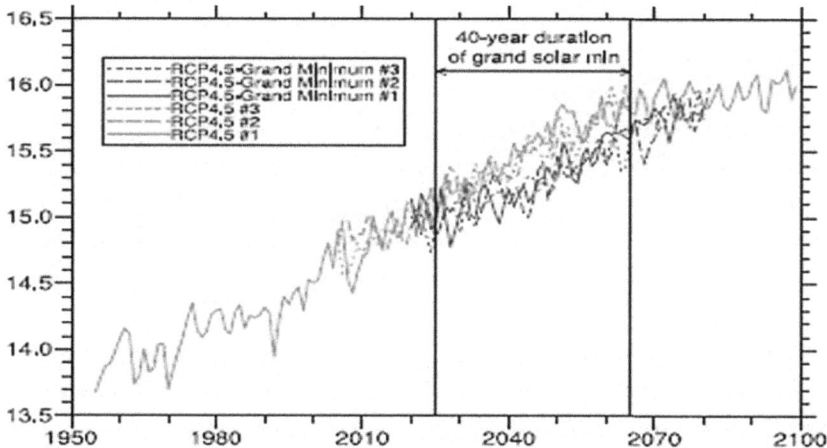

Figure 9. Time series of globally averaged surface air temperature for standard model projections (pale grey) and three grand solar minimum simulations (darker shade). The duration of the grand solar minimum is indicated from 2025 to 2065. Note that the standard models all show a projected rise of about 1.5 degrees C between 1950 and 2010 when the observed rise was only half of that. The revised model shows no further warming from 2010 to 2050 and an extra warming by 2100 of 1 degree above the present level, (Meehl et al, 2013).

My experience of those 'developing' countries most at risk from climate change (whatever the cause) is that they need resilient communities supported by ecological agriculture, clean water and sanitation. Two years ago, in an analysis for the *Lifeworks Foundation*, I discovered that less than 5% of all development aid reached these ecological grass roots.[11] The rest was aimed at creating clone economies in service to the developed world. The poorest and most marginal people to that global economy benefited hardly at all and the clean technology transfer programmes will hardly affect the climate and leave them just as vulnerable.

Notes

1. P. Taylor *Chill: A Reassessment of Global Warming Theory* (Clairview, Forest Row, 2009).

2. http://www.bbc.co.uk/blogs/paulhudson/posts/Real-risk-of-a-Maunder-minimum-Little-Ice-Age-says-leading-scientist

3. http://arctic.atmos.uiuc.edu/cryosphere/arctic.sea.ice.interactive.html

4. http://arctic.atmos.uiuc.edu/cryosphere/iphone/images/iphone.anomaly.global.pngAntarctic sea ice—global ice cover

5. There is a chapter in *Chill* on ocean cycles and how they peaked together in the global warming period from 1980-2005 (see temperature graphs for the previous 'hiatus' between 1945-1975).

6. It is not generally appreciated that predictions of the temperature response to carbon dioxide and other GHGs are based upon theoretical calculations and a wide band of uncertainty with regard to 'climate sensitivity'. Recently, a group of leading climate scientists signed on to a paper stating that only the lower bounds could be supported by actual data http://pubs.giss.nasa.gov/abs/ot03100r.html

7. For a detailed discussion see http://www.nature.com/news/climate-change-the-case-of-the-missing-heat-1.14525; and also, a more critical review: http://judithcurry.com/2014/01/21/ocean-heat-content-uncertainties/. The latter also addresses related issues of sea-level rise (not accelerating!).

8. N.-A. Mörner / *Global and Planetary Change* 72 (2010) 282–293

9. Mörner believes the driving force of surface current changes is related to acceleration and deceleration of the Earth's spin, but I think it more likely that magnetic and far-UV cycles are affecting the Jetstream as the proximal cause of the shift: see—Shindell et.al., (2001), *Science* 294, p.1491.

10. G. Meehl et al (2013) *Geophysical Research Letters*, VOL. 40,1789–1793.

11. See the report—Resilience (www.ethos-uk.com) {2024 update: this website is no longer current. Mail to: peter.j.taylor@protonmail.com for a free pdf}

2.2 Hothouse Earth

This article was published in Caduceus *Issue 99 (2019).*

We are assailed by warnings that the climate is now unstable—with record heatwaves, droughts, species facing the 6th wave of mass extinction, and a slippery slope toward an irreversible 'hothouse' Earth, not seen since the time of the dinosaurs. These are not just media concoctions but the words of some scientists writing in learned journals.[1] We are also told, especially by the left-liberal-green newspapers, that there is no longer any scientific debate on the reality of anthropogenic global warming.[2] Indeed, a professor of philosophy at East Anglia University when recently invited to a discussion on the BBC and, claiming the debate was over, added he was a lifelong 'green', and refused to participate on the grounds that a climate change 'denier' had also been invited.[3]

Denial is a strangely powerful term of our times. It surfaced first as 'Holocaust denial' and was taken up by the green 'climate coalition' as 'climate change denial'. Whilst there are a few who deny the globe has warmed or maintain that humans have made no contribution, they are largely ignorant of the science and not representative of the substantial body of 'scepticism' with regard to the conclusions of the so-called consensus.

Nevertheless, the term is used as a blanket defence to block debate with anyone who has any scientific criticism, particularly criticism of the use of computer simulations to predict futures. The issue is not whether global warming is 'real', but what percentage contribution do human emissions make? This question is central to any policy response that would involve human agency—if the human contribution is the main driver of change, then we have agency; if it is small, then nothing we do will alter the course of natural climate change and we should focus upon creating resilience to that change.

Currently, almost every government policy, with the exception of the United States, assumes that humans are the main drivers. Almost all climate scientists and the major science institutions act and talk as if this contribution has been well established. In my own work I went against this apparent consensus, publishing data and analysis that showed a *natural* peaking of warmth during the late 20th century and arguing that this rise had been used to (falsely) confirm the model predictions.[4]

There are now several new papers confirming my estimates made in 2008, that most of the warming is the product of natural cycles not accounted for in the models (I estimated 75–80%). In fact, the UN special panel (IPCC) in its 2013 (5th) Report, though somewhat unreported has already admitted that at least 50% of the centennial warming is natural. That a shift is under way can be seen in the briefings of the media and the goals of the Paris Agreement where the focus is now upon staying within a 'safe limit' of 1.5°C; whereas the early models had focused upon an expected and dangerous future 3°C. Very few scientists now include the more extreme temperature rises above 3 degrees and there is a large and growing body of science that argues a doubling of CO_2 levels expected on current trends by 2060, will lead not to 3°C but to 1.5–2°.[5]

When the 'expected' doubling effect was three or even four degrees (e.g. in models built for the 1st IPCC meeting), 1.5° would have seemed relatively harmless. The reason for this shift is that the real-world data upon which the revisions are based shows about half the warming compared to expected in the period 1990-2018 (Fig. 1). The much-feared feedback effects have failed to manifest and there is now a real debate on just how much the observed late 20th-century warming is man-made and how much is natural.

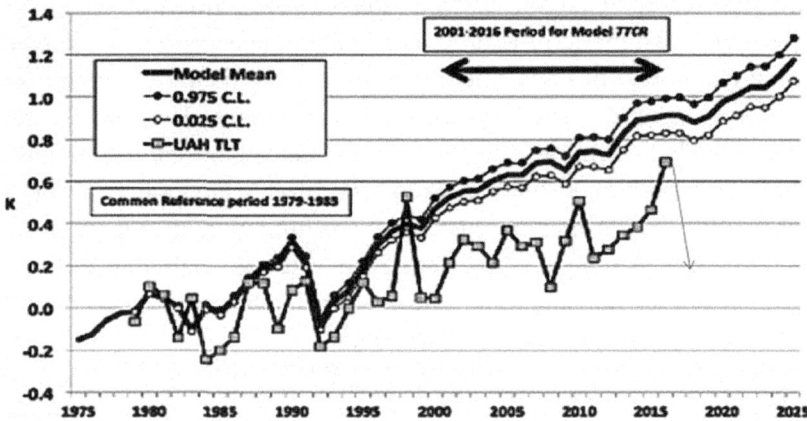

Figure 1. Mean of CIMP-5 Model Simulations and Observations of Global Lower Tropospheric Temperature (from Christy and McNider, 2017).
Note: I have updated the graph to 2018 (grey arrow and see also Fig 6 for post-2016 ENSO event).
{2024 Commentary: Christy's comparisons are regularly updated—the observed temperatures dived and then peaked with the recent El Niños of 2016, 2029 and 2024, touching the lower of the simulations, but as La Niña conditions return, the pattern of divergence will no doubt be maintained.}

New IPCC Report—moving the goalposts

It has been obvious for some time within the climate science community that global warming is unlikely to breach the 2 degree 'danger limit' by the end of the 21st century, a limit that they set in the first of their reports 28 years ago. That figure was always arbitrary, but it is clear from the rate of warming over the last 40 years, at 0.13 degrees/decade, with a slowdown over the past 20 years (0.09/decade), that the danger limit is unlikely to be reached. The addition of CO_2 to the atmosphere continues at a steady 2ppm per year, but the temperature rise has levelled off. It is therefore no surprise that the huge bureaucracy of alarm, both scientific and political, together with the multi-billion-dollar financial interests related to carbon trading, credits and derivatives, has now in the recent IPCC Report, *Global Warming of 1.5°C*, moved the goalposts to 1.5 degrees, in order to avoid reaching the former danger limit, which is now portrayed not as a threshold, but as a catastrophe.

These limits are quoted against a base-level of 'pre-industrial' levels, but no mention is made that that base-level is a natural trough in a wave of amplitude of 1 degree—and which is where we are now—or that the wave has had higher natural amplitudes in former warm periods, without catastrophic consequences for global ecosystems. For example, between 6-8 thousand years ago, the Arctic Ocean was ice-free in the summer; 2,000 years ago, the Romans cultivated vineyards in Northern England; and 1,000 years ago white storks nested in Edinburgh. Much recent published science shows that most (at least 75%) of the current warm period is part of the natural cycle. This means that the computer projections of the IPCC are erroneous by a factor of 2 or 3.

Geological history shows us that carbon dioxide does not have the power to prevent the natural cycle from turning downward, as it is expected to do by 2030.

As far as I am aware, there is no detailed critique of the IPCC projections. Such a critique would necessarily involve:

1. A close examination of the projections for the growth of carbon dioxide in relation to realistic projections of economic growth and exploitation of fossil fuels.
2. A review of recent science on the power of CO_2 to affect temperature; many recent papers have downgraded the 'sensitivity' of the atmosphere to an increase in greenhouse gases due to the 'saturation' effect.
3. An examination of the timescales for emission control to take effect based upon the lower power figures for atmospheric sensitivity.

The suspicion remains, therefore, that the IPCC, whose panellists' vested interests are not apparent, has become an industrial and financial lobby directed at UN funding programmes, most of which subsidise Western industrial production of 'clean' technology. The former, influential head of IPCC, Rajendra Pachauri, was also head of a major, renewable energy technology conglomerate in India. If nations were to aim for a zero-coal-emissions policy by 2050, for example, there would be a massive development of wind turbines and hydro schemes in mountain regions, biofuel plantations in tropical forest zones, tidal barrages on wild estuaries and solar arrays across vast areas of desert. These developments would have major impacts upon landscape, community, indigenous peoples and biodiversity.

IPCC has quietly endorsed my scientific analysis
My analysis showing 75% natural forces of warming is relatively easy to support by careful reading of the IPCC itself. Their models and data show that the world has warmed by approximately 1 degree Celsius since pre-industrial times (say 1750-1850). They agree that from 1900-50 the world warmed by 0.5°C naturally—there was a warm phase between 1920 and 1940 (driven, I suspect, by cyclic release of heat from the oceans). Then a standstill occurred from 1950-75 and the remaining rise of 0.5°C occurred primarily from 1980-2000 at the same rate as 1920-40. The IPCC argues, based entirely on computer simulations, that 'most' of the post-1950 warming is caused by human agency.

'Most' is not a precise term and is the result of consensus making. The actual percentage is hugely important. If, as I believe the data shows, the changes are 75% natural, then reducing global emissions by 50%—a tall order by 2050—will affect 12.5% of the driving force and have no significant effect on the natural climate cycle.

Several reputable specialists have recently come to the same conclusion as I—that the late 20th-century rise is largely natural, by factoring in the natural cycle known as the Atlantic Multi-decadal Oscillation or AMO.[6] This cycle was releasing heat from the oceans in both the pre-1950 period and the late 20th-century period. It has an amplitude from trough to peak of 0.4°C. Thus, this natural warming must have contributed to the post-1950 temperature rise and the data shows this; therefore the IPCC's use of the imprecise term 'most' (being of human agency) of the warming since 1950 does not tally with real-world data (Fig. 2).

One can readily see when the trend is removed that the AMO has driven a rise from 1980 to 2000 of 0.4°C. Source: The Climate Data Guide: Atlantic Multi-decadal Oscillation (AMO). Retrieved from https://climatedataguide.ucar.edu/climate-data/atlantic-multi-decadal-oscillation-amo.

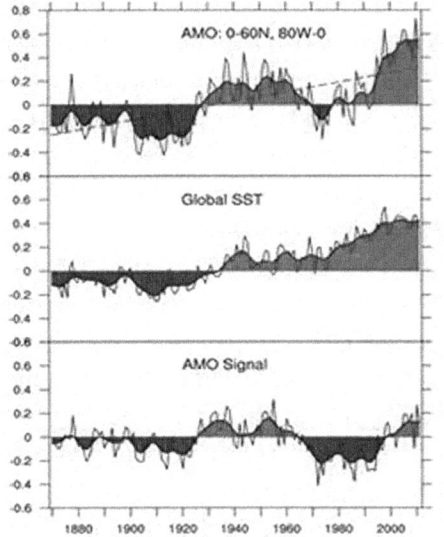

Figure. 2. Atlantic Multi-decadal Oscillation: 1870–2011
Note: *The Atlantic oscillation in surface temperatures influences the global temperature, here shown to have an amplitude of about 0.4 °C.*

{*2024 Commentary*: there is no clear methodology in the literature isolating the global effect of the AMO oscillation. Using a crude eyeball method—the lower panel indicates a 'signal' on the global Sea Surface Temperature (SST)—mid-panel, from a low in 1970 of -0.3 to a high of + 0.15, hence approximately a 0.45 rise from 1975; and the global SST mid-panel shows an amplitude of 0.2~0.4 or 0.6°C from about 1920 to 2020. In this case, the AMO could account for 75% of the global centennial rise in SST. The centennial rise in land temperatures is usually reckoned to 0.8°C from 1900~2000—but note that the previous oscillation of the AMO from 1910-1940 is of similar amplitude and at a time when carbon-dioxide levels were ten-times lower than during the second cycle. The recent 1~1.2°C total rise to 2024 is constituted of 2000~2015 with *no surface rise* and the extra comes from two strong back-to-back El Niño Southern Oscillations.}

Simple arithmetic shows that ocean cycles can account for 80-90% of the observed warming since 1900. {*2024 Commentary:* I should have explained that this figure includes other ocean cycles than the AMO, such as the long-cycle of Little Ice Age recovery from 1850 at 0.05°C / decade.} Even if we take the IPCC 'most' to mean any figure in excess of 50% but not more than 99%, then the lower figure of the consensus range at 51% gives 75% to natural forces—and this lower figure is much more in line with the observed amplitude of the AMO.

Is global cooling likely in a near future?
Furthermore, although I was lambasted by some environmentalists for suggesting that the Earth may cool in the near future, one leading team of modellers recently looked at the consequences of a pause in the solar magnetic

cycle, as I argued was likely to happen, and they anticipated a decline with a trough between 2030 and 2060 (see Fig. 3). Using a different technique, a team from the Chinese Academy of Sciences extrapolated cycles that were revealed in tree-rings on the Tibetan Plateau, and they expect a global cycle to now turn downward (Fig.4).[7] This does not mean we can relax and all is 'safe'; after all, climate change is causing problems *now* and historically a cooling phase is more dangerous to food supplies and health.

I visited the National Center for Atmospheric Research's labs in Boulder, CO, in 2010 and shortly afterwards they updated their model (see Fig.4) to simulate the Jetstream changes I discussed in *Chill*. These fluctuations are thought to be caused by variable UV light. What are the chances of a solar minimum and how will it interact with ocean cycles?

These latter factors are very hard to predict. The Sun's energy is certainly declining, most particularly the magnetic field and in the far-UV spectrum. The last 11-year cycle was 25% down on the previous (and wholly unexpected by NASA) and the expectation for the next cycle is another drop of the same magnitude. Specialists are split as to whether there will be a short, Dalton-type minimum of two low cycles, or a Maunder-type for five cycles (coincident with the Little Ice Age when glaciers advanced globally and the Thames froze over).

Whenever the IPCC dealt with solar influences they doggedly avoided the variability of the magnetic field and its potential to influ-

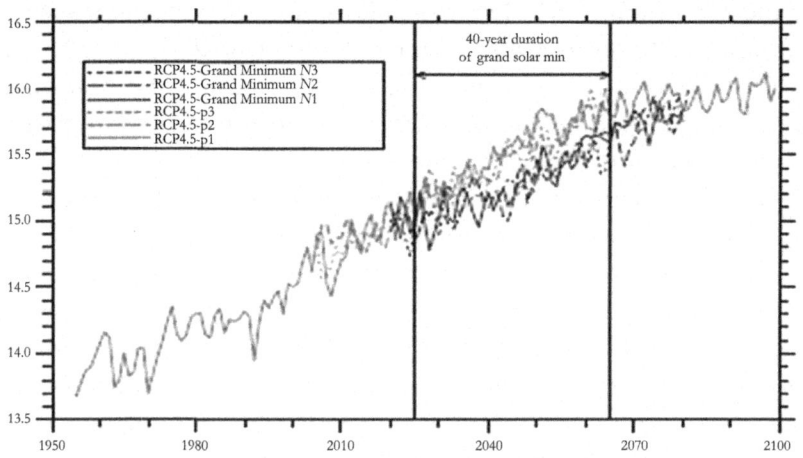

Figure 3. Predicting cooling.
From Meehl et al (2013): *two sets of simulations, the pale grey lines representing the usual AGW prediction using a standard model; the darker lines simulate the effect of a drop in solar activity commensurate with the Maunder Minimum and Little Ice Age period. Note: from about 2025 under the reduced solar scenario there is a pronounced cooling and temperatures do not recover until about 2050.*[8]

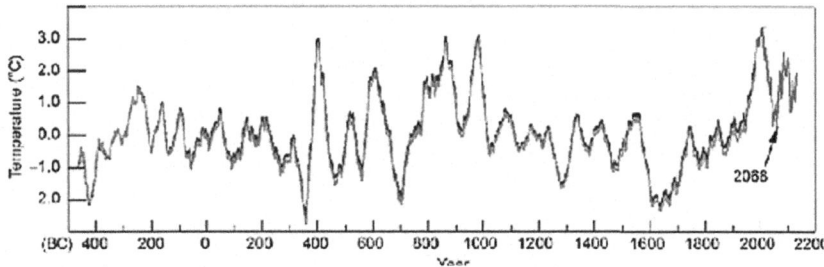

Figure 4. Extrapolated cycles from tree-ring data on the Tibetan Plateau. From Liu (ref.7).
Note: the extrapolation begins around 2010 and was marked red in the original.

ence climate—but now, it is a major area of research. Fig. 5 shows the progression of recent solar cycles, a fact upon which projections of possible future cooling are based. In the last three cycles, NASA, with its array of super-computers, failed in all it predictions, whereas German scientist Dr Theodor Landscheidt, a much-maligned outsider, predicted the post-1990 decline; and if there is a longer minimum, as he predicted is possible, it should be named after him.[9]

Cycles rather than 'Records' the real issue
There are now hundreds of papers in paleo-climatology showing correlation of cycles in tree-rings, peat-deposits, stalagmites, ocean and lake sediments, with solar magnetic cycles but the mechanical links were not known and only the latest computer models are now attempting to incorporate them. It is highly unlikely that this cyclic behaviour ended in 1950 and clearly it contributes substantially to the warming since then.

It should be obvious that the issue is not whether wildfires are at a record level, coral is bleaching, droughts and floods and hurricanes abound, and biodiversity has a problem—all of that is to be expected in a natural cycle that last peaked 1,000 years ago. The problem is that the cycle is now peaking, with 7.5 billion humans having sequestered the global ecosystem—and thus any climate change impacts are hugely amplified.

The ocean surface is also less alkaline due to enhanced levels of carbon dioxide (but it will never be 'acidic') and that may well cause shifts in ocean biodiversity and, although this has happened before at much higher levels of carbon dioxide and ocean life survived, extinctions did occur and it is an issue that needs more study.

However, substantially reducing emissions would be very expensive, raise energy prices and affect the poorer sections of society. The cost of emission reduction has to be weighed against the risks and clearly what

68 | CLIMATE, COVID AND CONSPIRACY

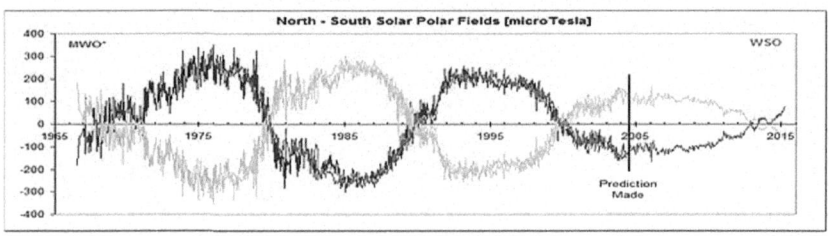

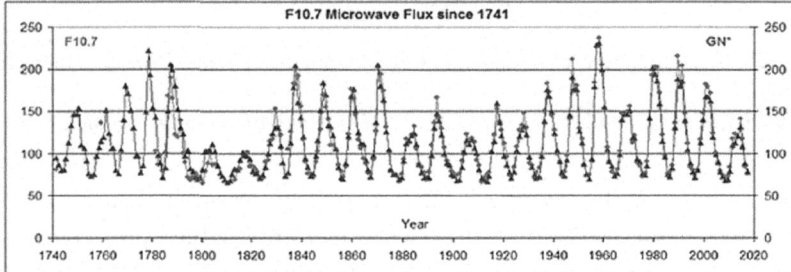

Figure 5. Here are plotted sunspot numbers (GN) in upper graphic and the 10.7cm radio flux, a proxy for UV activity, since 1741 (lower graphic). It can clearly be seen that the Sun's energy is declining from its peak in 1990. Solar specialists expect the next cycle to be lower, a repeat of the 1800-20 low cycles; but some also think the low cycle could extend for a longer period. The upper graphic shows the last four sunspot cycles and the declining polar difference—WSO.

is required is for a substantial percentage of the money now being spent on hopeless 'mitigation' to be refocused on resilience to change. This especially applies to agricultural ecosystems, forests, water supplies, coastal marshes and wildlife reserves, all of which are now under massive pressure.

In whom can we trust?
Shortly after publication of my book, *Chill*, prominent 'greens' challenged my credibility as a 'climate scientist'. This is only right; we have to know whom we can trust. However, my work never claimed to be original science—in this field I am primarily an analyst (and have a good record of accurate analyses). Few 'greens' ever read my work, but I did get a call from the environment correspondent of the BBC, Roger Harrabin, who had read the book and was about to interview Professor John Christy, whose impeccable data and analysis I had quoted.

Christy is chief custodian of NASA's satellite measurements of the global temperature. Harrabin wanted to know what questions he should ask. Well, not: 'Is global warming real, or do humans contribute?', inanities on which 97% of scientists will agree, but 'What *percentage* of the warming is natural?' Christy replied: 'About 75%' and this was broadcast, only then to be buried, but perhaps to resurface in the discussion which the green professor refused to attend.

Though, then again, perhaps not; such media-orchestrated debates tend to drag in real 'deniers' to make for a better spectacle. Who wants to debate percentages? Well, actually, the former Trump appointee at the US Environmental Protection Agency, Scott Pruitt who, after hearing Christy's testimony to Congress, openly stated that the 'human contribution was under debate', for which of course, he was lambasted by the world's campaigning media.

Since that time, I have, in fact, published a climate science paper, jointly with my colleague Professor Jackson Davis at the Environmental Studies Institute in the USA.[10] Our work re-analysed ice-core data, looking more closely at the relationship of CO_2 to temperature and, in doing so, we documented an undescribed cycle of centennial magnitude that seems to trigger warming in the northern hemisphere—and we could extrapolate to show that the modern warmth is right on time.[11]

Media hype and scientific collusion
An illustration of just how far from science the media hype can drive debate and how far scientists can collude by knowing the facts but not raising their heads above the parapet is the recent 'record' warmth, with coral bleaching and global ice meltdown, as temperatures peaked in 2016. The peak was a record 1.2°C above the long-term mean of the instrumental record, but it was caused by the well-known ocean heat-release cycle, the El Niño Southern Oscillation (ENSO), and it has a well-attested amplitude of 0.6°C. Figure 6 shows clearly that global temperatures have now returned to their long-term 'warm period' high by shedding 0.6°C within a year, despite the presence of anthropogenic carbon dioxide! The 21st century is thus far about 0.6° above the mean for the 20th century and about 0.8–0.9° above pre-industrial levels. Incidentally, those levels were in the trough of the Little Ice Age and the current high is within the normal amplitude of that cycle.

{*2024 Commentary:* Note that this graphic ends in 2018. There followed in 2023/2024 another large ENSO peak—an unusual event in the 45-year satellite record, that reached +1.2°C in the anomaly.}

ENSO is instructive: it is a cyclic process in the central Pacific whereby the top 200m of the ocean stores and releases heat over a 3-4-year period, with larger peaks approximately every 12 years. The AMO seems to do the same over an 80-year period and there are at least three

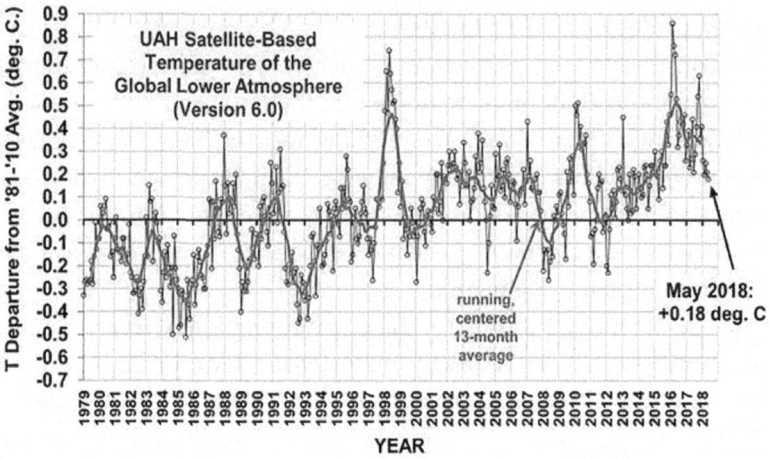

Figure 6. Temperature of the lower atmosphere, which closely follows the surface temperature. This is the only completely global surveillance. Note: from 2000–2015 there is no significant warming (the 'pause'). The record heat in 2016 is due to natural ENSO peaks riding on top of a steady, general warming rate in the 40-year satellite record of 0.13°C per decade, which, if continued, would add 1.04°C by 2100. Note also: this anomaly is calculated with reference to the 1981-2010 average, as recommended by the World Meteorological Organisation.

other cycles in other ocean basins—the north Pacific, the Arctic and the Southern Ocean around Antarctica. Their varying phases interact on a global scale but the mechanisms are poorly known (and cannot be readily incorporated into models).

These decadal cycles must involve heat storage and release phases of the shallower waters and they play out on top of a much longer cycle of about 1,000 years from peak to peak and with a global amplitude of about 1 degree C. This long cycle, which appears to involve deeper water masses, rose to the present peak from a trough roughly 400 years ago. In the last peak, the Vikings colonised and raised cattle in Greenland and white storks nested in Scotland (the species is prospecting now for nest sites in England). In a significantly higher previous peak (at 6000 BC and about 1°C higher than today), the lake-dwellers of Somerset ate pelicans for breakfast and the Arctic Ocean was ice-free. There was no global meltdown and no 'tipping points' were breached.

The heat is on—and then off

So, what of the current heatwave? Perhaps it is that which has galvanised the somewhat moribund, post-Paris campaigners? First, it is a repeat of previous waves—in the USA in 2013 and Russia in 2010, when the Jetstream maintained 'blocking high pressure systems', preventing moist, cool air-flow from the oceans. Continental air then becomes very dry and cloud-free, soil moisture falls and forests become incendiary.

Wildfire becomes an issue because another factor has changed: there has been widespread conversion of old-growth forest to young, single-species plantation, with suppression of natural wildfire. Young trees have thinner bark and branches close to the ground, which itself has accumulated flammable debris. The US Forest Service highlighted these elements[12] as central to previous devastating fires (thus far, 2018 is below several previous burned acreages measured in millions).

Media commentators, however, rapidly abandon science in favour of the carbon dioxide demon, when a little research on greenhouse effects would tell them that the enhanced greenhouse effect has little impact on daytime temperatures and is mainly observed at night.

To the non-specialist reader, the situation I describe might appear unbelievable—how could the world's science institutions become so biased, even corruptible? A little reflection on the phenomenal level of corruption, malpractice and even criminality within the banking system provides a parallel. Add to that the Catch-22 of prior commitment: models have to be believed because so much investment has been based upon them; and when real-world data contradicts the models, the data is disbelieved or even doctored to agree with the model expectations!

It is easier now to see the political process in action. Under Trump and deregulation, funding for the simulators is cut and critics invited to speak. Here in the UK, as Jeremy Corbyn and Labour seek the high moral grounds of climate mitigation, renewable subsidies and increasing regulation, the science funders will take note and critics will not be welcome.

One final factor: in 2016, I presented a paper at the World Congress of Anthropology (unpublished as yet) {see link in Appendix}. I work these days more as an anthropologist than an ecologist on why it might be that cycles, irregular periods, spiral mathematics (the longer millennial cycles display Fibonacci series) and 'chaos' theory present such enormous problems to the climate science community, most of whom are men?

Science itself is, of course, a largely left-brain activity. Add to that the mission to predict and control Nature, even human nature, and we have a heady, masculine cocktail—could there be gender issues in climate science? Our discussion was aided by anthropologists 'embedded' in the climate science community—all of whom were female! They are reflecting upon the issue, but constructing a testable hypothesis is not going to be easy!

Notes

1. The idea that we are approaching a 'tipping point' has resurfaced in a push by the Stockholm Resilience Centre in a paper by Will Steffen and signed by a dozen scientists from institutes with a history of alarmism. The paper, 'Trajectories of the Earth System in the Anthropocene' and supplementary material can be accessed: https:// tinyurl.com/y82rw3fk The arguments that human activity could alter the trajectory of the planet toward a 'hothouse' state similar to conditions tens of millions of years ago are weak and the authors display poor knowledge of the Holocene (the last 10,000 years); for example, when, 8,000 years ago, the Arctic Ocean suffered a warm-period meltdown and was ice-free in the summer, but 'tipping' points were not breached.

2. In a letter to *The Guardian*, 27 August, Jonathan Porritt and various campaigners and journalists, including George Monbiot, state: 'We will no longer debate those who deny that human-caused climate change is real' and '…we urge broadcasters to move on—as we have done' (gu.com/letters). Note how the term 'real' is used—no critic of the science debates the reality of a human contribution, but there is a real debate to be had on the percentage contribution, which these signatories now appear desperate to avoid.

3. Rupert Read, a philosophy professor at East Anglia University, refused to take part in a BBC local radio debate on the grounds that a 'climate change denier' had been offered an 'equal' platform (i.e. one of several speakers, the 'denier' Philip Foster, a Cambridge University Natural Sciences graduate, pointed out the natural rise of temperature since the Little Ice Age). The debate can be heard on Radio Cambridgeshire; note in particular the way the accredited expert from the British Antarctic Survey talks of the 1°C rise without any reference to natural cycles: www.youtube.com/watch?v=V3lSRh-I2ZQ

4. In *Chill: A Reassessment of Global Warming Theory* (Clairview, 2009; reviewed in *Caduceus* issue 78; articles in nos 78 and 91). I point to data showing that during the main global warming period of 1980–2000, increased solar insolation, i.e. the amount of sunlight that gets through to the surface, accounted for three times the radiance effect of the increase in atmospheric greenhouse gases and this was due to a 4% reduction in cloud cover.

5. For example: Otto A. et al. Energy budget constraints on climate response. *Nat Geosci* 2013;6:415-16. For a specialist discussion see: https://tinyurl.com/y9a82qpr

6. See: Christy and McNider (2017) *Asia-Pac J Atmos Sci* 2017;53(4),511-18, DOI:10.1007/s13143-017-0070-z; this paper subtracts the effect of natural forces from the observed rise to arrive at an estimate of climate sensitivity and projec-

tion to a doubling in 2060 at about half the IPCC expectation: the maximum rate of anthropogenic warming is derived as 0.096 °C/decade.

7. Liu Y et al. Amplitudes, rates, periodicities and causes of temperature variations in the past 2,485 years and future trends over the central-eastern Tibetan Plateau. *Chinese Sci Bull* 2011;56:2986- 94, doi: 10.1007/s11434-011-4713.

8. Meehl A et al. *Geophys Res Let* 2013;40:1789- 93, doi:10.1002/grl.50361

9. Landscheidt T. 'New Little ICE age instead of global warming', *Energy & Environment* 2003;14(2-3):327-50. See also his book: *Sun, Earth, Man: A Mesh of Cosmic Oscillations: How planets regulate solar eruptions, geomagnetic storms, conditions of life and economic cycles*, Urania Trust, London, 1989.

10. ESI: www.environmentalstudiesinstitute.org/

11. The Antarctic Centennial Oscillation: a natural Paleoclimate Cycle in the southern hemisphere that influences global temperature (*Climate* 2018;6(1): 3); https://tinyurl.com/y7vh54rg and can be downloaded free at: https://tinyurl.com/ ybrhr4lx

12. See the US National Inter-Agency Fire Center for an objective breakdown and comparisons of severity: https://tinyurl.com/8y5zprm .

2.3 Heatwaves And Wildfires

This article first appeared as 'Climate Watch' a regular commentary on climate news in New View *magazine, no. 104, Summer 2022, p. 13*

It is the season of heatwaves and wildfires. The mainstream media now begin their trolling of record temperatures and acres burnt. They don't deal in context. In fact, they are paid *not* to deal in context. Supposedly independent newspapers have teams of 'senior climate correspondents' as part of a global network paid for by billionaire 'philanthropists' following the Bill Gates model of investing money in projects that make money for the overall philanthropic fund. And so the money spiral continues, whether in pharmaceutical solutions to pandemics or the technology of carbon-free energy.

The Independent newspaper kicked off with reports of record highs and heatwaves in Europe and India. The unexplained context is that carbon dioxide contributes virtually nothing to daytime highs—its effects, well-known to the climate-science community, are to raise night-time temperatures. Record daytime temperatures are caused by persistent high-pressure systems and clear skies. Science knows this because the additional radiative flux from carbon-dioxide emissions amounts to about 2.5 watts (per square metre), whereas the natural daytime solar flux at the surface in mid-latitudes lies between 500 and 1,000 watts. The average all-latitude surface flux is 240 watts, and thus the human emissions contribute a non-scary 1 per cent of that. Some scientists think that the Earth has a built-in stability mechanism that easily handles this extra flux.

Concentration of carbon dioxide in the atmosphere increases linearly, but the power to heat falls off rapidly above 300 parts per million. We are at 420 ppm, a 'scary' 50 per cent rise since pre-industrial times and according to *The Independent*, a level not seen in four million years.

So what about the 'global warming' scary 1° rise in temperature since that pre-industrial period? Such an increase is very far from 'unprecedented' as *The Independent* journalist claimed. There is a solid scientific record of a 1,000-year cycle repeating for hundreds of thousands of years evident in the ice-core analyses, and the current warm period is exactly on time. How, then, does the planet engineer its own global warming (and subsequent cooling)? The obvious candidate is changes in cloud cover—and sure enough, there is good data for clouds reducing during the main global-warming period, and by quite enough to account for the warming.

Precisely how the clouds are influenced is still under investigation—though by very few research teams. My best candidate is the fluctuating flux of ultraviolet light during a long solar cycle, this affecting temperature changes in the stratosphere that then work their way down to affect the Jetstream and the displacement of cloud.

The current extremes of heat, wildfire, floods or drought—and less reported, cold snaps—are a consequence of a changing Jetstream. Again, very few people are working on this. One Russian team has just reported statistical effects of such a natural cycle for the Arctic.

The Arctic Ocean is, contrary to media hype, beginning to cool, as is the North Atlantic, and many Arctic stations recorded their highest temperatures around 2010–2016. The whole region has an 80-year cycle with amplitude of 3° (i.e. in the natural course of events it rises from a trough to a peak of this magnitude, exactly as observed from 1940, the last peak one 80-year cycle ago; this is something I have never seen reported in the media).

With regard to global temperatures, they peaked in 2016 under the global effects of a 'super' El Niño cycle (the normal low-amplitude Niño cycle is 3–4 years, but every 12–15 years the amplitude is much greater). Since then, they have fallen back to levels of 20 years ago.

In total, five regional and global cycles interplay, and all are turning downwards, cancelling the most recent warming. It is an open question as to whether the dominant cycles can over-ride the carbon-dioxide effect, and take us step-wise and on-schedule into the next ice age. Ironically, if the greenhouse gas has the power ascribed to it in models, it could save us from the next ice age. And all this hype about temperature actually obscures the most important element of climate change—that of wind direction. The winds are changing and, with them, rainfall patterns—and with that comes crop failures. Not one member of the mainstream media has their eye on that ball. Though they are reporting often enough the 'drought' in Europe and the blocking high-pressure systems in the Atlantic that reduce the westerly rain-bearing winds. That is what happens approaching the 'little ice age', according to the fossil record. My colleagues and I expect that event by 2300, and an ice-age slide over the following 3,000 years, and we don't think carbon dioxide has the power to stop it.

See the above figure (p.135) for the latest satellite record of atmospheric temperature—the only metric I trust (the compiler, Professor John Christy, from Alabama University, had his offices machine-gunned—by assailants unknown; but he has steadfastly refused to adjust his data to fit the mainstream model).

PART 3: SUBTERFUGE

3.1 Heating Power Declines with CO_2 Concentration

This article originally appeared in New View 'Climate Watch' No105 (2022)

There is a curious phenomenon evolving in the climate debate and one that is intensifying. We have become used to the mainstream media and campaigners deferring to the 'science', but what they are actually deferring to is *the authority* in science, as expressed by the National Academies and their selection of governmental representation at the United Nations (UN) binding treaty on climate change. The Intergovernmental Panel on Climate Change (IPCC) is largely made up of government-appointed scientists, and they make a five-yearly science report. The report is liberally distributed to the broader science community in an apparent peer review, but the authors decide how much notice to take of any comments received. It is this apparently authoritative process that has captured almost every government, parliament and all of the mainstream media. We have also seen the intensification of 'exclusion', as media platforms such as the BBC have openly stated they will not present critical views of the UN stance. Even science journals such as *Nature* have stated the same policy.

Rational minds across the political spectrum—conservative, left, liberal and 'green'—assume that such a process could not get something badly wrong. Science, after all, has checks and balances such as peer review and the debate of positions. 'Follow the science' has been a clarion call of disturbed youth (led by campaigner Greta Thunberg), none of whom know how science actually operates. The media and government bodies are not so innocent: they know there is an exclusion process going on, but it suits their political stance.

However, in the last couple of years something new and disturbing is emerging. A 'truth movement' has coalesced and begun to focus on climate change. Hitherto the movement was concerned with a number of issues: from 9/11 and the 'war on terror' through 'chem-trails' to the Covid pandemic, with further-out revelations of alien-contact, faked moon-landings and the imminent return of the Anunnaki.[1]

This heady mix was always problematic, but recently the Covid issue has been supplemented with apparently scientific arguments from fringe 'experts' that not only does the Sars2 virus not exist, but viruses themselves have not been proven to exist and certainly not proven to be causative agents of disease. And now the climate debate has seen the use of fringe characters—far outliers in scientific circles, given exposure with their own theories and facts. Since I have been called a 'climate-change denier' and could easily be described as a fringe character, I want to clarify here that the issue is not about consensus, fringe individuals or science; it is about how the disagreement is handled.

For me, 'truth' in science is not an absolute; it is a process. Truth emerges from process, and changes with time—not only from new facts being discovered, but also from social priorities and perceptions changing. The social world of politics and psychology determines what kind of data is gathered and the extent of funding, as well as the nature of hypotheses. There is a *sociology* of science, and the paradigm shifts that have taken place clearly show that 'truth' is an evolutionary process.

Thus it is that an emergent theme in the 'truth' movement is that the undeniable rise in carbon-dioxide (CO_2) emissions (nobody disputes the atmospheric measurements) is largely natural, and that human emissions constitute a mere 4 per cent of the increase in atmospheric CO_2—which now stands at just under 420 ppm compared to the pre-industrial level of 280 ppm. The 4 per cent figure has been aired on TV channels in Australia and in the UK-based monthly *Light* newspaper. {*2024 note*: and in the political campaigns of the Reform Party}.

In the UK, this recent (2020) 'free' paper has already given pages to the 'viruses do not exist' faction, and now to the 4 per cent theorists. I would suspect that hardly any readers or watchers can even approach the science behind these claims. The problem is that these alternative facts suit the narrative of manipulation by scientific, medical and economic elites—that 'they' lied to us and want to control us etc., and hence provide something to 'believe' in as a truth. And although I have spent most of my professional life exposing false narratives—for example, that nuclear power is cheap, safe and 'green'—I cannot see this 4 per cent figure being correct.

The 4 per cent argument is available (but you have to pay to access it on the internet) in two complex papers by well-qualified, but decidedly fringe physicists, and depends upon flow-rate models and their reading of carbon-isotope data. I was an anonymous reviewer of one such paper for a respected climate-science journal. I had to admit my limitations regarding the flow-physics (I am a biologist), but argued that the authors would have to come up with a source of the increased atmospheric CO_2. I recommended publication for the purposes of exposing their model to peer review, but the editors turned the paper down. Since then, the author has published in a little-known new journal of limited peer review.

In my view this fringe scientific argument founders upon one fact—the only source for short-term increases in CO_2 has to be release from the ocean surface waters. As oceans warm, they release more CO_2 and as they cool, they absorb—it is partly chemical solubility, partly the action of plankton and respiration. There is a seasonal flux (what comes in and out) that is well quantified and relatively stable at about 90 Gigatonnes/carbon/year. This is about ten times the annual emissions from human activity, and as the natural seasonal flux balances out each year, it has always been assumed that it is those human emissions that accumulate over time. In fact, the rate of accumulation of CO_2 in the atmosphere is half that expected from emissions, and the assumption is that the oceans are absorbing the other half—and incidentally, turning the upper waters less alkaline (scarily called 'ocean acidification').[2]

If the IPCC scientists are wrong about 'flow' rate and solubility—a valid line of debate—then there needs to be a mechanism for the observed 130 ppm increase in the industrial era. Could it simply be a release from the oceans due to the undeniably warmer water? One would expect some proportion of the observed increase to be due simply to reduced solubility.

The best check is the past swings of CO_2 over the main temperature changes of the Earth system both during the ice ages and in the lesser swings between ice ages (interglacial periods). In seven such ice-age changes (over the last 700,000 years) for which we have ice-core records, the swing is from 180 to 280 ppm. The latter is also taken as the base-level of pre-industrial times. Over the last 10,000 years of this current interglacial period known as the Holocene, CO_2 has varied little, whereas temperature swings of 1–2° have been a regular feature.

The Holocene optimum temperature (about 8,000 years ago) was about 2° warmer in the northern hemisphere than it is at present—and the recent swing of 'little ice ages' every 1,000–1,500 years involves about 1° amplitude (up or down). So, in terms of ocean temperature, nothing unusual is happening today. None of these Holocene swings have increased the CO_2 levels much above 280ppm. So, ocean out-gassing is an unlikely explanation for the accumulation of 130 ppm of CO_2

to the current 420 ppm, which, unless I see data to convince me otherwise, I think must be due to those accumulated human emissions. And yet concentration of CO_2 is the wrong issue—a red herring, one I suspect was deliberately fed to the media rather than the real issue, which is the power of CO_2 to raise temperature, which falls logarithmically as concentration increases. Thus, above a certain level, CO_2 has a minimal effect on temperature, no matter how much the increase above that level. This is a typical media-related issue where a perceived vital policy is

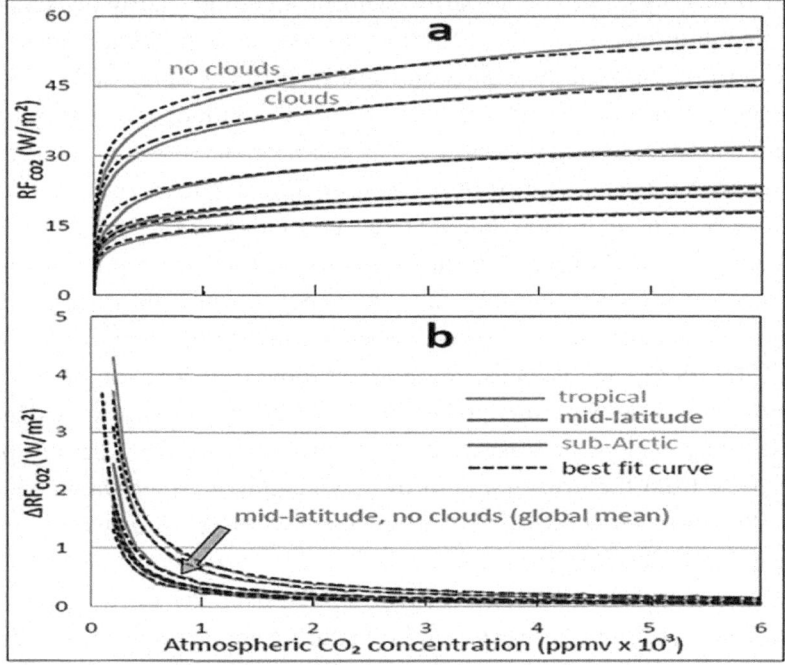

Figure 1. Computer-generated changes in Radiative Forcing [RF] (watts per square metre) with atmospheric concentration. Source: Davis (2017), see reference list.

Note: the inflection points occur between 200 and 300ppm. The power of CO_2 to affect heating diminishes with its concentration in the atmosphere. Above concentrations of around 300 ppm, CO_2 loses its ability to heat. This graphic shows that: the curve begins around 200 ppm, and by 280 it is almost flat—and each additional 100 ppm adds only a tiny amount. This amount—somewhere between 1–2 watts/square metre of Earth's surface—is nevertheless a lot of energy in total, but the ecologist in me wants to know how it compares to the natural flux. The 'natural flux' (how much radiation comes in and out) needs to be measured at the Earth's surface, which then stores the energy as heat. We are talking about radiative power, and the convention is to reduce all types of radiation—visible, ultraviolet and infrared to one unit of watts. The natural flux at the Earth's surface is 240 watts and is made up of sunlight (visible and ultraviolet parts of the spectrum) and heat (infrared radiation) mostly from clouds and water vapour (90 per cent), with CO_2 and other trace greenhouse gases adding the rest.

concerned: a message, in this case 'the climate emergency', must rest on 'settled' science, and the public must not be distracted by arcane details.

Here are those details. From 0–180 ppm CO_2 is a potent greenhouse gas and its potency is measured in watts (the power to heat). But as the curve of power in relation to concentration rises (see Fig. 1 above), it starts to curve and flatten.

This 240 watts is what keeps the ocean and land surfaces warm and habitable. The energy is absorbed by the oceans and released as latent heat, evaporation of water vapour and formation of clouds, all of which in concert make the climate.[3]

Until recently, the human contribution was so small that it could not be measured—as infrared radiation, separately from the other sources—and had to be computed. Between the years 2000 and 2010, the first spectrally resolved measurements were made—showing an increase of radiation from CO_2 of 0.2 watts/decade. The change in concentration over this period was 22 ppm. The researchers claimed that this validated the computer models; but if you divide 130 ppm as the human contribution by 22, and multiply by 0.2 watts, you get 1.2 total, and the models assume closer to 2 watts. The curve is slightly steeper at the beginning of the 130 rise, but it looks flat for much of it; however, let us take the IPCC figure of 2 watts for the human CO_2 effect.

As is obvious, 2/240 (2 watts as a proportion of the natural flux of 240 watts at the Earth's surface) is a less than 1 per cent rise in warming power. But you will never see this figure outside of the arcane scientific group reports of the IPCC. A 46 per cent rise in concentration constitutes a 1 per cent rise in heat flux, yet it is the 46 per cent figure that is trumpeted widely—and this sounds quite scary. And for most scientists—including, I would think, the majority even in the IPCC—this discrepancy does not register. Both figures are 'true', but they have entirely different contexts, so why bother the public with the wattage! But it is the increase in wattage that counts most, not the concentration.

Thus, neither the mainstream media, nor the IPCC, nor the science institutions proclaim the whole truth (including the 1 per cent wattage change); they only use the seemingly scary partial truth of the 46 per cent change in concentration.

There is also another issue. The same caucus of half-truth-sayers completely avoid talking about cycles in the climate. Here, it is the shorter-term decadal, centennial and millennial global temperature cycles, not the longer-term 100,000-year ice-age cycles. It is clear from paleo-climate science that even during the Holocene period, temperature cycles are regular, relatively predictable and of a rate and amplitude that can easily explain the current warming. (I append to this chapter references of my work on cycles in the published science literature and at a major science conference.) And furthermore, the IPCC readily admits to a poor understanding of the dynamics of natural 'variability' (they don't like to talk of cycles!), in particular, changes in cloud cover—the most obvious way of amplifying the relatively small variations in light originating from the Sun.

In addition, one often hears from the 'consensus' that the basic science is settled. That is far from the truth. The wattage has to be converted into resultant temperature, using a conversion factor, at the Earth's surface or in the atmosphere. On this simple physical conversion factor there is a rather large uncertainty, ranging from 0.3 to 1.2, depending upon the constituent atmosphere (see Fig. 1, above).[4]

When we are dealing with complex systems—especially a relatively homeostatic (self-correcting) system like the Earth—a 1 per cent fluctuation is i) hardly detectable above background variabilities, ii) likely to be rebalanced. In scientific terms, if one hypothesised that humans have zero effect—the 'null hypothesis'—and then martialled evidence to disprove that hypothesis, as would be normal practice in environmental science, one would have great difficulty in doing so from observable real-world data. One would have to look at the natural expectation—of sea-level rise and rate, ice mass, glaciers, heatwaves, wildfires, hurricanes etc.; and the evidence is equivocal—all of these phenomena peak with the regular warm cycles. Furthermore, changes in wind direction, water vapour and cloud cover are the ultimate cause of all of these phenomena—yet the IPCC admits that they cannot model them accurately. Often, they are simply assumed to be constant.[5]

These are real issues in climate science—the subject of conference debates and many published papers, but tricky territory for public involvement. This is where the 'truth' movement must take care. It is blustering about the wrong things—about supposed facts, rather than the process by which 'truth' can emerge. I am convinced that on climate issues (as with Covid and the origin of the virus), the edifice of UN-based 'science' is corrupt—and that has been said plainly by former presidents of National Academies in the USA and Russia, so I am not alone. And my work goes back to the days of Britain being the 'dirty man' of Europe with regard to toxic emissions and dumping at sea—all under the auspices of the UN regulatory bodies. We spent 20 years reforming the system—but alas, old habits die hard.

Many expert dissenting climate scientists have fallen foul of the UN's latest process of exclusion of these dissenting voices—on hurricanes, droughts, sea-level rise, atmospheric physics and ocean cycles. Additionally, the modern academies are corrupted by their own self-interest, ignore relevant papers and do not invite cogent critics. But at the lower end of the scientific establishment, there do exist courageous editors of up-and-coming journals and science conferences who are willing to listen. I have been able to debate openly with the top UN IPCC scientists in these forums, though to date to little effect. The upper echelons just keep their heads down, repeat their mantras—which they 'believe' are true—and cultivate their relations with government, funders and the media.

Finally, a cogent example to close this chapter with. Top lawyers, experts in choosing their facts to suit their clients, are now getting on to the stage and tackling governments—thus far, not challenging the process, rather amplifying it. For example, Client Earth (see the link appended to this chapter) recently sued the Australian government on behalf of the Torres Strait Islanders (North of Queensland) who, according to their own testimony, suffered from sea-level rise. The UN agreed with Client Earth's case, and ordered Australia to pay damages for breach of human rights. Australia is a main supplier of coal to China and hence in the eyes of these radical lawyers contributes to 'ecocide'. Client Earth gave no figures for sea-level rise in the press release seeking funding for the court case. I checked. There has been no significant rise in the last 20 years at Cairns on the Queensland coast. At Sydney, also on the Pacific, the rise is 0.65 millimetres per year, steady since 1860, the first hundred years of which, by common agreement of CO_2 science, must be natural—65 millimetres per century or 2.5 inches! The Pacific rises and falls according to El Niño conditions,[6] and the Torres Islanders may have suffered from two unusually large El Niño storm surges back-to-back instead of 15 years apart, as normal. Ocean warming since 1860 is in line with expectations of recovery from the last 'little ice age'. But then, once again cycles complicate the message of 'truth'.

These forms of myopia besetting modern science and environmental law demonstrate an aversion to cycles, irregular periods and other factors revealed in the cycles data of ice cores but never commented upon—and an aversion to being open and inclusive. If one acknowledges these fundamental elements of nature, it becomes less amenable to strategies of control, and the observant would note that these elements would normally be ascribed to the feminine polarity of thought and reality.

There is a reflection of these issues in the Covid saga. A complicit media does not focus upon the origin of the virus and its possible accidental release but, rather, on controlling the spread. The scientific institutions and the UN collude, thus the key issue of safety—whether laboratories should be harvesting and genetically manipulating wild viruses in the first place—is sidelined, as also is the issue of global investments in the science of manipulation. Climate will now replace Covid in this scheme of things—with no focus upon the origin of change, but rather on lucrative investment strategies of control such as 'The Green New Deal', 'Net Zero' or 'The Great Reset'. In all this 'the truth movement' is alone in a very complicit political world.

Notes

1. The Anunnaki are a group of deities of the Ancient Sumerians, Akkadians, Assyrians and Babylonians. In the earliest Sumerian writings about them, which come from the post-Akkadian period, the Anunnaki are deities in the pantheon, descendants of An and Ki, the god of the heavens and the goddess of Earth, and their primary function was to decree the fates of humanity. See https://en.wikipedia.org/wiki/Anunnaki—some people are convinced they were actually technologically advanced visitors from outer space who modified human DNA to make a slave labour force.

2. I will report here that my colleague in the US, Jackson Davis, Professor of Biological Sciences, has been studying the relation of ocean acidification to biodiversity loss, and his conclusions—which I am reviewing at the present time—are that we are heading for a serious oceanic extinction event within the next 50 years. His work calls for emissions reductions as a matter of urgency. Clearly, more research is necessary.

3. The Earth has a stable but bipolar climate: for 100,000 years the 'normal' is an ice age, with much water locked up as ice at the poles, lower sea levels (200 metres lower), stronger winds, much dust and much drier overall. Deserts and savannah grow, tropical rainforests shrink by 80 per cent. Then, some kind of 'tipping point' occurs with regard to ice cover, the winds die down, and the planet warms (land by 5°, oceans by 3°, poles by 15°) and sea-level rises. However, a mystery exists. The overall amount of radiation from the Sun does not appear to change enough to cause these shifts, and the current theory is that where the sunlight falls is crucial, and here a long cycle concerning the varying angle of Earth's tilt and precession causes more light to melt the snowfields, exposing dark light-absorbing earth, and thus a feedback sets in. Within these cycles, the energy-absorbing oceans behave rather like 'flow-forms' in basins—

i.e. they develop internal oscillations of warming and cooling on decadal, centennial and millennial timescales. Thus, there are long-term changes, most especially in water vapour in the atmosphere and cloud cover. Unfortunately, this is all too complex for computer modelling (the cycles are not exact enough), and so the default position is a static flow—and from this is developed the 'flux' model of what comes in and out. That flux can be measured most accurately at the 'top of the atmosphere' above the shifting cloud layer, and the measurements appear to show a 'net' flow of energy into the planet (more in than out equals 'global warming'). There is a problem, however: the instruments have an 'error margin' of about 5 watts when measuring the influx of 1,360 watts (almost entirely visible spectrum) from the Sun at that height above the Earth, and the balancing outgoing wattage—reflected sunlight plus outgoing infrared (heat). Some scientists argue that even the 'sign' (whether it is a net plus or minus) cannot be reliably established. On top of that, 5 watts as net influx is far too high, and it is corrected by looking at how much the oceans accumulate heat—to a figure of about 0.5 watts. And on top of that, the surface data, more accurately measured, is constantly shifting because of cloud behaviour—which reflects sunlight (about 30 per cent) but has been assumed constant over decadal timescales. Data from 1980 to 2000, when the Earth gained a lot of warmth, show that cloud cover diminished substantially over two decades—by more than enough to dominate the flux equations (that was the basis of my argument in my book *Chill: A Reassessment of Global Warming Theory*). Critics argued that the clouds got thinner as a result of 'global warming'—i.e. they amplified the effect of CO_2. For reasons I haven't got space for, that argument is readily debunked by new data.

The conclusion here is that 'natural flux' varies and by several watts at the Earth's surface, and this is obscured by the official use of an average figure that takes account of average cloud cover.

4. The conversion of watts to temperature is not simple—though a single conversion factor is required in most mathematical models. If you imagine shining a light on a clear atmosphere of mostly oxygen and nitrogen, the atmosphere is transparent. The same is true for infrared, except for water vapour and carbon dioxide—the main 'greenhouse' gases which absorb that wavelength and heat up. Atmospheres on Earth differ: the poles are very dry, land has a lot of natural and man-made aerosols, and of course, there are clouds. When radiation shines upon atmospheres, the constituents determine whether and by how much it heats up. The same radiative power does not heat up empty space (on its travels from the Sun). Fig. 1 is a computer calculation of wattage according to concentration of CO_2—it would still require converting to temperature.

5. If we take the period 2000 to 2016, cloud cover varied little and surface temperature 'flat-lined', and we then had two very large El Niño events where huge amounts of heat are released from the surface waters of the Pacific, changing wind direction and cloud patterns. The resultant global temperature changes (increases of about half of one degree) are temporary, and global temperature returned to pre-Niño levels after 2020. Recent research indicates that all the temperature change can be explained by cloud changes. The same is true of the 1983-2000 period. We don't have data before that.

6. El Niño is key to global weather patterns: it has far-reaching effects over 2–3 years on rainfall, wind direction, droughts, floods and wildfires, as does its sister, La Niña—when the Pacific goes 'cold' and absorbs at depth (down to 300 m). Global temperature rises and falls from Niño peak to Niña trough by 0.6 degrees (the whole of global warming over 120 years is reckoned at 1.2 degrees—if the latest El Niño 2016-2020 episode is added, and 0.8 degrees if it isn't). A new paper connects the current Niña phase to the droughts in Europe, the USA and China. During global warm periods—Minoan, Roman, Norman and this one—Niño phases outnumber Niña phases, and vice versa in cold periods (dark ages of famine and mass migration). The phenomenon is what is known as 'a charge/discharge oscillator'. For reasons unknown, easterly winds off South America die down and the central Pacific warms up because those easterly winds have kept the surface waters cool by dragging cold water up from the Pacific depths to the surface. During such cold Niña conditions of strong easterlies, cloud cover diminishes and thus more energy from sunlight is stored in the top 300 m. Then the winds dies down, and the surface gets warm and releases heat to the atmosphere. Somehow, this increased heat then triggers the next shift in winds, and so on.

Additional links and references

Link to Client Earth: https://tinyurl.com/2j45dfpm

Ice-core analyses by Environmental Studies Institute, Santa Cruz, Calif.

W.J. Davis, 'The relationship between atmospheric carbon dioxide concentration and global temperature for the last 425 million years', *Climate*, 5 (4), 2017; 76; doi:10.3390/ cli5040076, available at https://tinyurl.com/3f97nfd8 (accessed 15 May 2024).

W.J. Davis, P. Taylor & W.B. Davis, 'The Antarctic Centennial Oscillation: a natural paleoclimate cycle in the Southern Hemisphere that influences global temperature', *Climate*, 6 (1), 2018, 3; doi:10.3390/cli6010003, available at https://tinyurl.com/54cu25fh (accessed 15 May 2024).

W.J. Davis, P.J. Taylor & W.B. Davis, 'The origin and propagation of the Antarctic Centennial Oscillation', *Climate*, 7 (9), 2019, 112; doi:10.3390/ cli7090112, available at https://tinyurl.com/ywtjyvnf (accessed 15 May 2024).

W.J. Davis & W.B. Davis, 'Antarctic winds: pacemaker of global warming, global cooling, and the collapse of civilizations', *Climate*, 8 (11), 2020, 130; doi:10.3390/cli8110130, available at https://tinyurl.com/2rf8ebt3 (accessed 15 May 2024).

3.2 Clouding the Mind

This article was published in New View *Issue 108, 2023*

We take them for granted. We don't see how they nourish us. The world would be a desert without them. They are, of course, an extension of the ocean, without which there would be no life for complicated carbon lifeforms like us. They carry water and their water would not rise from the ocean without the power of the Sun's element of fire. They are moved solely by the wind, these very elemental beings without which our earth-gardens would not grow and our fields would lay barren. Water, fire, air and earth have an elemental purity, but clouds… they come and go, wax and wane, rain or hail or snow.

It seems odd to me as a scientist interested in the climate that clouds are so neglected. There are few studies yet they represent the biggest acknowledged uncertainties in supposedly sophisticated climate models. I was not suspicious at first. I am an ecologist and I can readily understand when science simply does not notice something of great importance—a blind spot and often, as I once argued at a conference of anthropologists looking at climate science, because science has gender issues.

There may be plenty enough top women scientists (though currently I think no men *identifying* as women), but they are *all* caught up in a male paradigm. First, they studied the air and then the light from the Sun (archetypally male elements), only later coupling the ocean to their models of reality and they didn't see Earth as playing much of a role at all.

The number one rule in ecology is that *everything* is related, connected and changing in cycles small and great. Ecologists focus on change, connection and continuity, rather than any individual object within that web. And in that web time is cyclic not linear and it is never at all clear what causes what. Ecology is a more feminine science.

Sixty years ago, ecology did not have much influence—the fashion was all political sciences, economy, technology and eternal growth. One might think nothing has changed. The Economy still rules, of course, but now ecologists sit on the boards of all the major banks, they advise departments of government and have their own political parties. Even I have been sought out for my advice and offered a desk in the City [the financial district of London]. 'I already have a desk,' I said, half-joking, whilst quietly mulling over that alternative future with a Porsche and my daughter's happy face at my new-found financial status!

My work began advising Donegal in Ireland—in its fight against uranium mining; then regional and national government; the European Commission and Parliament; several countries outside of Britain and the United Nations (UN) itself, but that all changed in the early parts of this century. Governments (and even Greenpeace) began to believe the staff scientists they employed directly and not to invite the critics, especially where ecological models of the Earth and ocean were concerned—and pulling apart models that justified pollution was my specialty as an analytical scientist.

I had once built a team of scientists with incredible minds—with mathematical and computational skills far superior to mine—in order to pick apart the government-appointed scientists' models. Science and government were speaking with one voice. Freedom in academia had been severely compromised by the financing system and few from the academies would risk going against a government or intergovernmental scientific finding.

That trend has gotten much worse in the last four years—since Covid. We have seen how the 'follow the science' mantra rules the show. We now have a global Climate Emergency—with legislation and any critics are branded as irrelevant and ignored. There are professors, globally, standing up—but we can perhaps count them on two hands—for each of those fields of Covid and Climate whilst so many others keep their heads down not publicly questioning the output of the government's modelled futures.

The almost laughable thing is that those models have one huge error. It is obvious even to the men (and one or two women) who built them—and they confess this as such in the latest UN report—that *clouds* are the biggest uncertainty in the models.

Nobody really understands the physics of how they form, nor their trajectories, which are subject to chaotic factors that totally confound the mathematicians. They don't fully understand what causes clouds to rain and, as I quickly discovered, they haven't studied *cycles* of cloudiness, related of course, to cycles of wind, related ultimately to cycles of solar energy.

There is one notable exception, a Danish scientist working in a relatively small laboratory of the Danish Space Programme, by the name of Henrik Svensmark. He studied cloud cycles in relation to the 11-year magnetic cycle of the Sun. Over the two decades he observed and logged the data, clouds increased across the globe when the solar magnetic cycle was low and then thinned as the solar cycle moved upward to the peak. This would not ordinarily have been controversial, but the temperature change, though small, would be significant if the solar cycle went flat, i.e. no peaks, simply a long trough when the magnetics are very low. The Earth would then naturally move to a colder state because it is the clouds obscuring the Sun that lower the temperature. This is one explanation for the Little Ice Age (LIA) (from the early 14th to mid 19th century) and several Little Ice Ages before then, about one thousand years apart.

Earth should have been called Ocean—water covers 70% of the planet, which is blue not green, and our life is made possible by the fact that water stores solar energy as heat—land cannot do that to the same extent and the atmosphere itself holds a thousand times less heat than the oceans. Most of that oceanic heat is stored in the upper three hundred metres. The equatorial regions accumulate more solar heat than they re-emit at night and this heat is then carried North and South by winds and wind-driven ocean currents to poleward regions which lose more solar energy than they gain—they are zones of permanent heat loss. Clouds in the equatorial zone cool the ocean by blocking sunlight, clouds in the extra-tropics and especially polar regions, block heat leaving the planet, and hence are warming in their effect.

When Svensmark published his correlations, another scientist, Drew Schindell—at the much more prestigious labs of NASA—was studying winds and rain and storms from a period when the solar cycle appeared to disappear (a prolonged trough) for several decades, (roughly 1600-1650), sunlight dimmed a little and, also relevant, the solar magnetic field carried by the solar wind also lessened. This period was known as the Little Ice Age in Europe and Schindell was looking at evidence for shifting extra-tropical wind patterns and storm tracks along the western coasts of North America. Sure enough, the storm tracts moved south during the cooling—which would mean less cloud in the polar regions and hence more heat loss from the planet. Other members of the US labs were logging how the southern tropical El Niño[1] oscillation slowed down and became less extreme in its global effects.

There developed a lot of interest in Dr Svensmark, particularly from environmentalists who could see where his work was leading. He found it difficult to finance his work in Denmark, but suddenly he was offered a lot of money to relocate to the CERN laboratories in Switzerland, where he could explore the cloud microphysics of the whole issue of the Sun's energy, whether light-wave, electric or magnetic (they are, of course, a continuum meaning they all work and act together) and there he floundered. The theories persist, that the Little Ice Age was caused primarily by a repeating solar cycle, but the microphysics didn't deliver.

If I had known Svensmark, I would have whispered in his ear—'Don't go' and urged him to stay local and study cloud distribution, as there was a huge bank of new satellite data that was being ignored. I was more interested in Schindell's work—the observation that during the LIA cycle the winds changed and that would have had strong effects on regional climates. As the solar energy dropped—and it drops more in the ultraviolet spectrum than in the visible bands—the oceans cool and wind directions change. There would be less water vapour and hence less cloud and the clouds would alter their distribution. The poles would cool more than the equator. There would be changes in the Jetstream[2] and hence surface winds, which became more meridional (describing north-south 'loops' across the equatorial latitudes) than zonal. In warm periods, the Jetstreams move north and become more zonal, in cool periods, the reverse happens.

My own theory, developed initially for the Antarctic by my colleague Jackson Davis at the Environmental Studies Institute in Santa Cruz, California, is that an oscillator mechanism is at work. In the Antarctic stronger Jetstreams and surface wind speed drive ocean currents which cause warmer water beneath ice-capped chilled surface waters to 'upwell' and melt summer sea ice, thus liberating more heat. These waters are driven towards the equator at the surface, but then pull hydrostatically on a massive global 'conveyor belt' of heat held at depth in the oceans. Professor Davis thinks that this dynamic *initiates* all the regional ocean cycles of warming and cooling (called oscillations) which vary from 60 years to 100 years and ultimately the long (1,000 year) cycle of which the LIA was the last cooling trough of the cycle.

In the Arctic, and of more relevance for us peoples in the northern hemisphere, in warm cycles such as the one we are now in, warmer ocean currents bringing with them more cloud melt the sea ice at the poles from above and below liberating heat stored in the waters below. This heat leaves the planet rather quickly warming the air on its way to space, hence the rapid rise in Arctic air temperatures, so beloved of the media's headlines: 'Arctic is warming four times faster than the rest of the planet'.

However, beneath the surface, Arctic Ocean temperatures are falling—as is the heat-content of the North Atlantic Ocean basin—after a century of warming. This oceanic heat reduction causes the Jetstream to lose power as it is driven by the difference between polar air and equatorial air where it meets at high altitude. As it slows, it becomes wavy, up and down in altitude, and more north-south (meridional) episodes occur (the cause of weather extremes)—and my own conclusion is that this starts to cool the planet.

Our work has been published in a leading climate journal, in particular, the hypothesis that warming-leads-to-cooling, and cooling-leads-to-warming. My part of the theory is that when the Jetstreams lose power they become loopy in their movement. Warmth equals power, cool equals loopy—with loss of warmth, comfort, abundant crops etc.

Now the paleo-ecologist, if not the government-appointed ecological advisors, should get very interested in the *amplitude*—i.e. amount of temperature change—of this cycle as well as the periodicity. Whilst a few have studied the period—and upwards of a couple of hundred of them have published findings—very few have tried to calculate the *amplitude* and the rate of change.

I wrote to Schindell, complementing him on his work and asking how much more data he now had, but he did not reply. I later discovered he had (been?) moved to another department and had also become a key advisor to the UN. He was now working with orthodox models. No one else worldwide has shown much interest in following up this avenue of research. Nonetheless, one can make a rough estimate of the temperature change: globally it lies between 0.5 and 1.00 degree Celsius—the upper level coinciding with the modern warming that we have observed since the LIA (known by the UN advisors as the 'pre-industrial' period). Also, the International Panel for Climate Change (IPCC) no longer uses the word 'cycle' or even 'oscillation' referring instead to 'variability' (which doesn't imply a repeating cycle).

So far, most of the scientists I have mentioned have not occupied very senior positions in climate science. One such, however, is the distinguished Japanese geophysicist, Syun-ichi Akasofu, who was director of the International Arctic and Antarctic Research Center at the University of Fairbanks in Alaska. He, more than any other scientist, should know about climate cycles because they have profound effects upon the polar regions, especially the Arctic. Among his staff was Russian academician and Professor Igor Polyakov, who published the seminal paper on the 80-year Arctic Oscillation and its amplitude of about 2 degrees Celsius. The significance of this work is that the hyped-up melting ice and high temperatures at the poles is *cyclic* and the Arctic always heats up more strongly than other regions.

On his retirement, Akasofu spoke to the press—telling them that he and his colleagues saw a *natural cycle* dominating the global warming signal (which at this time was about 1 degree globally). He also said he feared 'assassination' for saying this! I think he meant, political assassination—which happens in science. He then published his estimate of the 'recovery rate' from the LIA, estimating 0.05 degrees/per decade, and this, by the year 2000, came to 0.8 degrees, about 80% of the observed warming. Hitherto, nobody talked about the long recovery rate from that trough in global temperatures—and the recovery started around 1850, with many glaciers beginning their retreat at this time.

He *was* duly 'assassinated'. The mob was led by a journalist from *The Guardian* newspaper Dana Nuccitelli, actually a former very junior climate scientist, who wrote to the editors of the climate journal that published this finding claiming the paper was deeply flawed and that it compromised the status of the journal and should be withdrawn. They also persuaded a colleague to resign from the journal's editorial board on the issue. No up-and-coming journal can afford this kind of publicity, but they stuck with Akasofu at the time and refused to withdraw a peer-reviewed paper. However, no one has revisited the issue since 2013 and it is the subject of a paper I have just now submitted to that same journal.{2024 *Commentary*: see Appendix 5}

I presented the issue of cycles at the Third Global Summit on Climate Science in Prague 2019, and challenged the top IPCC modeller presenting their cycle-less models. He admitted there was a problem with cycles. I wrote up my presentation and sent it to five journals. All of them referred me to the 6th report of the IPCC released in August 2021, asking that I update the paper by critiquing their approach.

In short, the IPCC airbrushed the long-cycle (1,000 years) and hence the Little Ice Age, out of existence altogether, claiming its amplitude—and hence recovery phase, was small and global effect negligible compared to the 'unprecedented' modern warming.

Now let us return to clouds
During the post-1950 warming period (and half the warming since 1900), climate science developed satellite surveillance and could measure cloud cover and hence any changes. The data runs from 1983 to 2005 under the International Satellite Cloud Climatology Programme (ISCCP) based at NASA. I reviewed that data for my book *Chill: A Reassessment of Global Warming Theory* (published in 2009) and I also archived many graphics and made them available

freely on my Ethos website. In my view it was a superb set of data that was also independently corroborated by scientists working at ground stations across the planet—and it showed a global drop in reflective cloud cover of about 4 % from 1983-2000. Ground surveys published in 2005 showed the effects of increased solar radiation at the surface—and their figures were high, at 4-6 watts/square metre. This compares to a meagre 1.8 watts from carbon dioxide's radiation. Watts are a measure of radiant 'power'—how much they heat things depends on the nature of the thing—zero for a vacuum, for example—and then power is absorbed by water vapour and carbon dioxide and any particulate matter and is absorbed also by the Earth and the ocean.

Global cloud cover then recovered in 2001 by 2% and has remained relatively stable until major deviations caused by very large ENSO (El Niño Southern Ocean) events in 2016/2019. Global surface temperatures actually stopped rising from 2000-2015 in line with the stable cloud regime, but El Niño disrupted that regime, temperatures rose by 0.6 degrees Celsius, and then by 2022 had fallen back to where they were before.

I wanted to follow up on the original ISCCP data and in particular data since 2005. I called their office in NASA, because try-as-I-might, I could not navigate their website. The custodian was apologetic. They had been closed down. The data is no longer held at NASA—rather at the National Center for Environmental Information (which was even less accessible). In its place was data from a new programme at NASA named CERES (Clouds and the Earth's Radiant Energy System and Energy) and not at all in the same graphic format. It requires computer programming skills to read it. It consists of graphs of radiation fluxes from 2001 onwards when clouds varied little. Here I should add that when James Hansen, then a director of NASA, had been asked about the trend of low cloud over two decades, he had belittled the ISCCP team and what he called untrustworthy data, citing changes in satellite orbit geometry that could account for the trend. The specialist team had actually dealt with those issues in the open science literature and had resolved them to the satisfaction of their peers. However, in the course of writing this article, I hear that the ISCCP project has been rejuvenated, it seems almost single-handedly, by the retired former custodian gaining support within the satellite science community and refunding from NASA (James Hansen retired recently to become a full-time activist against fossil fuels). The extensive checking and re-evaluation has confirmed the 4% decline in cloud cover over the critical global warming period.

CERES may be largely indecipherable without a degree in radiation physics, but we can look to the work of a team that studied the cloud effects and what happens at the surface in terms of sunlight and warming of the two recent super ENSO events (that bumped up global temperatures to 'record' highs in 2016). They show clearly that ocean-heat release and storage phases *are controlled by clouds*. Their work does not make it through the UN vetting process to the final conclusions of the report.

Coincidently, after ISCCP closed and my website then became *the only source* of the valuable cloud graphics, some dark force (how else to describe it) coincidently repeatedly destroyed my website—which otherwise contained only my rather inoffensive conservation work.

And so it is, that all the way up to the UN's special advisory panel, clouds get a raw deal—they are ignored, as are cycles, irregular periods, spiral dynamics of wind and water and the operation of chaos (where even cycles disappear).

Clouds are still defying even the super-computers to understand and model them, thank goodness, because whatever their operators say about having solved the dynamics, those computer models will be impenetrable to understand. It is hard for scientific critics to challenge these models using different parameters because they would have to obtain and use comparable computer equipment and fund the enormous costs involved unaided by industry and government.

I have often bemoaned the fact that compared to the Covid 'emergency' no professorial-level paleo-climatologists had stood up against the UN. This group of scientists is essential for piecing together the past, its dynamics and its limits—they know, for example, that the Arctic was naturally ice-free in summer during some previous, but quite recent, warm periods. I have just been sent a paper published late last year in the leading journal of paleo-climate studies wherein 22 experienced specialists detail the *level of bias* in the IPCC's latest report and call for a specialist, more balanced review team at the UN. The revolution has begun!

This graph in Fig. 1 (over) looks complicated (ignore the P's and B's in the writing between the top and bottom graphs as this is different analyses of much the same data) and I will draw attention to something quite simple. The upper figure represents a compilation of the different proxies for temperature, such as tree-ring width. You can see that over 2000 years there was a lot of variability and it takes signal-pro-

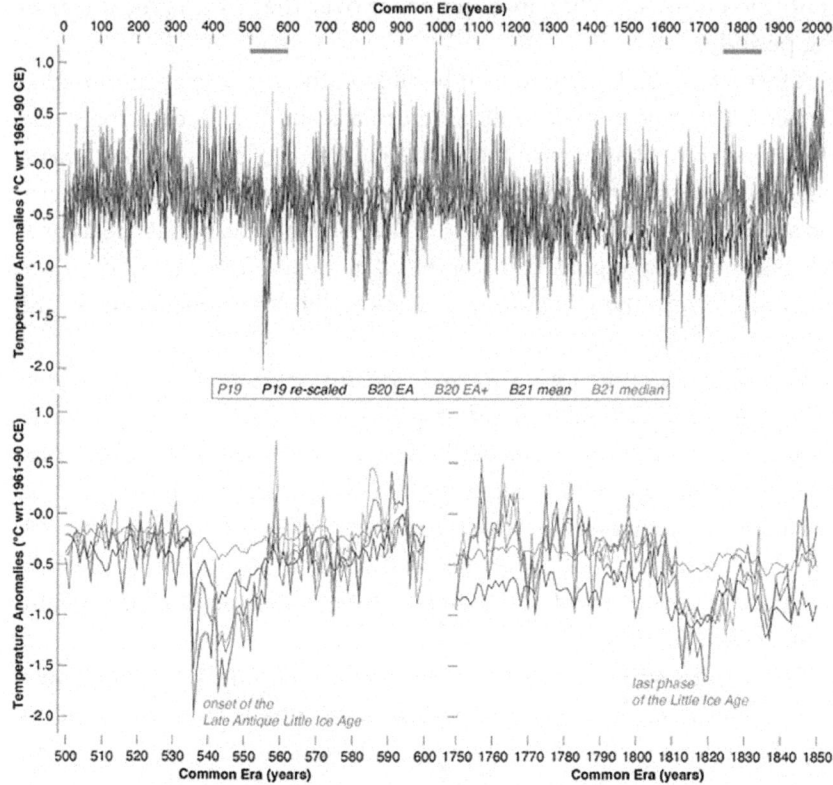

Figure 1. Various proxies for temperature change based on tree-ring data. (from U. Buentgen, et.al. Dendrochronologia 74 (2022) 125982.)

cessing software to extract any cyclic pattern. However, there are three clear warm periods—the present, the Viking/Norman and the Roman. Closer analysis of the 'low periods' shows two: the Late Antique Little Ice Age and the last phase of the Little Ice Age (note the two different age periods top and bottom marked in the top graph by blocked horizontal lines and these periods are shown in greater detail in the lower graphic).

Now the crucial point here is that by applying particular statistical techniques that amplify the importance of a relatively stable equatorial region and downplay the polar extremes, you can get a graph that will follow the pale grey line in the mid-point of the lines in the upper diagram—that is a 'Hockey Stick', where nothing much happens until the end.

And when you stick on the recent temperature rise as measured by instruments, the uptick (of the 'stick') is amplified (taken out of its proper context). This technique has been highly criticised but is used by the IPCC to label the present situation as 'unprecedented'—a word duly picked up by the Media Circus that follows the major UN climate meetings.

Now, at last, a group of senior specialists are calling them out on this biased approach. The extra-tropical cycles have huge implications for the northern land mass and its inhabitants. And from the plethora of post-Little Ice Age studies, you can see how far back the recovery phase began, in the mid-1800s, *well before the high emissions of carbon dioxide.*

Notes

1. El Niño Southern Oscillation is an alternate warm phase and cold phase of the central Pacific equatorial region. During the warm phase there is a pulse of water vapour into the atmosphere multiplying the greenhouse effect (and sometimes raising global temperatures by half-a-degree Celsius), thereby creating much cloud and heavy rain globally; during the cold phase, equatorial skies become clear and the colder ocean begins to absorb more heat from the sun, which is a recharge ready for the next pulse.

2. The Jetstream is a high-level high-speed ribbon of wind that encircles sub-polar and sub-tropical latitudes. It has two modes: zonal (horizontal from West to East) and meridional (longitudinal, meandering over hundreds of kilometres). The former predominates in warm periods, but then induces the meander, since the power of the wind depends upon the equator-to-pole gradient and in warm periods the poles warm faster, hence reducing the gradient. My own sense is that more meandering leads to a general cooling of the planet and also that the ultimate cause of Jetstream variability is the changes in the solar cycle.

3.3 Encountering the Modelling Mentality

This article first appeared in New View *No.103 (2021)*

My initial involvement with climate science was in 1996, when I was asked by the then Countryside Commission, a UK government agency, to review a report they had commissioned from the University of East Anglia, one of the world's leading climate science centres. This somewhat academic report was not of great use to the Commission, since the authors had little understanding of countryside issues—such as farming, biodiversity, forestry, recreation and water supplies, all of which the Commission needed to integrate into countryside policy. I was brought in as an expert on these issues, having advised the Commission on energy policy and its impacts. This was then my first contact with the 'modellers'—a subset of climate scientists with little experience of the 'real' world. Their world was inside a box—a set of mathematical relationships actually known as a 'box model' with calculated flows from one box to another.

I took time to study the structure of the models—which was not easy for an outsider. I had done similar work for ocean models and for atmospheric dispersion, in both cases concerning the disposal of toxic chemicals to the environment and where the models predicted 'acceptable' impacts. Regulation of discharges would be based upon the predictions. However, in those cases, I had a team and funding to replicate the models and vary their inputs using the growing real-world oceanic data. At this juncture with the climate models, all I could do was examine the inputs and output. It struck me immediately that the model outputs were very linear and without any *cycles*.

As an ecologist with a great interest in past environments and evolution, I knew that climate was always changing in a cyclic manner—that is, in *repetitive* patterns, and that phase-changes occurred, often abruptly, especially where the northern hemisphere and the Arctic were concerned. I told the Commission they could not rely upon predictions that Britain would steadily warm toward a climate rather like northern Portugal in 50 years' time—it could get colder, wetter or drier in places. Everything depended upon ocean currents and potential changes in wind patterns—a colder Britain was possible even in a generally warmer world. Moreover, the average temperature was a relatively useless measure—of greater importance to agriculture, forestry and biodiversity, would be the extremes.

I was not to revisit the issue until 2002—when the renamed Countryside Agency had a role in a project to integrate community renewable energy into the landscape, settlements and nature conservation. I pioneered and developed a computer visualisation technique with the graphic designer Richard Fraser that provided all the regional councils and authorities with a visual tool to weigh impacts of the different energy choices available. During that project I rapidly realised that Britain's strategic plan for renewable energy would devastate the countryside. The sheer numbers of turbines, hydro-schemes, biofuel power stations and solar farms needed to power a densely populated industrial society would create a soulless electro-technical landscape where integration was all but impossible if the values of community, tranquillity, landscape quality and biodiversity were to be respected. But my role was not to campaign, rather to outline the consequences of democratic choice.

However, recalling my initial sense of the inadequacy of models and computer predictions, I decided to examine the model more closely. I wanted to know just how much time we had to make decisions and prepare integrative strategies. I had just completed another project for the British Association of Nature Conservationists and published a book in 2005—*Beyond Conservation*, which was part of an awakening *rewilding* approach to biodiversity. I had some time, but no funding, and it took three years to review the science of climate change—looking at paleo-climates, current temperature, sea-level rise, glacial melt, and most importantly, the apparently settled physics of carbon dioxide and anthropogenic greenhouse gases. Again, I noticed a massive disjunction—paleo-climatology talked of *cycles*, but the word never appeared in the modellers' vocabulary. It did not take long to discover why. Nature's cycles are not *exact*. Their waveform may be repeated, but their period was generally irregular. And the longer the cycle, the longer the 'variability' of the period—for example, the 1,000-year cycle varied between 800-1200 years. Amplitude—that is the temperature from trough to peak, also varied within what appeared to be a 'beat cycle' of about 10,000 years—the closer to the end of the beat cycle, amplitude might increase and period shorten. Early studies by climatologists would simply take the average over tens of thousands of years of data (e.g. ocean sediment records), coming up with a cycle of 1,500 years throughout the ice ages and also into the interglacials, where they are much fainter but still present. The distinguished Sino-US scientist, Kenneth Hsu, produced a study showing the 1,000-year cycle over the last 5,000 years and highlighting the rise of major civilisations at the peaks, and 'dark ages' where empires crashed down. Herein lies a problem for the modeller who would predict the next 50 or 100 years: you have a long cycle of 1,000-years, with an amplitude of 1 degree Celsius in the northern hemisphere (maybe half that in the southern, where there is more ocean); and then a 100-year and 200-year centennial cycle riding on top of the long wave; then several multi-decadal cycles ranging from 20-80 years; all topped by a thunderous El Niño Southern Oscillation (ENSO) of 3-4 years, but with a super ENSO at about 12-year intervals. ENSO is a major oscillatory event in the central/south Pacific driven by changing wind patterns that periodically pump vast amounts of water vapour and heat into the global atmosphere and can raise global temperatures temporarily (a year or more) by more than 0.5°C (remember the *whole* of global warming is 1°C). Between 2016 and 2019 there were *two* large events at the end of 15 years of no significant trend in global surface temperatures. The likelihood is that the trend will turn downward—already the global surface temperatures have dropped 0.5°C since 2019.

How to put that lot into a model? And as I highlighted in my book *Chill* [1]—*all* of these cycles peaked in the latter half of the 20th century. It can't be done, simply because you do not know *where* you are accurately enough in the longer cycles, which have much more variability in the periods. The long-cycle is variable 800-1,200 years! Its last trough was around 1600AD and last peak around 1200AD, but both troughs and peaks trundle along at the bottom or plateau at the top for hundreds of years. Moreover, the *mechanism*—what drives these natural cycles, is not known! But they are very well established and have been stable for hundreds of thousands of years—the record is there in the ice cores. And despite the media hype—when all of these cycles are taken together, the modern 'global warming' is still within normal variability.

However, not knowing the mechanism means you cannot adequately programme the box model to represent reality. And not knowing the period exactly, means that you cannot with any confidence *initialise* a century-long 'run' of the model.

What to do? Especially when there are hundreds of paleo-climate scientists watching the exercise with great interest. As modellers, to gain traction (and funding) you have to gain the upper ground. This means to attain some kind of authority as well as a funding stream to develop the models. Up until 2001, the modellers did not hold much authority. During the 3rd report (2001) of the UN special committee set up to examine the science, its Russian Vice Chair, a respected geo-scientist, told the world that Russian scientists think 'anthropogenic global warming' is over-hyped—they think it is mainly a natural cycle. The retiring director of the International Arctic Research Center at the University of Fairbanks, a distinguished Japanese geophysicist said the same, and even calculated and published a 'rate of recovery' from the Little Ice Age that so afflicted the Arctic during the period 1450-1850.

Serious corruption of science at the UN
Despite this clear dissent, the UN appointed Professor Michael Mann, who had developed a computer algorithm that airbrushed away all the offending cycles! And the IPCC published this to great fanfare (Fig. 1). The 'imprint' of anthropogenic warming was made clear from what became famous as the 'Hockey Stick'—a flat shaft where nothing happens for 2000 years, and then the 'uptick' at the end....

The former chairman of the US National Academy of Sciences said at the time, he had never seen a more serious corruption of the peer-review process. But the world's paleo-climatologists, authors of thousands of studies on cyclic patterns in tree-rings, ocean and lake sediments, pollen in peat bogs, stalagmites and ice cores, kept their heads down. Dissenting scientists had been severely attacked—not so much by their fellows, but by the media and above all, environmental campaigners. Such publicity would endanger research grants.

It fell to a retired mining engineer with a long-standing interest and knowledge of tree-ring data, and the tenacity to go against the grain and demand the release of the data used by Mann along with his computer coding. It took three years. Normally, scientists are obliged to provide this data—but the modellers (and the UN) closed ranks. Steve McIntyre analysed the algorithms, publishing his analysis concluding they would create a 'Hockey Stick' even from random data. But the damage (to scientific integrity) was done and the UN was committed. Nevertheless, Mann's graphic disappeared from the 2007 4th report and has not been seen *until August 2021*.

Miraculously, the 'Hockey Stick' has been resurrected in 2021 for the 6th report. Here it is in the following graphs (p.102).

In the reconstruction the last 2000 years is represented by global proxies of temperature (such as ice cores, ocean sediments and tree-rings) and the algorithms 'reconstruct' the past, ironing out the Medieval Warm Period and Little Ice Age. The 'observed' instrumental readings are spliced in—a very questionable scientific procedure.

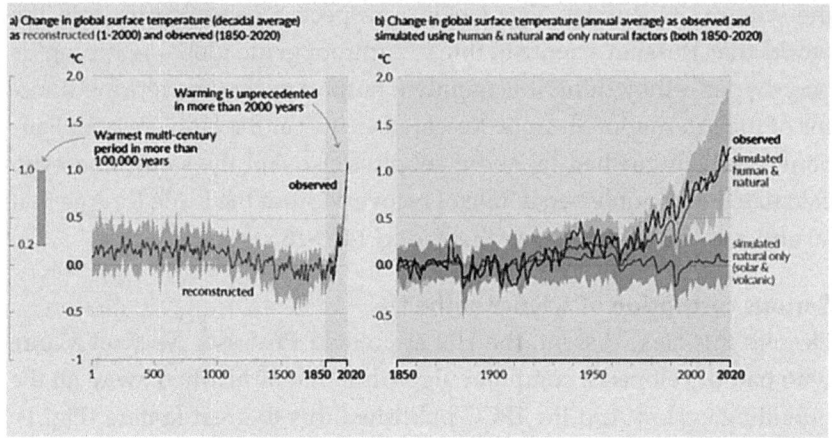

Figure 1. The Hockey Stick Resurrected (IPPC 6th Report, Summary for Policy Makers).
Left: Change in global surface temperature (decadal average) as reconstructed (1-2000)—grey line; and observed—black line (1850-2020) °C.
Right: Change in global surface temperature (annual average) as observed and simulated using human & natural—brown shading; and only natural factors—green shading (both 1850-2020)

Note in the right-hand graphic the final temperature stops at the height of El Niño, whereas global temperature has since fallen back from this peak by 0.5°C {*2024 Commentary*: However, another El Niño followed in 23/24 and the expected decline is underway in 2024}; and note that the 'natural tendency' (as simulated in the model) is depicted as remaining 'flat' with no peaking cycles since 1950—so not only has the 1000-year cycle disappeared, but the centennial and multi-decadal too!

The 6th report—in its citable entirety is not fully available, but the Hockey Stick definitely is part of the press package and Summary for Policy Makers. This Summary is the basis for the UN's 'code red' statement of alarm. Any scientist who now objects to this graphic will be accused of undermining the urgent message. There is actually no revelatory new science in the Working Group's reports. We know the world is warmer now than in 1850. There is a lot more energy in the system—stored in the oceans and ready for cycling. We can expect all manner of climate/weather changes, though not entirely predictable. However, it is far from proven that these changes are 'unprecedented'—that claim depends upon the knowledge of past cycles. And that knowledge has again been airbrushed out of existence. You can find cyclic evidence for all of the following in the paleo-climate literature: wildfire extremes, the complete retreat of Arctic Sea ice cover, extensive drought, episodes of flooding, heatwaves, migration of ocean organisms and land animals even the collapse of overstretched empires. And so far, the scientists involved in those studies have gone very quiet.

I will take one example: a strategic factual point that undermines the whole of the UN's document and their alarmist predictions. It concerns the Working Group 1 graphic (Fig. 2) for Arctic climate change and is set among dozens of vignettes of change throughout the globe. This region is key, as everyone knows, because the rate of temperature rise is greatest and apparently 'unprecedented'. If this graphic is faulty, given the weighting of Arctic impacts on the global index, then the whole global warming argument is faulty.

The first thing to note is: only the last half of the century is shown. All the published graphics of past cycles, especially in the Greenland ice cap, have been relegated—no longer visible to the media. These documented cycles have been supported by careful spectral analyses showing the periodicity and amplitude of past peaks and troughs, and there is a larger set of studies of synchronous events across North America, Eurasia, South America and even in Antarctica. In fact, the century-long graphic of temperature for 1900~2010 (they chose not to show) has a *double* peak like a camel, with the last maximum on the

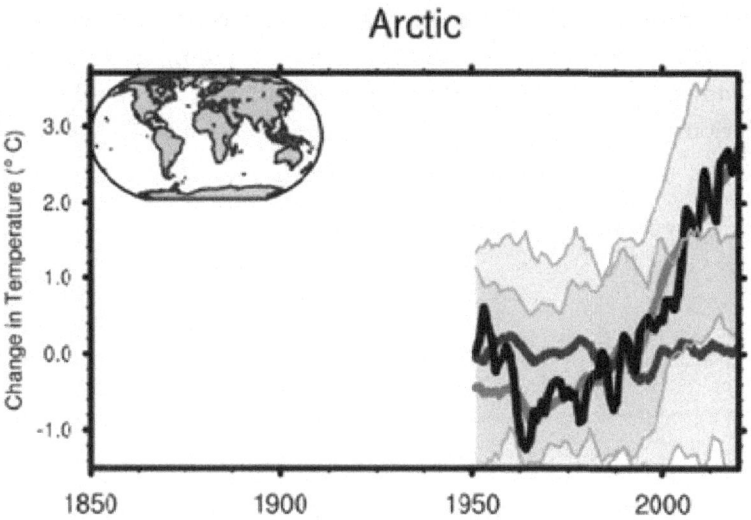

Figure 2. The 'unprecedented' Arctic warming
The graphic depicts precipitation which is strongly linked to temperature, and it rises from 1950 to 2020—the black line. The grey line represents expected natural 'variability' with the average in dark grey and the upper and lower bounds in light grey. It can be seen that all three grey lines stay relatively flat for 70 years. The black lines represent the spread and average of the observations—in this case precipitation in the region.

Greenland ice cap, or in Iceland, Canada and Alaska, in the 1930s and early 1940s. Temperatures in the Arctic are accurately recorded over this period.

Some records from that previous warm spell stood until the last decade, and are now only marginally exceeded. However, references to this work are buried in the as yet 'not citable' and very dense (3,000 pages) Working Group reports.

The next thing to note in Fig. 2 is the thick 'grey' line—this represents *average* 'variability'—i.e. what would be expected *by the models* without human influence by greenhouse gases—in other words, the natural 'forcing', and as you can see, the trend is depicted as effectively zero over this period. The thin grey line represents the 'outer bound' of the variability. It is not presented as a *recurrent cycle*—the one known as the Arctic Oscillation with a period of about 80 years and an amplitude of 2-3° Celsius. As is well known by the Arctic specialists who published on aspects of the cycle, it was *expected* to rise from 1920 to 2000, peak and then eventually to fall. *And* the second 'hump' would be expected to be higher because the long-wave of 1,000 years is likely still operative. Thus—as the Arctic now warms in 'unprecedented' ways, Viking graves are being uncovered by the retreating land ice! All Arctic scientists know this fact, yet no one tells David Attenborough as he frets about the ice falling into the sea, to look downward at the dissolving permafrost and the smelly graves underfoot.

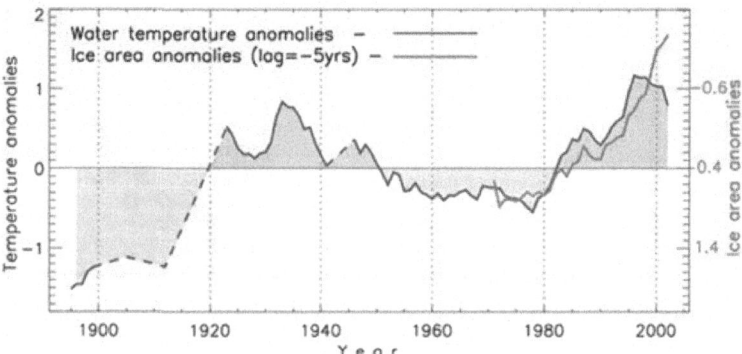

Figure 3. Arctic water temperature.
This shows how Arctic water temperatures rose in two peaks some 70 years apart, with the later peak preconditioning the massive ice-losses in 2007-2012. The changes were caused by influx of warm Atlantic water—a cyclic pattern. (from Polyakov et al., 2010, DOI: 10.1175/2010JPO4339.1). The dark grey line beginning 1975 is ice-area anomalies.

I have examined this Arctic cycle carefully (from the published literature *and* the available station data) and concluded that recent temperatures are *at most* only 25% higher than might be expected (see Fig. 3). That might sound alarming—and there are real changes in the Arctic, but it means 75% of the warming is likely *natural*. If emissions are held responsible—and of course, the consensus is that they do contribute to the warming, then halving them by 2050 (a huge global task) will deal with only 12.5% of the *driving* force, and that will not materially affect what the climate does.

When I state that the 'consensus' in science is that greenhouse gases contribute to the warming, I would add that a few respectable scientists have serious questions which remain unanswered from within the ensemble created by the UN and academic institutions—for example, that there is *zero* correlation of CO_2 levels with temperature when the whole history of life on the planet is analysed over 500 million years. Levels have been much higher than at present, but not necessarily correlating to higher temperatures (proxies such as sediment cores and isotopes in shells are used to estimate global temperatures of the past). There is a clear correlation during the last 2 million years of ice-age cycles, but always temperature rises *before* CO_2 (which is released from the warming oceans).

My own key question goes unanswered—it is somewhat technical and relates to the equivalence accorded to carbon dioxide infrared radiation and the visible wavelengths of solar radiation. All the models make the flux of both infrared radiation and visible radiation at the Earth's surface *equivalent* in terms of wattage—and this can be measured. However, this only represents the *power* to heat. The actual *temperature that results* depends on a number of factors to do with absorbing that energy. For example, land surface does not store much heat—as one can attest by going barefoot in the morning after a previous hot day, especially if the night is clear. The heat absorbed is radiated back to space. If cloudy, that heat energy is absorbed by clouds and water vapour and the atmosphere stays warm (for a while). The atmosphere *stores* very little heat. There is an unquestioned consensus that 80-90% of 'global warming' is registered in the oceans, where the heat is first stored and then released. However, long-wave infrared (IR) and short-wave (SW) visible sunlight are *not* equivalent where water surfaces are concerned—SW radiation penetrates to 100m or more, after which the oceans are dark, and *all* the energy is absorbed, to be redistributed by currents and very clear *cycles* of heat release. IR radiation cannot penetrate deeper than 1-2mm of the surface—hence, it is not stored, but contributes to surface evaporation, which *cools* the surface, but transfers heat and water vapour to the atmosphere, thus contributing to warming. A warmer atmosphere and the presence of CO_2 will *slow* the radiation of Earth's heat back to space—that is the greenhouse effect, but the effect is primarily to raise *night-time* temperature and that raises the *average* which is what is presented. All the daytime extreme temperatures and their effect (including wildfires and drought) are caused by prolonged lack of cloud.

The problem in answering the question of 'how much warming' is caused by greenhouse gas emissions lies with the nature of models—the effect is *so small* it cannot be readily measured and hence complex 'black box' models churn out the result as a single global figure. As an ecologist I ask—what is the simulated input from CO_2 and how does it compare to the normal and natural average net flux figure? The answer is 2 watts/square metre, compared to a flux of 240…or less than 1%. That is not as scary as the 40% increase in carbon-dioxide *concentration*—the graphic of which is ubiquitous. Neither the UN documentation nor the media show the relevant graphic of wattage against concentration—it is not linear, but logarithmic and the effect tails off at 300 ppmv (concentration in parts per million). We are now at about 410 ppmv for CO_2 in the atmosphere, with the wattage increasing at 0.2/decade.

The issue then develops further. If CO_2 increases water vapour and clouds, these can either warm or *cool* the planet, depending upon disposition. Clouds in the tropics cool by blocking sunlight, clouds in the polar region insulate and warm the planet. Thus, the behaviour of clouds is *crucial*. This is admitted in all the science literature as the greatest uncertainty in the models. You would expect therefore the maximum amount of research—in particular, whether cloud cover varied—by what percentage, how it affected the surface flux and whether there were any *trends*.

This was the main subject of my book on climate dynamics.[1] At the time of its writing, NASA held satellite data-sets and they clearly showed that over the late 20th-century warming period, clouds thinned by 4%. Surface radiation stations also registered wattage increases of the order 4-6 watts/square metre—all SW radiation due to increased sunlight reaching the surface. This is 3x the computed influence of CO_2 over a period of two decades. There was some discussion within NASA—some thought the clouds thinned because of global warming, some thought the thinning *caused* the warming. I wrote that the test of which was in 2001, when cloud cover registered a 2% recovery from that

4% loss and global temperatures stabilised for the next 15 years, thus not supporting the hypothesis of 'feedback'. If thinning clouds were a feedback from increasing greenhouse gases, then they should carry on thinning as carbon dioxide output continued to rise. The most obvious conclusion is that thinning clouds *drove* most of the warming from 1980-2000. This conclusion would then shift the focus to mechanisms for affecting cloud cover.

Now it gets darker. All such discussion ceased. NASA effectively 'disappeared' the data-sets, and supporters of the consensus position—key appointees of the UN, questioned the surface data record as well as the cloud trends. There are clear results in papers as recent as 2015-2018 to support the data, but the IPCC report only mentions them and the questioning, and not the implications, despite admitting clouds are still *the* major uncertainty. This demonstrates active bias but one that few scientists, even co-authors of the giant 3,000-page 6th report, are aware of.

This is how the IPCC operates its smoke-and-mirrors. It gets the majority of scientists 'on side' in the Working Group reports, but then spins everything—without their prior agreement, for public consumption. And few object. Historically 'awkward' characters have simply been omitted from the Committee.

They also use selective 'citations' and the omissions are hard to spot unless you know the field. In February of 2019, following publication of three papers jointly with a team at the Environmental Studies Institute in California, I was invited to present our work at a major international climate science conference (none of our papers on cycles have been cited by IPCC). On submission of my abstract, I decided not to pull any punches: my paper argued that 75% of global warming was natural, and that dealing with 50% of human emissions would not materially impact what the climate did over the next century when the cycles are likely to turn downward. I also quoted several recent modelling studies that also predicted no future surface warming. I expected to be dis-invited. Instead of being shunned, I was asked to present a 'keynote' address. Present at the conference, was the UN's modeller-in-chief, who defended their graphic—Professor Venkatachalam Ramaswamy, director of Princeton's Geophysical Fluid Dynamics Laboratory. When challenged by the real-world data I presented, he readily admitted that IPCC 'did not do cycles at all well'. It was a friendly and open exchange. I did not say—'Then why don't you tell the public that!' As a scientist, and one from outside the fraternity, I was encouraged and Ramaswamy invited me to Princeton for discussions. Then Covid intervened.

It is a shame, because I detect a change. This happened before with the UN—over ocean pollution, acid rain, x-raying pregnant women—all of which it had licensed against the advice of a few critics and with 'models' to back up their decisions on regulatory control (I have documented this in the science and policy literature). The UN special committees eventually respected the data—but they had to be pushed into it by outside pressure—the science alone was not enough. And therein lies our problem. There are *no* environmentalists prepared to get involved—they have *all* taken the King's Shilling. And the major science journals—and we have a paper trail, have said they *will not publish* any criticism of the IPCC.

In political reality, there is a huge global prior commitment in terms of carbon finances, without which a green techno-revolution, hailed by the World Economic Forum as the 'Great Reset' and fundament of a New World Order, could not be funded. And although some environmentalists are now playing catch-up on the impacts of 'renewables' and a rejuvenated zero carbon nuclear option, there are no strategic impact assessments of the Great Reset (nukes, turbines, hydro, biofuels, rare-earth mining etc.) on biodiversity, landscape, forest cover, indigenous communities, water resources and food-supply lines.

Adaptation or Collapse
As climate changes, and if human population increases, stress on ecosystems becomes greater—but all eyes are not on this ball, they are focused on the carbon goal. That has to change. Mitigation will not work. If carbon dioxide is already causing the current 'emergency' the levels will not drop within the next 30 years, no matter what happens in Glasgow this November, when the parties to the Climate Convention (COP 26) meet and try to gain agreement on emission reductions. Adaptation is therefore essential—most especially for poor nations and poorer people in the developed world. The rich can buy their way through the crisis—but not out of it, not at the end. Inclusivity and equality are now rising up the agenda. Eventually, the UN will be reformed—the corruption is now rather obvious. I am sure we will see a major change in policy, but at the outset, a lot of hardship will not be shared equitably.   It is worth pointing out that the most important 'adaptation' concerns food-supply lines. There are 97 countries that cannot feed themselves and rely upon the World Food Programme and global surplus of grain. As Kenneth Hsu pointed out—the down-phase of the cycle coincides with famine and collapse of overstretched empires. We could yet see a UN initiative to control and ration food supplies—and that would need a re-organisation

of international commodity markets. Already there are behind-the-scenes plans for carbon accounting, crypto-carbon currencies and intervention in the markets. Not everyone welcomes the post-Covid hand of the UN and its allies in the World Economic Forum.

I believe the human spirit will triumph in the face of such adversity—and not in perpetual *fear* of climate change, rather in a more humble acceptance of Nature's cycles of abundance and scarcity. In a strange way, the 'Bat Virus' crisis—such as it is, faces us with the same dilemma of whether to accept the constricting powers of Nature, or fight against them with an army of technicians. Resilience of the natural human immune system needs to be rebuilt just as solidly as habitations, food-supply lines and biodiversity, but the focus as ever is upon funding the technicians. In terms of natural cycles, the times of abundance that have allowed so-called advanced or developed societies to vastly increase their numbers, and especially numbers of elderly, unfit, overweight and variously vulnerable people, with all the demographic and economic stresses that has entailed, have created what some epidemiologists have called 'dry tinder'—a breeding ground for viral plagues. It is the same with modern factory-farming food production—with the same opportunities for vast profits in pharmaceuticals to keep the technology productive.

Concepts of resilience may thus have to be extended to the spiritual and emotional realms in order to cope with increased mortality and loss. Instead, with both climate and Covid, there is promulgation of fear—now involving programming children with an advocacy of techno-protection (always expensive and highly profitable for some) and faith not in the human spirit, but in scientific and engineering expertise. The history of previous failures is not part of the educational process, of course—and the mass media are complicit, allowing no dissent or branding critics as 'deniers' of the science. The next two decades will see how this all plays out. Many fear a 'techno-fascism' of control. Power is being handed to technocratic elites and history shows us handing away power does not end well. However, we all too easily forget that 'Nature' has its own rules, and thus far, though it might take a while, no civilisation has survived the cycle of rubble and dust.

Notes

1. *Chill: A Reassessment of Global Warming Theory* by Peter Taylor, Clairview Books, 2009

3.4 Climate Change: Cloud Cover Evidence Challenges Flawed IPCC Model

This article first appeared in Caduceus No196, 2021.

In 2009 I published a scientific review of climate science that demonstrated that the claimed consensus on the causes of global warming was falsely constructed—largely by scientists within the UN framework. More than 10 years on, other scientists are now producing proof that cloud-cover changes drive the warming, not the relatively minor effect of carbon-dioxide emissions. Here I rehearse the long-standing issue of corruption at the UN.

The power of authority in science
If you want to influence your government on environmental policy, you have to go to the UN. They set the standards to which all governments must adhere.

This was my experience in Britain 40 years ago concerning ocean pollution, especially toxic chemical and radioactive discharges and dumping at sea. That experience is relevant to the issues of climate science and the role of the UN today, especially in the run-up to the COP26 'climate summit' just past, upon which vast investments and alterations to lifestyle depend, and with wide-ranging environmental impacts.

On environmental issues back in the early 1980s, there were few pockets of national dissent from UN standards, but the few were instrumental; in the USA, for example, their National Academy of Sciences carried out important critical reviews of radiation hazards that clashed with the standards proposed by the chosen UN scientists.[1]

There are vital lessons here for climate change policy and, as the role of the UN in the Covid saga has shown, every policy for our future environment, health and freedom. The first lesson relates to the power of *authority* in science. Unless you are a scientist, it is hard to appreciate how this operates but it is deeply ingrained in the scientific mind.[2]

Some 40 years ago the UN system had a scientific committee for every aspect of pollution: marine, atmospheric (especially trans-boundary such as acid rain), radiation and health, reactor safety, nuclear weapons proliferation; and these days we would have to add climate change, energy policy relating to carbon emissions, biodiversity and bioweapons. Crucially, national legislation and standards including what is *legalised* must, by law, kowtow to the relevant UN committee. And now that climate science (as well as Covid origin debate) has become a global, political issue, we are experiencing the mass media, Facebook and YouTube openly censoring posts that 'criticise' either the IPCC or the WHO on these issues.

UN's chequered protection history

If such committees represented the best science and were free from the corruption of vested interests, including those of the scientific community, a UN standard would be valuable guidance, especially for countries with poor scientific infrastructure. However, such committees have proven easy targets for vested interest. In the case of nuclear dumping, for example, the UN required that dumpers must consider land-based alternatives and provide detailed comparative risk assessments and the dumping nations, a consortium led by Britain, had not followed these guidelines.

However, the relevant UN committee, under the rubric of the International Atomic Energy Agency, had allowed the dumping without intervention. Similarly, when almost all national governments perpetrated the fiction that nuclear reactors could not melt down, the IAEA, knowing otherwise, said nothing—and worldwide, national governments licensed atomic power stations under parliaments that had been seriously misled as to the consequences of a major loss of containment.[3]

This turning of a blind eye applied to many fields. Under UN auspices, for example, the x-raying of pregnant women was a standard, licensed procedure and it took 10 years for one lone, brave scientist, Dr Alice Stewart at Manchester University, to change that standard.

In other fields, despite lone voices of warning, the UN licensed the production and free dispersal of CFCs, the chemical that nearly destroyed the ozone layer; likewise, the dispersal into the oceans of PCBs that now compromise the health of cetaceans and seals; the trans-boundary emissions of sulphur (acid rain); and the atmospheric and underground testing of nuclear weapons. All of these activities are now banned. They were huge environmental mistakes, apparently supported by science, which took decades of activism, led mostly by dissident scientists, to correct.

This dynamic operates in the current field of climate science and the drive toward Net Zero carbon emissions, with huge consequences for financial structures, investment, social changes and environmental impact of apparently renewable energy supplies. Yet, among environmentalists, there is no orchestrated dissent; they make common cause with the UN and with a panoply of vested interests, and all believing it for the good of humanity.

Impenetrable models
This cadre of vested interest, which includes global networks of scientists and their need to sustain funding, always had a *model* of the environment, one that backed their policy and was all but impenetrable, unless you could run it yourself and vary the inputs, for which you needed massive computer resources. Even Greenpeace could not do that; but our small group of scientists was blessed with dissenting insiders within academia and even, at one time, within the nuclear industry, who could run models, and eventually, under European Union legislation, we were given the relevant codes.

In the most important case these were codes to model the atmospheric dispersion of radioactivity in the event of a loss-of-containment accident.[4] We managed to change the safety standards, making reactors safer but formidably more expensive. We also halted the drift to a Plutonium Economy by limiting the spread of the dangerous reprocessing technology that separated plutonium from spent reactor fuel. The ability to critique models was essential.[5]

Rigging the game
These shenanigans were accompanied by a panoply of techniques to rig the game, which still operate within the climate issue:

- If data arises that contradicts the model, ignore it, and if dissenting scientists try to publish it, pressure the journals to prevent a review; and if that fails, get the reviewers to trash it; and if that fails, belittle the critics with ad hominem attacks accompanied by pressure on their security of employment at their institutions.
- And if all that fails, then the relevant committee will *cite* the work, but not the implications, or in some cases, not cite it at all.
- And if publication could not be blocked, then mount a combination of staged resignations of members of the editorial board of the offending journal, together with publication of a dissenting and readily citable paper that would challenge the competence of the dissidents, henceforth to be known as a *rebuttal*.
- But the most effective, was to rig the *collection of data* by not funding areas that might produce conflicting results, or defunding areas that were producing conflicting results; where UN funding was not

involved, this required a word in the ear of the relevant, national funding bodies.

The Intergovernmental Panel on Climate Change's Sixth Report

The Intergovernmental Panel on Climate Change has just issued its sixth report. Following past protocol, it has first issued a laypersons' 'Summary' for press consumption, with the actual scientific report still in draft form (and without integration of text and diagrams it is extremely time-consuming to wade through its 3,000 pages). The Summary warns that the planet is now in a 'code red' state of emergency.[6]

These UN climate reports have a long history of controversy, the third report in 2001 having been described by a former President of the US National Academy of Sciences as the worst example of corruption of the peer-review process he had ever seen.[7] Twenty years on, this and other failings are repeatedly ignored by the mass media and, of course, the Climate Coalition of environmentalist groups.

I have recently worked with Professor Jackson Davis in the US, producing four papers,[8] and now have a paper reviewing the whole history of modelling at the UN, showing how it failed to effectively consider all the key papers on ocean cycles of warming and cooling published over the past *twenty-five* years (!) and, most importantly, how the third report in 2001, used faulty algorithms to erase the crucial 1,000-year-long cycle that included the Medieval Warm Period (800~1200 AD) and the Little Ice Age (1450~1850 AD). That egregious act had been achieved by promoting an obscure, American climatologist, Michael Mann, Director of the Earth System Science Center at Pennsylvania State University, to lead author of the crucial UN Working Group on the past history of climate change.

The 'Hockey Stick' controversy

Mann had developed (impenetrable) algorithms that ironed out all previous climate cycles over the last 2,000 years, leaving the 20th-century warming as 'unprecedented' in the temperature record. This graph, known as the 'Hockey Stick', showed a straight line 'shaft' for 2,000 years and then an 'uptick'—the blade—for the last 50 years due, of course, to carbon-dioxide emissions, (see Fig 1a). This influential graphic featured in media reports worldwide.

In (a) the last 2,000 years is represented by global proxies that iron out the Medieval Warm Period and Little Ice Age, and then instrumental readings are spliced in—a very questionable scientific procedure. Note in (b) the IPCC graphic stops at the height of El Niño Southern

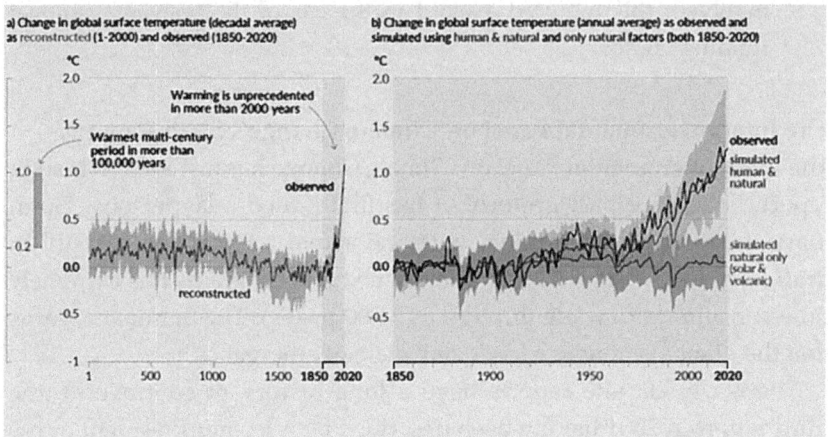

Figure 1. The Hockey Stick reprise—IPPC 6th Report, Summary for Policy Makers.

Oscillation (ENSO), whereas global temperatures fell by 0.5°C from 2016 to 2020, see (c), from University of Alabama/NASA, as it has done regularly; all the major peaks and troughs are natural ENSO events. Note also that the 'natural tendency' (as simulated in the model) is depicted as remaining 'flat' with no peaking cycles since 1950; so not only has the 1,000-year-cycle disappeared, but the centennial and multi-decadal Atlantic and Pacific cycles are compressed into a range of 0.4°C, with no indication of a cyclic peak.

Critics immediately tried to find out how Mann had concocted his record and were initially denied access to the data (against all scientific norms). After much use of Freedom of Information legislation, effective criticism prevailed in the scientific journals and this misleading graphic was dropped in the fourth 2007 report and not revisited in the fifth (2013).[9] Since, however, there has been a steady build-up of modelling results that totally ignore the issue of the long cycle and a team has been busy re-supporting Mann's work.[10]

This is a crucially important issue. Many papers on the long cycle attest to the fact that we are not yet beyond the natural variability of the climate—no *unprecedented* rates of change, nor drought or wildfire, sea-level rise nor glacial melt.[11] Moreover, the expected natural rate of recovery from the trough of the cycle (from about 200 years ago) *can* explain at least 75%, and perhaps all, of the 20th-century, warming pattern. However, the number of scientists funded to work in this area is miniscule compared to the cadre of modellers and 'Hockey-Stick' enthusiasts.

SUBTERFUGE | 115

Thus, I have now read the sixth report published 9 August and, to my utter astonishment, the UN has *resurrected* the discredited Hockey Stick. It takes a bit of reading to see how but, essentially, they picked a new hockey team!

Background to the debate
It is worthwhile reviewing the Hockey Stick controversy before its resurrection. Mann's invented algorithms that smoothed out all the varying proxy-indicators of regional temperature, such as tree-ring data, downplayed classic, ice-core records and a plethora of 'spectral analyses' of proxies across the globe that showed a millennial cycle in the data. He was immediately brought into the UN system, from wherein he promoted his own assessment and downplayed other work.

The world's large assortment of paleo-climatologists said nothing. It took *one* man, a retired geologist, Steve McIntyre, with a passionate interest in tree-ring chronologies, to challenge Mann and request his data and algorithms. As noted, Mann refused to share his data but, as it was publicly funded work, was eventually forced to release it under FOI legislation. McIntyre tested the algorithms and found they would produce a 'Hockey Stick' even when applied to *random* data![12] Mann remained in post, but the issue seemed closed.

Mechanism driving natural cycles suppressed
There is a parallel issue here. It concerns the *mechanism* that drives natural cycles capable of altering global temperatures by one degree Celsius (which is the rise we have seen over the last 150 years). It was central to my thesis published in 2009 as *Chill*[1] and concerned the fact that NASA satellite data showed clearly that over the crucial, global warming period (1980-2000), thinning, low-level cloud provided more energy input to the surface—about *three times*—than the computed energy input from carbon emissions.

In 2010 I had taken this data to challenge one of the top US modelling laboratories—and *they had not seen it!* Jackson Davis had accompanied me and it was this encounter that convinced him the models were wrong (note: he had hitherto been an advocate for the Pacific Island States at the UN Framework Convention on Climate Change and a co-author of the Kyoto Protocol).

Shortly thereafter, as I have only recently discovered, the international satellite cloud climatology programme (ISCCP) at NASA was wound up and the team disbanded. Furthermore, the key graphics on falling cloud levels were buried in another data centre and no longer readily available. In fact, my website at ethos-uk.com then became the *only* public source of those graphs, but the website is destroyed by hackers as soon as it is repaired, so we have given up.[13]

Fortunately, there *has* been recent cloud analysis by scientists outside of the usual teams. In 2015 a group of Israeli specialists led by Gerald Stanhill,[14] with work published by the American Geophysical Union, reiterated the finding that thinning cloud was the most significant driver of the warming. And in 2021 effective confirmation of the effect has been published.[15] The first paper was *cited* by the IPCC, but with the simple comment that 'clouds were still a major source of uncertainty in the models', thus burying the implications. The recent published work is outside the timeframe for the sixth report.

The UN report also contains citations of ocean cycle papers that clearly show there is no unprecedented rise in ocean temperatures,[16] but the UN does not represent the detailed figures or any comment that this work challenges the otherwise disappeared, 1,000-year cycle. Almost for sure, the mechanisms for these cyclic changes relate to varying cloud cover—driven, we think at the Environmental Studies Institute (ESI), by changing wind patterns. This is the subject of our sixth published paper which, needless to say, is not cited in the UN report—see Davis & Davis, ref.8. {*Commentary 2024*: ESI wound up its climate work and relocated to Santa Barbara under a new director and programme}.

The future is Green—dark Green
The lessons here are clear: the UN's structures regarding science and the environment have been seriously corrupted and for some time. It would take a monumental effort to clean them up, but it is not impossible. With time and resources it can be done; in the old days, we had Greenpeace, but in modern times *all* environmental groups are paid members (or paid up!) of the *Climate Coalition*, not just Greenpeace and Friends of the Earth, but the Royal Society for the Protection of Birds, Oxfam and even the Red Cross!

We, the dissidents, would have to turn to various organs of the right-wing, free-marketeers—organisations that believe in nuclear expansion (proliferation of 'modular', off-the-shelf, submarine reactors courtesy of Rolls Royce) and GMOs aplenty to underpin planetary 'business as usual'. These interests are anti-environmental, hate the Precautionary Principle and are vehemently opposed to any kind of supra-governmental regulation.

But then, the UN has a Total Solution on the horizon, courtesy of the World Economic Forum (WEF). That organisation has been meeting for the past 25 years in Davos and gathering all the world's governmental and corporate leaders, including UN functionaries, to solve these growing, planetary problems. As WEF's head, Klaus Schwab, writes openly in his book, *The Great Reset*, climate will become the greatest of all emergencies, requiring new levels of UN-sponsored control.[17]

We can see other lessons from the Covid emergency: rampant censorship by the key social media channels controlled by Facebook and Google, with a complicit mainstream media where even the BBC have stated they will no longer represent criticism of the UN on climate issues (they recently broadcast programmes focused on debunking the 'Hockey Stick' scandal, just as they suppressed any critique of the origins of Covid, its treatment or the testing and efficacy of the vaccine). Governments and parliaments have rolled over in the face of UN-sponsored 'science'.

There is, however, one big and hopeful difference—the number of doctors, scientists and virologists who have stood up against this authoritarianism, far more than have done on environmental issues, and their use of alternative channels of social media.[18]

Compromised campaign groups and the COP26 agenda

Unfortunately, our own environmental campaign groups are now so heavily compromised by their prior commitment to faulty models, despite warnings, and to the agenda of COP26 (global carbon emission reductions), that they cannot carry out any kind of review and are programmed as campaigners to attack all dissenters as co-conspirators with the Trumpian anti-environmentalists.

The greatest casualty is now scientific integrity; the environmentalists are forced to ignore the *data* on the *impacts* of the policies they are adopting—and not just environmental, but social and political also.[19] The WEF are preparing their plans for an electro-technical, GMO-enabled, highly controlled, green economy, with most of the relevant technology made in the global workhouse that China has become. Corporate investment houses, such as Vanguard and BlackRock, where all the billionaire beneficiaries of the Covid lockdowns have placed their future bets, will make all the key decisions as to what gets built and where, and with appropriate input from their 'green' advisors.

There is no real rebellion. Even the massive public concern at the extinction of wildlife, the forests, the beauty, landscape and fate of remaining indigenous peoples, gets captured and channelled into the maw of the Climate Coalition, rather than focusing on the real threats of over-consumption, agricultural intensification, invasive species, poaching and pollution.[20] We can hope at best, that the system collapses, though that too will have some dire consequences; in which case we need to seed the future with positive examples of a balanced and sustainable life. Or perhaps, the climate itself will further an awakening, for we are at the end of a much longer cycle and things *could* get significantly colder.[21]

The jury is out on the ultimate driver of the 1,000-year cycle but solar activity has been shown to vary at this frequency, with early work on North Atlantic, ice-rafted debris finding a cycle shortening over the last 10,000 years from 1,500 years average to 1,000 years and a correlation with proxies for solar magnetic activity. The last trough of this magnetic cycle coincided with the Little Ice Age (LIA) and the rising magnetic field from 1900~1995 has coincided with the global warming period. But the mechanism is not understood and may involve solar-UV affecting the Jetstream as well as cloud-seeding effects.

Some solar scientists are projecting a coming solar 'minimum', as solar activity has been dropping with each 11-year, sunspot cycle since 1995. My and Davis's understanding is that an LIA would be expected in 2300, but that the centennial cycles within the millennial would be expected to cool the planet by 2030.[22]

Notes

1. See: *Chill: A Reassessment of Global Warming Theory* (Clairview, W. Sussex, 2009) which summarises my policy work on Clean Production Strategies.

2. Whenever a science paper is written, the reference list itemises the *authorities* in the field and the hardest job of a critical review is to spot the *omissions*; all authors are subject to 'confirmation bias', often citing their own work or their colleagues' and ignoring critics. A good paper is one that references and answers valid criticism.

3. In 1988 I published the first paper in the science literature that showed the potential land contamination impact of a major reactor meltdown: 'Taylor, Land-use implications of radioactive contamination' *Land Use Policy* 1998;5(1):62-70.

4. See: P. Taylor, 'Large Consequence Low Probability Accidents'. *Standing Conference on Health & Safety in the Nuclear Age*, CEC, Radiation Protection, Report EUR 11608 EN, 1988.

5. This is documented in a PERG report—available from the British Library. P. Taylor (1985) *The disposal of nuclear waste to the deep ocean* PERG RR-15, Political Ecology Research Group, Oxford.

6. 'UN IPCC 6th Report, 2021: Summary for Policymakers'. In: *Climate Change 2021: The Physical Science Basis. Contribution of Working Group I to the Sixth Assessment Report of the Intergovernmental Panel on Climate Change* (V. Masson-Delmotte et al).

7. See *Chill*, p 269.

8. W.J. Davis & W.B. Davis 'Antarctic Winds: Pacemaker of Global Warming, Global Cooling, and the Collapse of Civilizations', *Climate* 2020;8:130 doi:10.3390/cli8110130; W.J. Davis, P. Taylor & W.B. Davis, 'The origin and propagation of the Antarctic Centennial Oscillation', *Climate* 2019;7:112. doi:10.3390/cli7090112; W.J. Davis, P.Taylor & W.B. Davis, 'The Antarctic Centennial Oscillation: a natural paleoclimate cycles in the Southern Hemisphere that influences global temperature'. *Climate* 2018;6:3; doi:10.3390/cli6010003; W.J. Davis, 'The relationship between atmospheric carbon dioxide concentration and global temperature for the last 425 million years' *Climate* 2017; 5:76, doi:10.3390/cli5040076.

9. S. McIntyre & R. McKitrick, 'The M&M Critique of the MBH98 Northern Hemisphere Climate Index: update and implications', *Energy and Environment* 2005;16(1):69-100; S. McIntyre & R. McKitrick, 'Hockey sticks, principal components and spurious significance', *Geophys Res Lett* 2005;32(3), L03710 10.1029/2004GL021750 12 February 2005 and see: Montford AW, *The Hockey Stick Illusion*, Anglosphere, 2015, and *Hide the Decline*, Anglosphere, 2012 .

10. Abrams led the Pages2k consortium with a paper in *Nature Geoscience* 2013;6:339-46 that appeared to show unprecedented modern warmth, but when later corrected by McIntyre, showed no significant difference between medieval warmth and modern warming.

11. For the correction see: www.nature.com/articles/ngeo2566.pdf; and see also: www.NoTricksZone: Pages2k rebuttal by Pierre Gosselin for a critique of the new 'hockey team'.

12. See 9 above.

13. One reason for the discontinuity, apart from the constant criticism of ISCCP data from NASA's former head, James Hansen, an active alarmist on the global political issue, is that new satellites were capable of measuring the cloud effect, known as CERES; however, only in the last year have relevant analyses been performed (see 14,15).

14. Stanhill et al, 'The cause of solar dimming and brightening at the Earth's surface during the last half century: Evidence from

measurements of sunshine duration', *J Geophys Res Atmos* 2014;119(10):902-10,911, doi:10.1002/2013JD021308.

15. N. Loeb et al., 'Satellite and ocean data reveal marked increase in Earth's heating rate', *Geophys Res Lett* 2021;48; e2021GL093047. https://doi.org/10.1029/2021GL093047

16. G. Gebbie, 'Atlantic warming since the Little Ice Age', *Oceanography* 2021;32(1):220-30, https://doi.org/ 10.5670/oceanog.2019.151.

17. Schwab K., *Covid 19: The Great Reset*. WEF, Switzerland, 2020.

18. For example, Dr Robert Malone, one of the inventors of the mRNA technology. https://www.youtube.com/watch?v=9E2UkhCWosg

19. In fact, there is no comprehensive environmental impact assessment of the Green New Deal, in particular the renewable energy/decarbonisation component.

20. In the 2019 UN biodiversity report a detailed reading shows climate changes ranked fifth in terms of impact: www.un.org/sustainabledevelopment/blog/2019/05/nature-decline-unprecedented-report/refs….2019.

21. Temperatures in the northern hemisphere have been falling since 2016, having lost almost 0.5°C from the peak caused by a super-El Niño, and are now back where they were in 2000. The long cycle would be expected to produce a plateau of warmth that might last several decades, but projection of past centennial cycles, which we did in our papers referenced above, shows a dip to 2060 and an eventual return to LIA conditions by 2300. But in the Holocene we are now at the end of what I have called a 'beat cycle' of 10,000 years, largely ignored by the climate science community (an exception: Yiou: *J Geophys Res* 1997;102:441-5). This cycle could 'reset' the clock and take us steadily down into the next real Ice Age. In this case, human emissions of carbon dioxide become a potential saving grace!

22. There are several ways of projecting future patterns—looking at peaks and troughs in proxies for solar activity (e.g. beryllium isotopes) and projecting sine waves forward (not easy due to harmonic patterns); projecting patterns in oxygen isotopes as proxies for temperature in ice cores, which we have done, and in tree-rings, which has been done in Tibet. In each case there is a potential natural drop to 2030 and it will be interesting to see how this interacts with the greenhouse gas increases. Professor Nicola Scafetta at Naples University has a long history of analysis in this field, having found correlations between Saturn-Jupiter cycles, aspects of the solar dynamo and climatic signals; his work also projects a Dalton minimum of lower solar activity, which then competes with greenhouse-gas forcing. Scafetta N, 'Multi-scale harmonic model for solar and climate cyclical variation through-

out the Holocene based on Jupiter-Saturn tidal frequencies plus the 11-year solar dynamo cycle', *J Atmos and Solar-Terrest Phys* 2012. doi:10.1016/j.jastp.2012.02.016; Scafetta, 'Reconstruction of the Interannual to Millennial Scale patterns of the Global Surface Temperature', *Atmosphere* 2021;12:147. https://doi.org/10.3390/atmos12020147

3.5 Adjustments to Reality

Originally published in New View 2022-23 Issue 106

I have argued often enough—including in leading scientific forums—that climate change cannot be effectively mitigated and that we need to adjust to this reality. However, adjusting to reality doesn't sound profitable, nor may it involve new technology, or give positional advantages to scientific funding streams, nor does it help build reputations or support the aspirations of the United Nations to regulate matters on behalf of the world. Adaptation to climate change is a subsection for action under the Paris Accords (and was also under the Kyoto Protocol) but of the billions of dollars spent globally, less than 1% has been allocated to adapting to the changing climate.

What we get instead is a belief system of alarmists that scare the life and happiness out of a young generation that then fosters nihilistic activists quite willing to break the law, cause disruption to daily life and risk imprisonment—all in the belief that nothing is being done to save the world from 'climate breakdown'. Contrary to activists' claims of 'nothing', vast sums of taxpayers' money are devoted to the cause of mitigation—by emission control, and huge changes are afoot in technology fields related to carbon-free fuels. Despite the expense, carbon-dioxide levels continue to rise—however much the technology is deployed, the global model of growth demands fossil fuels.

But what happens when despite all the apparent climate extremes, the globe does not warm as expected? From 1940 to 1980, there was no net warming despite the huge increase in carbon emissions. From 1980 to 2000, the globe warmed at the rate of 0.2 degrees Celsius/decade—the same as the rate from 1920-1940. And from 2000 to 2015, there was no surface warming. These inconsistencies have been brushed aside with the assertion on scanty evidence that the 'missing heat' has been buried in the deep ocean layers.

Since 2016 there have been two 'super' El Niño events—a natural global recycling of surface waters in the Pacific that bumps up global temperatures by as much as 0.5°C, after which they drop back to pre-Niño levels. Such 'super' big El Niño events—the usual Niño cycle is 3-4 years with a much smaller impact on global temperature—are usually a decade or more apart, but there were two 'back-to-back' from 2016-2019. Many scientific commentators have used this to claim that global temperatures are now 1.2°C above 'pre-industrial levels' implying the whole of this rise is anthropogenic. This is unsound—the Niño-effect needs to be subtracted, and this means the rise from 2000-2022 contains no significant anthropogenic signal. Furthermore, the pre-1950 rise was 0.4-0.5°C and before CO_2 could make a significant impact. That leaves the 1980-2000 rise of 0.4-0.5°C as the only reasonable anthropogenic claim—except there are several other ocean cycles peaking in that period, which in my estimation can contribute at least half (0.2°C). The UN's Intergovernmental Panel on Climate Change (IPCC) themselves only claim that this late 20th-century rise is 'mostly' anthropogenic (51-99%?). I now expect a further hiatus, or an obvious decline.

The scientists' response to these blips is, as I will explain, to get busy adjusting it—that is, doctoring the data. This is an issue that the mainstream media ignore. The media have become heavily compromised by foundation money as well as the psychological prior commitment that results from endless scare stories, and it now selects only those 'stories' that fit the narrative.

Herewith, a recent example. The BBC sent a team—which included their science editor—to Svalbard (Norwegian for Spitsbergen), to investigate a story floated by Norway's top climate laboratory that the archipelago was the 'fastest warming' place on Earth. According to the Norwegians' data, it had warmed by 4°C. The BBC team interviewed various natives who all agreed that they were in new territory with permafrost thawing, walruses behaving like seals and hauling out on sand-spits instead of on floating summer sea ice—the latter having all-but disappeared. Polar bears did not get a mention (as it happens, their population in the region is stable and, elsewhere in the melting Arctic, actually increasing).

Four degrees of warming didn't sound right—the globe has warmed by about one degree, but the Arctic does have steeper cycles. In research for my 2009 book, *Chill*, I made an in-depth assessment of Arctic temperature and summer-ice data. There were 35 stations above the Arctic Circle, with long-term and reliable measurements, situated in Canada, Alaska, Greenland, Iceland, Norway and Russia. In data up until 2008 and going back to 1900, 30 of those stations recorded the highest temperature around 1935-1945, and of the remaining five, two exceeded the previous peak around that time, and three matched it. There was a clear peak-and-trough cycle with amplitude of three degrees across all Arctic stations and the trough occurred around 1960, the last peak around 1940. This was well-known among Arctic specialists—with the lead authorities in the field based at the International Arctic Research Station at the University of Fairbanks, Alaska. The team there was led by a distinguished Japanese geo-physicist, Syinichi Akasofu, and included the Russian Professor Igor Polyarkov, the leading climatologist. Polyarkov described this 'Arctic Oscillation' in research papers noting it is caused by warm and cold periods alternating according to variable inflow of warm water mainly via the North Atlantic. When it comes to long-term centennial warming, Akasofu, on his retirement, wrote a paper on 'recovery from the Little Ice Age'—a cycle of 1,000 years with its last trough about 400 years before present.

It is worth exploring treatment of this 'long cycle' in current scientific circles. Prior to the hype over global warming, there were hundreds of published papers in the field of paleo-climatology on this 1,000-1,500-year cycle, but the IPCC published one graphic (the infamous 'Hockey Stick') that did away with the cycle entirely. This was heavily criticised and the IPCC withdrew the graphic for the next report, only for it to resurface in the latest 2021 report's summary—without *any* treatment in the main text. Furthermore, if you look up Akasofu, a distinguished geo-physicist, on the internet, you will be guided to 'deSmog.blog' which calls his paper on the recovery issue 'flawed' and highlights an apparent critique (a letter to the editors) by the part-time *Guardian* newspaper journalist Dana Nuccitelli and other 'warmist' climate scientists—who claim the paper is flawed but provide no analysis of their own.

I came to update my database on the Arctic Stations around 2014. In the previous research I had found ready access to graphics for all the stations. They exist as part of a network known as the Global Historical Climate Network (GHCN) and are compiled by US specialists—initially at the Goddard Institute of Space Studies (GISS—part of NASA), but also by the US National Oceanic and Atmospheric Administration (NOAA) and shared then worldwide. In this later review, I could not readily locate the graphics. When I did navigate the links, I was puzzled to find that many of the graphs did not accord with the previous graphs. Checking with NASA, I discovered the station data had been 'adjusted' according to a quality appraisal programme that filled-in gaps, took account of shifts in instrument location and technology, and 'homogenised' the raw data.

I was surprised by the scale of the changes which have occurred worldwide, and in almost all cases they lower the past, thus emphasising the long-term rate of warming. In the case of the Arctic, the change is doubly significant because by lowering temperatures prior to 1950, they reduce the peak that is part of the Arctic Oscillation, an 80-year cycle from peak to peak. This makes the Arctic align with the rest of the global pattern imposed by NASA and importantly, makes the Arctic warming since 1960 (4 degrees) look much worse than it is because the 2020 peak is actually only 1 degree above the previous peak in 1940.

I complained to NASA and asked for access to the 'unadjusted data', which they facilitated as it was not so readily accessible. One other person, a climate blogger—Paul Homewood—followed these changes and alerted the world, pointing out that some stations with impeccable scientific credentials, such as the Irish station on Valentia Island, had been adjusted to reflect the 'new reality' that the world had been warming at the same rate since 1900.

This was my background knowledge when I first saw the BBC story—and I was certain that a) the Arctic had *not* warmed by 4 degrees since 1900, b) the faster rate of warming (as part of a 60-80-year cycle) was well-known, but no different than the previous warming from 1920-1940. So, I did a quick check for Spitzbergen on the World Data website: from 1900 to 2020, *it had warmed by 1.3 degrees*. That is to say, the second peak was 1.3 degrees above the previous peak—about what I would have expected, since the whole century was experiencing a 'recovery' from the Little Ice Age, since 1850, by about 0.05°C/decade (from the paper published by Akasofu in 2013).

There is a compilation of global stations by the independent team known as Berkeley Earth—though they use the same station data and combine data from Spitzbergen and Jan Mayen, a nearby island. It shows clearly the long period coincident with the Little Ice Age and then the 20th-century warming with the two peaks of the Arctic Oscillation. We should note that all computer models of CO_2 influence show no significant effect until after 1950, so the first peak and the steep rise *is natural*.

As if in response to my complaint about data availability, NASA now provide the original 'raw' data as well as their adjustments. You can see how the well-attested Arctic Oscillation all-but disappears from the adjusted data (the black line in Fig.1)—and also how the warmth has peaked and, in line with other stations, is now falling, as is the seawater temperature of the Atlantic inflow. Sea ice has been recovering over the past five years.

Homewood complained to the official BBC watchdog regarding their recent Arctic foray on the grounds that they had only looked at the rise since 1960—which, as you may readily work out, would give 4 degrees of warming. But only one degree and a half is actually relevant, and it is *not* out of keeping with the global rise nor the centennial rate of warming. The BBC watchdog responded that they had taken the whole story from the Norwegian climate lab, including the term 'fastest rate of warming on the planet' and hence could not be held responsible.

The lessons I take from this:
1. Climate labs the world over—and Norway is unlikely to be an exception, need funds and need to draw attention to their work.
2. Science editors should know this but are not minded to check the data if the hyped story contributes to the already instigated media campaign of alarm, nor are they likely to do much in the way of simple scientific background checks on the real data.
3. The biggest climate labs are quite capable of doctoring real-world data and adjusting them to fit the expectations of their computer models.

I would gladly offer a free seminar to the BBC on Arctic realities—which would include the Holocene Optimum about 8,000 years ago, when for

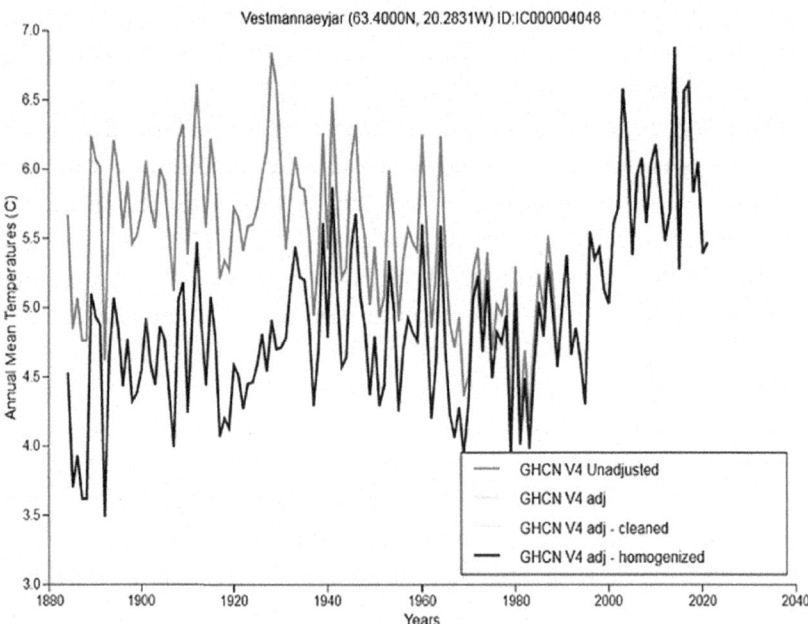

Figure 1. Adjustments made by NASA to the station data off the southern coast of Iceland, which lower the significance of the 1940's peak. The two peaks occur between 1920-40 and 2000-20. Note: the caption refers to four options to display and for clarity only the two most relevant ones are shown. Unadjusted is the grey line.

two thousand years the Arctic Ocean was ice-free in summer, and clearly its wildlife adapted; and then the Little Ice Age Cycle of 1,000 years, which saw previous warm periods—Roman and Norman, for example, in the western temperate region, and Norse colonisation and farming on Greenland (800-1300AD), all then declining into the trough around 1650 AD. Pelicans nested in Somerset 3,000 years ago, and white storks in Scotland at the time the Vikings farmed Greenland. This information is not hard to come by.

In conclusion, we can look at the poster-child for 'global heating'—the Arctic meltdown, beloved of David Attenborough and Greta Thunberg—and scratching the surface reveals that not a great deal unusual is happening. Carbon emissions have not accounted for the greater part of the warming, which began 150 years ago, and hence, are not likely to stave off the descent into the next cold period. Time will tell, of course, but we have to keep a wary eye on the data-keepers and the reporters, as they are not entirely trustworthy. We may see another long 'warm period' as in Norman and Viking times, but my own feeling is that we are at the end of a 10,000-year 'beat cycle', which is discernible in the long series of ice ages. It consists of a 'bar' like in a musical score, with 4-5 beats (where the temperature shoots up rapidly) and these vary from 2,500 to 1,000 years apart, with the period shortening toward the end of the bar, and then a new cycle begins. Climatologists have noted the peaks, but not the pattern of the beat-cycle. During the interglacial period, there is a 'ghost' of this pattern, and most interglacials, such as our current geological period, the 'Holocene' period, last only 10,000 years before a gradual descent into an Ice Age.

We are now at that point. And if CO_2 had the strength that IPCC models claim, it might stave off the Ice Age! But the data does not show that. At the end of every interglacial, CO_2 levels were high and stayed high whilst the descent took place.

Until these realities are faced, we will not see the necessary investment in adaptive response, in particular, infrastructure and agricultural adaptations that are robust to any change in temperature, whether up or down. A country such as Sweden has had to adapt to strong seasonal changes—warmer summers and colder winters—and we could learn much from them with regard to housing, transport and food production.

3.6 World Climate Declaration Challenges 'Adjusted' Data Supporting IPCC's Flawed Models

This article first appeared in Caduceus No.108, 2022

In August this year a group of Belgian and Dutch scientists launched the World Climate Declaration, now signed by 1,400 professional scientists, many of them professors, in which they declared: 'There is no Climate Emergency' (https://clintel. org/world-climate-declaration). There have been several such declarations over the past two decades, some attracting tens of thousands of signatories—all to zero effect.

Tens of thousands of signatories—all to zero effect
Does anybody listen? Certainly not every single science academy, all the mainstream media, every UN body (following the IPCC), the EU and as far as I am aware, all governments who signed up to the Paris Accord aimed at limiting global warming (or 'heating' as now preferred, by the media, along with climate 'breakdown'). The aimed-for 'danger' limit is 1.5°C and according to the MSM [mainstream media] we are now at 1.2°C and rising at 0.2°C/ decade. Hence the 'emergency' declared by the UN's Secretary General at the recent COP27 gathering of governments party to the Climate Convention.

As readers of my articles will know, there is a reasoned, scientific critique of the climate change science that these policies and targets are based upon, several of which the Declaration draws attention to: future projections are based upon computer *models* of reality and these have been shown in published papers to produce about twice the future warming that data show is the likely reality; there are no long-term, climate cycles in the models that incorporate the data on natural changes, such as cloud cover, which brings significant uncertainty into future projections, including potential cooling; and historic global temperature data has been 'adjusted' to match expectations from the flawed models (Fig 1)!

A classic example of 'adjusting' raw data, from the Arctic (Iceland/Greenland), where the unadjusted (yellow line) and hitherto dependable data (before 2011) assimilated by NOAA and used worldwide, has been 'adjusted' and 'homogenised' by NOAA (black) to give the impression of a much cooler period from 1880 to about 1995 (see Fig. 1, section 3.5, p.126). NOAA and other centres have explained generally how they adjusted 1,500+ stations' data but no one had the time or funds to check their calculations.

Note how the typical, Arctic 'double hump' in the unadjusted data shows, compared to the post-1995 adjusted data, two peaks, with the 2019 one only marginally greater than the 1935 one, in contrast to the apparently much larger difference in the two peaks based on the adjusted data. The BBC recently reported from the Arctic but only referred to the temperature rise since 1960, which looks like 3 degrees across the region, hence misleadingly calling it the 'greatest rate of warming on the planet' at three times the global rate.

This deliberate 'adjustment' issue is very controversial and concerning. It seems to have begun in 2011, when climate blogs debated it, but it has been ignored by the media. The scientists, based in the USA involved in compiling global station data, independently 'cooled' the past on many station records, thus enabling them to emphasise an apparent, long rise and rate of change, while in the Arctic they removed evidence of historic highs that match the recent peaks. They obfuscate the issue by only publishing general rules, which needs an in-depth, independent investigation visiting each station to reveal how the various, national recorders have had their data 'adjusted'.

The MSM is complicit in the scientific sleight of hand, claiming that global temperatures now stand at 1.2°C above the pre-industrial level. By the year 2000, the acknowledged warming over 150 years was 0.8 plus/minus 0.1°C. From 2000~2015 there was no surface warming trend. In 2016 and 2019 there were two successive 'super' El Niño events—a natural cycle in the Pacific which temporarily bumps up global temperatures—since the peak in 2016, global temperatures have been *falling*—down by about 0.5°C. If those two natural peaks are removed from the data, there has been no significant surface warming in two decades!

Another sleight of hand relates to the target 1.5°C itself. It is entirely arbitrary—but politically convenient for the global 'emergency' mongers—which, as we saw with Covid, need to declare an emergency in order to give them the controlling role in coordinating global action. It is evident that the original projection of 3°C or even 2°C would not likely be reached by 2100. And, of course, none of the signatories to the Paris Accords, no academies, nor any MSM journalists discuss the natural cycle of warming expected as recovery from the 'pre-industrial period' (used as a baseline for change), which coincided with the trough of the long-cycle known as the Little Ice Age. The amplitude of this cycle in the northern hemisphere is about 1°C—hence we are not yet beyond the norms of the last few thousand years and not beyond the Holocene peak temperatures two degrees higher than today only 6-8,000 years ago, when the Arctic Ocean was naturally ice-free in summer and the lake-villagers of Somerset were eating pelican for breakfast.

Anyone who makes these criticisms is instantly labelled a 'denier' and aspersions cast on their affiliations and funding. The problem is that *some* critics, even professors, though not of climate science, *are* in denial, either arguing that warming is not happening, that the rise in CO_2 is not anthropogenic and that in any case both warming and more CO_2 is good for the planet and agriculture in particular. This makes it easy to dismiss the real critics by lumping them all as deniers. And then begins the assault on freedom to speak and to publish, with campaigns to de-platform heretics.

This process of labelling and censorship is directly paralleled by the Covid saga. In order to enforce compliance and market an unlicensed, experimental procedure based on gene-editing, the UN, under pressure to act globally, declared a pandemic 'emergency' in which the normal, safeguarding procedures could be legally abandoned. It was clear early on that the WHO acted in the commercial interests of vaccine manufacturers. Only under significant pressure from acknowledged professionals in virology did it backtrack on the zoonotic 'origin' story and consider an escape from the Wuhan Institute of Virology lab and its 'gain-of-function' research.

Currently, all of the policies of 'vaccinating' people not at risk, denying off-the-shelf and cheap treatments, masks and lockdowns, are under expert scrutiny, including in leading science and medical journals, yet the MSM and most governments still parrot the UN storylines. The label of choice for critics with a lesser profile than virology professors (who are simply ignored) is *conspiracy theorist*. And once again, there are plenty of commentators who see the hand of a global cabal intent on reducing world population. Very few people talk of an *economic* bioweapon and of the military lab down the road from the WIV that had access agreements to all their genetic coding from the manipulated bat virus.

The recent COP27 meeting in Egypt focused largely upon capital flows. The 'developing' countries, who apparently suffer most from climate change, are demanding $100 billion/year in reparations from the industrialised, carbon emitters. This sum is largely aimed at acquiring 'renewable' sources of energy. In reality, most of the money will bring jobs and profit to the industrialised producers of wind- and hydro-turbines, solar panels and electric vehicles—most of which are made in China with Western capital, or for biomass plantations that export fuel (as in Brazil). Some small sums will go to flood defences—again, likely with Western contractors. In actuality, despite pledges, only a few percent of that figure will be made available for adaptation to a changing climate.

The reality is that climate change cannot be influenced by emission reductions, at least not in this century, even if the models were correct and 'net-zero' by 2050 were possible (it isn't). Developing countries, which in the Kyoto Protocol definition *included* China, cannot *afford* renewable energy (where even the rich countries now struggle) and they will continue to want industrialised goods designed and built in rich countries—as they have all along the years of climate 'injustice'. But, like the Emperor with no clothes, nobody (of repute) dares to say anything! Paradoxically, 'developing' India and China, in pursuit of Western levels of prosperity, are following essentially the same industrial and economic growth model and relying heavily on new coal plants.

It is for these reasons that I think declarations generally go nowhere—all except The Great Barrington Declaration with 60,000+ professional signatories, headed by top professors in virology and epidemiology from Oxford, Harvard and other universities (www.gbdeclaration.org). It got little MSM coverage but governments were forced to listen due to the eminence of the leaders speaking on the futility of lockdowns and mass vaccination.

What is needed is an exposé of who funds the MSM and how all-powerful editors, especially at the BBC, avoid awkward questions like adjusted data in their complicity to promote the monotonic, global message on climate change.

PART 4: SCIENCE AND PUBLIC POLICY

Preface

Policy is always a political process and science imagines itself as somehow separate and objectively feeding into that policy process, being in denial that the very structure of science and its institutions involves complex feedbacks from the policy arena. Policy makers do not like caveats, uncertainties and multiple choices. Scientists know this and in the case of the UN Intergovernmental Panel on Climate Change (IPCC) the Summary for Policy Makers makes the necessary adjustments in emphasis—over which the majority of scientists consulted in the scientific Working Group, have no sight of let alone editorial control.

4.1 Science and Changing Climates

This article first appeared in New View *no.110, Winter 2023/2024*

At the recent meeting of the Parties to the Climate Convention (COP 28) The Secretary General of the United Nations (UN) tells us the climate is 'breaking down' and we must accelerate the reduction of greenhouse, gas emissions or it will get much worse. At the meeting, the BBC interviewed Lord Brown, former head of British Petroleum, who warned of a 3°C increase by the end of the century and that the oil companies are part of the solution—there will have to be carbon offsetting as well as accelerated investments in renewable energy sources, including new technologies; and *The Guardian* newspaper tells us this year is the hottest in human history—with the latter time period not defined but presumably meaning *Homo sapiens* and the last 200,000 years. (One wonders how they know?) Actually, there *is* something unusual happening with the climate. Laid out in a graph (Figure 1) is the very latest satellite measurements of lower atmospheric temperature—the best measurement of planetary systems as it is above the more turbulent surface layer of the Earth and has tracked the evolution of the average monthly temperature since 1979. The data is taken from about 3km above ground and the 'anomaly' method means you compare each year to a base-period, so it shows up the changes from year to year.

NASA satellites collect the data by using microwaves to 'sound' each layer of air. These are microwaves that bounce back from the air molecules, like radar, and carry information on their temperature. The data is analysed at the University of Alabama at Huntsville—a unit directed by Professor of Atmospheric Sciences, John Christy, a noted expert who has heavily criticised the models used by the UN. In an interview with the BBC (that they immediately buried) he reckoned the warming was about 75% natural. The BBC's interviewer, the science correspondent Roger Harrabin, had read my book *Chill* (my critique of the UN science) and phoned me to ask what questions he should ask; I advised him to ask what proportion of the warming Christy thought was natural—a question seldom asked.

We can balance the hype of the mainstream media by looking more closely at this short-term NASA satellite record of 44 years (from 1979 to 2023) and then place it in context of what we know of planetary temperatures *throughout human history*. Prior to 1979, there had been no global warming since the rise from 1920 to a peak around 1945, in fact a global cooling is evidenced that led many experts to think the next Ice Age was approaching.

{*Commentary 2024*: since October 2023 the super-El Niño peaked and by May 2024, global temperatures had lost about 0.3C from that peak, with a likelihood of dropping further toward the baseline.}

The first thing to notice in Figure 1 is the pattern of peaks and troughs—particularly 1998, 2016, 2020 and 2023, and their amplitude (the variation from trough to peak). These peaks are caused by what is known as a 'strong' El Niño, an oscillation of temperatures in the Pacific southern equatorial region that has an impact across the globe, altering some regional temperatures by as much as 2°C and the global average by 1°C. This phenomenon, known as the El Niño Southern Oscillation (ENSO), is a cyclic storage and release of heat from the upper 300m of the ocean. What causes the 'strong' ENSO is not understood, but during 'warm periods' in another cycle of centennial and millennial length, the peaks are closer together—i.e. the cycle frequency shortens. Thus, in, for example, the 1,000-year-millennial cycles, during its peaks El Niños are closer together and stronger; during its troughs further apart and weaker with more La Niña periods when the oceans are cooler.

To get a better measure of the decadal warming pattern (such as the last 40-50 years), we draw a line connecting the bottom of the troughs or the tops, and compute the 'trend'—for example, it is currently running at about 0.15°C/decade—and this is the figure given most attention

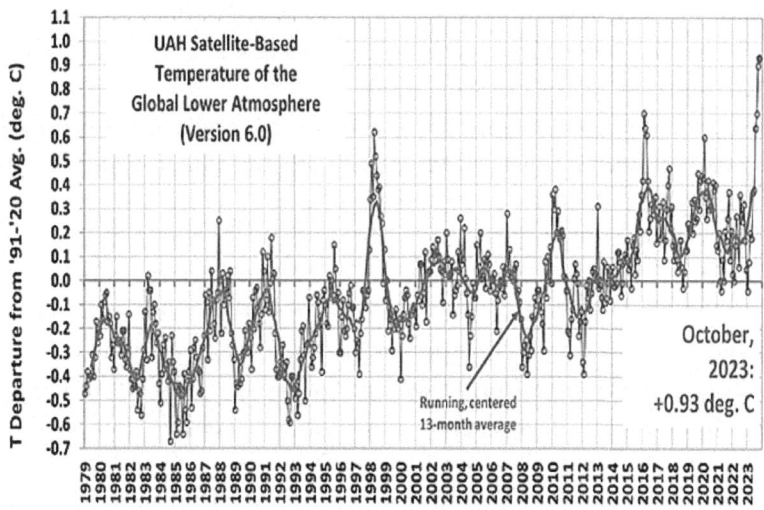

Figure 1. The satellite record of atmospheric temperature, 1979–2023. Source: website of Roy Spencer who with the University of Alabama (UAH) processes the NASA data. https://www.drroyspencer.com/latest-global-temperatures/

in the media; but a closer look shows many troughs and peaks with a global warming of 1°C within a single year. If we extrapolate 0.15/decade rate of warming to the end of the century, we will increase the global average by a further 1.3°C on top of what is generally recognised as a centennial rise to date (since 1900) of around 1°C. This is in line with the latest model predictions for a doubling of CO_2 levels—levels that now stand at 420ppmv above the pre-industrial baseline of 280 parts per million by volume (ppmv). Levels are increasing by about 2ppmv/year and this has remained unchanged throughout the 28-year history of COP and all the efforts to control emissions. On current emission trends this doubling would reach 560 ppmv in 70 years' time (2093) and produce, according to the projections of the models, 2.3°C of *apparently anthropogenic* global warming.

However, as I have argued in previous articles, this modelling assumes *all* the warming is due to human emissions. And it also assumes that the recent decadal rate is representative. If the previous 40 years were looked at (1940-1980) the rate of warming would be zero, due to the decadal cycles' cooling phase. What is missing is the long-term cycle that places the current warmth *in context*—all other cycles ride on top of that. It last peaked around the Viking colonisation of Greenland and they left when the cycle turned down; moreover the modern warm period is only now uncovering their graves! Figure 2 shows data derived from ocean sediments and published in the journal *Oceanography* and we can see the long cycle and the decline into a trough around 1600 AD—known as the Little Ice Age.

In a previous article [see: 3.2, Fig.1], I showcased the work of 22 paleo-climatologists and the existence of two such troughs—the one previous to this being known as the Antique Little Ice Age (see *New View*, issue 108, p.58). The authors of that work actually complained that the IPCC was biased in its choice of paleo-reconstructions, ignoring analyses that contradicted its preferred 'Hockey Stick' where nothing much happens for 2,000 years until the last 100. The term 'Hockey Stick' arose as a jest when a relatively unknown paleo-climatologist used bizarre (and later discredited) algorithms to iron out the cycles, leaving the last 70 years as an uptick due to greenhouse gases. The IPCC promoted him to 'lead author' of the paleo-climate group!

We can note from Figure 2 that current global temperatures are about 0.2K (effectively 0.2°C) above the previous peak and the amplitude of the previous wave is about 0.8K—thus on this data, modern warming could be about 80% natural. This data was published in a 2018 paper, but ignored in the IPCC 6th report in 2022. Closer reading of the science

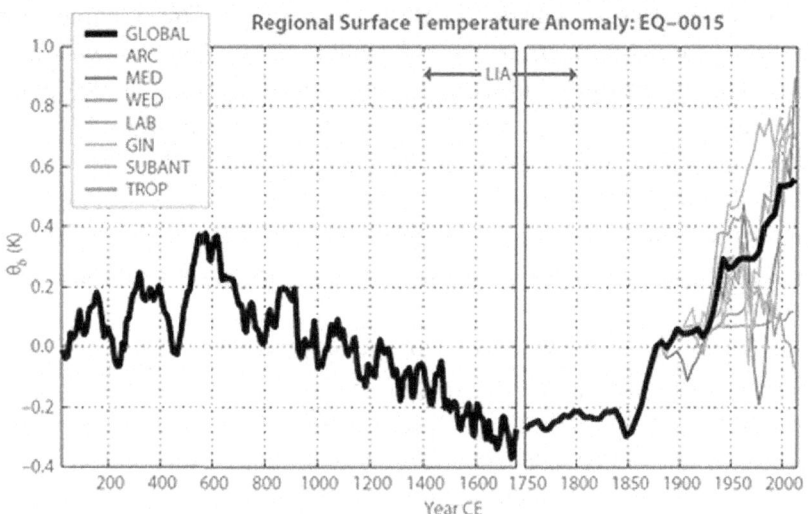

Figure 2. Ocean temperature proxy records: global, Arctic (ARC), Mediterranean (MED), Weddell Sea—Antarctic (WED), Labrador Sea (LAB), Greenland (GIN), Sub-Antarctic (SUBANT) and Tropics (TROP).
Source: Gebbie G. 2019. 'Atlantic warming since the Little Ice Age', Oceanography 32 (1) 220–230, https://doi.org/ 10.5670/oceanog.2019.151.

SCIENCE AND PUBLIC POLICY | 137

Working Group reports shows that IPCC only regards the post-1950 warming as 'mostly' anthropogenic—and we can see why, as it is only after about 1979 that global averages rise above the previous peak. The Panel realise that pre-1950 rises must have been largely natural and they rose 0.5°C in a 20-year period—which is half of the rise they are concerned about—so they don't talk about it! If we study Figure 2 we can see that at most the world is above the previous (natural) cycle peak by about 25% and thus, it could be concluded, this would be the signal for the human-induced effect.

We can take a closer look at this issue by looking at the most recent satellite data from the Clouds and the Earth's Radiant Energy System (CERES programme) in Figure 3.

Here, CERES logs temperature trends in the *rate* of warming in °C/decade but according to latitude. *This is what I would call a 'killer' graphic*—it was Einstein who said that however fancy a scientific theory built upon collected data, it takes only one contradictory fact to demolish the theory. This is such a fact.

We can note that from 30°South to 60°North, the rate varies from just above zero at 15°South to about 0.2°C/decade in mid-latitudes. However, the southern hemisphere from 55° South to 80°South is *cooling*

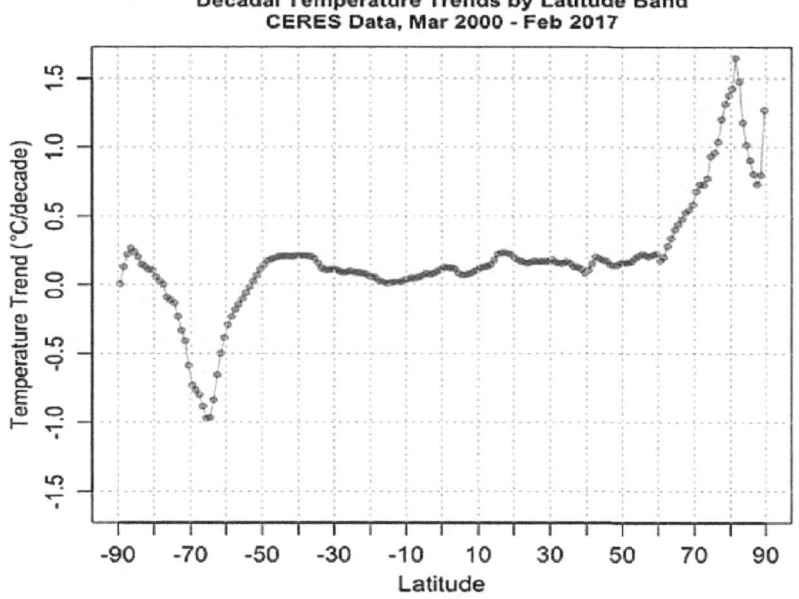

Figure 3. Decadal trends by latitudes from Clouds and the Earth's Radiant Energy System (CERES) satellite data from NASA for the period 2000-2017, processed by Willis Eschenbach.

and mirrors the higher rates of warming in the Arctic regions from 60°North. The warming is largely in the northern hemisphere and most particularly in Arctic regions. This pattern contradicts the global warming models, all of which predict the same global pattern—the Antarctic should warm at the same rate as the Arctic, because carbon-dioxide emissions are rapidly distributed evenly across the globe.

This simple graphic is completely at odds with the UN's preferred global warming theory (i.e. the effects of CO_2 on the Earth's radiant energy budget) where both poles should warm at the same rate. The pattern is, however, entirely consistent with the natural centennial cycles of change: when the northern hemisphere warms, the southern cools. This fact is well-known to specialists studying the ice-core data, but is ignored by the UN's special panel (IPCC).

This 'bipolar' see-saw effect is well attested in the paleo-climate literature and can be seen in ice-core records going back 200,000 years. The bipolarity is a multi-decadal pattern that is overlain by a *millennial* phenomenon that synchronises the peaks in Antarctica—which build up slowly over centuries to their peak, with a peak in the Arctic that is slower to rise but peaks at the same time (at least during warm interglacial times such as we are still in).

My colleague Jackson Davis, Professor of Physical and Biological Sciences at the University of California, and I proposed a detailed mechanism where ocean dynamics and wind patterns in the Antarctic were the drivers for global warming and cooling patterns. We published in a reputable climate journal—but again, this work is ignored by the UN specially chosen panel {2024: see Appendix 5 for links}

So—where does this leave the media/UN hype of 'hottest *ever*'? We can look at the Antarctic ice-core record of the last 200,000 years of human history—which is what we did in some detail in our papers, as well as the Greenland record of about 120,000 years. Greenland was undoubtedly warmer than present between 6000 and 1000 BP. We have good data for the northern hemisphere fauna over this time—pelicans in Somerset, England; white stork in Scotland; cattle farming in Greenland; vineyards in Northumberland (Northern England) etc. The paleo evidence simply does not support a modern 'record' temperature for the planet as trumpeted by the media. The conclusion from all these 'climate watches' is stark—the scary climate story is driven by politics at a UN and mainstream media level and *not* supported by good science, but a few carefully appointed scientists with a distinct scientific bias who ignore inconvenient facts presented by other scientists.

There is obviously something rotten in the State that includes government, the media and the science professions in collusion, such that critical discourse is sidelined and the media-message kept simple. Certainly there are vested interests in the scientific world—of reputations as well as government research grants, but why are the media so biased? Somebody needs to investigate the funding of mainstream media. Perhaps it is as simple as bad news *sells*. But I suspect there is more to it. The political, emotional and psychological climate is changing and this will, I think, soon expose the bad scientists and their, and others' vested interests. We know, of course, from an analysis of the proposed 'solution' to man-made climate change—known as Net Zero—that huge investments are being made, as well as 'lockdown-style' restrictions on basic freedoms. Somewhat bizarrely the 'resistance' is led in the UK by 'conservatives' (with a small 'c'), not the Conservative Party, who are at one with Labour, Liberals and Greens. All political Parties are signed-up and committed to a world led by unaccountable UN structures and 'expert' committees. I have yet to see *any* 'green' critique of either the World Health Organisation's planning and role in the control of pandemics, or the Net Zero plans of the World Economic Forum and the IPCC or the clear role of international investment banks and the industrial expansion of China as the workhouse of the 'Western' economies. Why is it that only conservatives—labelled 'right wing' by their opponents/detractors—call out the workplace human rights issues of China, such as the suppression of spiritual development, the oppression of Muslim minorities, poor environmental and health protection, and all supported by mass-surveillance and social credit structures?

China has benefited by increased capital flows from the West (doubling during the Covid years) and an 80% control of renewable energy technologies. These facts are ignored when Net Zero policies are supported throughout Europe and MPs blithely announce thousands of jobs for their countries in renewable energy industries, such as wind turbines, solar panels and electric cars. There will be maintenance work, but no manufacturing—even the car industries of Europe are bracing for a Chinese takeover of the market as their models are more 'competitive'.

In actuality, 'China' is a conglomerate of Western companies as well as capital—Volvo, BMW, Peugeot, Vestas… there needs to be a detailed inventory of Western companies now manufacturing in China. Perhaps it is simply a combination of vested interests—for example, pension and insurance funds and 'sustainable' portfolios hooked upon Chinese industrial expansion (and exemption from the Kyoto Protocol's emission controls!). Perhaps the global economy cannot maintain its 3% growth (below which some economists argue a collapse is likely) without the China factor—and all the investment houses (Vanguard, BlackRock, Soros et.al.) who invest all those pension funds, know this full-well. The 'system' (world banking underpinning economic growth) cannot 'grow' without this China factor and if it does not grow, it collapses as a result of its own internal contradictions as for some reason unknown to economists, anything below 3% causes instability in the financial system.

Faced with this sort of internalised memo, our decision makers seem mesmerised and thus support the hype of fearful climate changes (as well as rampant viral plagues)—by which 'emergencies' are declared and democratic rights take the back-seat. Whatever the nature of this beast, I continue to be surprised at the long reach of its tentacles and am dismayed in the cause of science as well as humanitarian rights—reason has been clouded over and the emotional climate of fear prevails.

At least a large measure of fear prevails among the masses, including, sadly, our schoolchildren. I can't say the oligarchs and their bankers look worried. Much as they purvey the doom, I think they know the climate threat is not real. They don't seem concerned either about the possibility of nuclear war or the next accidental release of a lab-virus. Could it be that they too are mesmerised into a false, but all pervading, sense of security by their own spellbinding ways?

4.2 Where the Truth Lies

This is an extract from an article in New View, *Autumn 2024, pp.74~80.*

As mentioned in the previous section the CERES project now has over 20 years of data and analysing these led to science papers clearly showing that the spike of warming from 2016-2024 was due almost entirely to ocean cycles *releasing* stored heat from the upper few hundred metres, primarily down to two major El Niño events in succession. The data show the effect of less cloud over the equatorial regions and greater surface radiation—dwarfing the measured (and modelled) decadal increase of carbon dioxide's radiation.

Carbon Dioxide—not the culprit?
Thus far, the *data-driven* science does not support the dominant role of carbon emissions in *driving* global warming—i.e. that it is the *main* cause. There are enough peer-reviewed published science papers clearly showing this. So, again, one can ask: What is the response of the UN's IPCC?

Firstly, there is no admission that the computer model is clearly wrong and that natural processes are the probable driving agency of the warming. But further, in August 2024, controversy arose when two scientists published a review of the UN's latest treatment of the CERES data—which the UN team presented without significant comment.

The IPCC appears reluctant to delve into the CERES data. My guess is that this is because it does not readily confirm the CO_2 main-driver model. The crucial confirming evidence would be to demonstrate a *reduction* of infrared emissions to space (i.e. heat is retained, or its exit significantly slowed, by the 'greenhouse effect'). Instead, the data show a *rise* in those emissions of radiation to space.

At this point, it is important to note that only a handful of specialists garner and represent work such as the CERES data-set and they pass this on for review by many largely non-specialist reviewers. There are two important trends in the data—the flux (increase/decrease) of short-wave (SW) radiation (sunlight) measured in wattage (heating power) at the Earth's surface; and the flux of longwave (LW) radiation (heat) leaving the planet. If they are in balance, the climate is stable. If the LW is diminishing (and the source of sunlight is relatively constant), then the planet is warming. As we know from all the surface and satellite measurements, the planet *has* warmed by about 1° C.

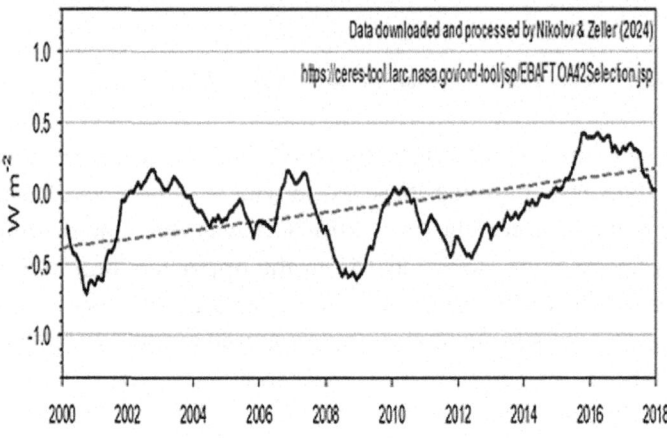

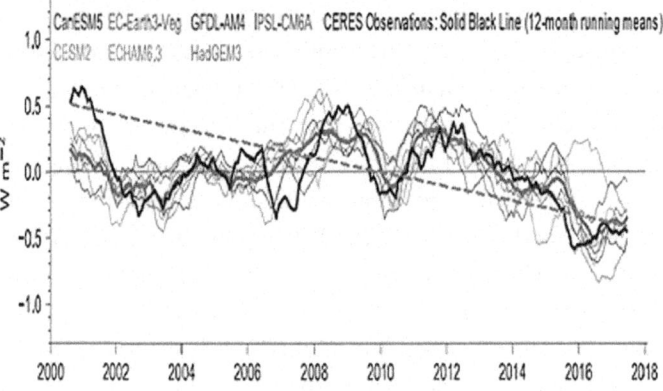

Figure 1. Upper: this data is the original data on Long Wave radiation leaving the planet. If the CO_2 greenhouse effect is strong, this graph should slope downwards. It doesn't—instead it shows the expected rise as the planet warms from absorbed solar radiation (see Figure 2 below) and hence provides no indication of the presumed extra greenhouse effect, and shows instead that natural forces are driving the warming without hindrance. The data is graphed from the IPCC repository of raw data by Nikolov and Zeller (2024). Lower: this is the IPCC published graphic using the same data, but reversing the 'sign' by the simple trick of multiplying the raw data by -1. The graphic then appears to confirm the anthropogenic GHG effect where outgoing long-wave radiation should decline. Ignore the coloured lines—they are model results; the black line is the actual data. Quoting Nikolov and Zeller: '…if the IPCC AR6 had acknowledged the increase of Earth's sunlight absorption during the 21st Century measured by CERES (Fig. 2), this would have invalidated the Report's central assertion that human carbon emissions were the main driver of climate in recent decades'.
Data graphed from original sources by Nikolev and Zeller (https://www.mdpi.com/2673-7418/4/3/17).

If the enhanced greenhouse effect is the cause, (i.e. anthropogenic carbon dioxide) then the LW radiation of heat out from the planet's surface must decline indicating that heat is being held there, thus increasing temperatures.

If one draws two graphs from the CERES data it will show SW (raying down onto the planet) *increasing*; but it also shows LW heat radiation leaving the planet as *increasing* too. This is exactly what would be expected from the quantity of wattage (the heating power measured) as a warmer planet emits more heat out towards space; the additional carbon-dioxide effect hardly shows at all. This rather confounds the 'official' narrative, to say the least, as, in other words, *natural processes are the dominant factor*.

But that is not what appears to be in the IPCC report. It seems to suggest the opposite of what I have just stated. Curiously, one of the scientists who prepared the report (formerly trained at the UK MetOffice computer centre in Exeter), now at Bristol University, *reversed* the 'sign' of the LW data. To the untrained eye (many on the IPCC review team) the LW graph shows a decline (as the graph goes *down*)—but the down is deceptive because it is the decline of a *negative*. LW radiation lost to space is therefore rising and any inhibitory effect of CO_2 is not visible.

On questioning by the team that criticised this way of interpreting the findings, the scientist from Bristol University simply said outgoing radiation was termed 'negative' and so he simply multiplied the data-set by *minus* 1 (see Figure 1).

What does this mean?
In mathematical terms, this changing of the positive to a negative by simply multiplying the data-set by -1 is actually a mere *convention* for showing energy lost to a system—going out—being expressed as a minus. But it gives a false impression to non-specialists—it looks as if the data *confirms* the GHG hypothesis (the Green House Gas hypothesis of carbon dioxide being the driver of global warming and therefore climate change) when in fact it does not. What it actually confirms, when read correctly, is that the natural processes of heat storage and release from the oceans, mediated by clouds, *dwarf* the GHG effect.

All that really changed, of course, was the *impression gained by non-specialists* from the two graphs—seeing one goes up, the other down... but the 'down' is actually up but non-specialists might not realise this and think—'therein lies the increasing greenhouse effect'—i.e. *an apparent decrease in outgoing LW radiation* because more is 'trapped' in the greenhouse. But the truth is the outgoing radiation is not decreased at all but

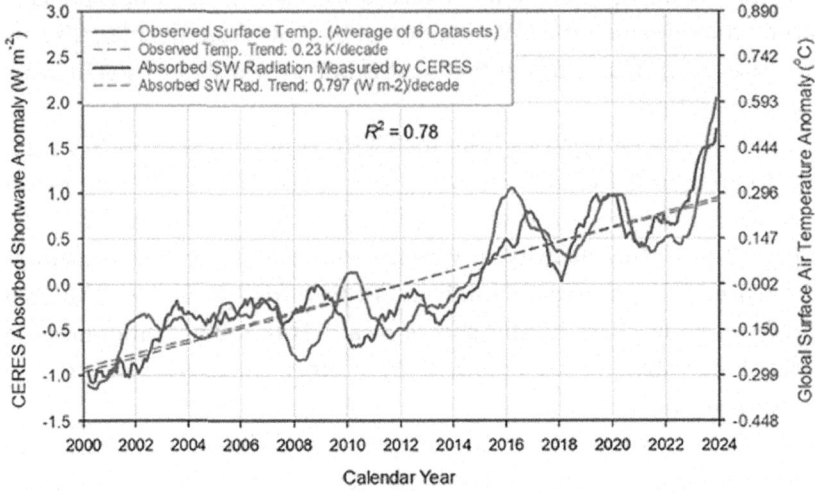

Figure 2. The relation of surface temperature (red) with incoming Short Waves solar radiation (blue), with temperatures lagging slightly the absorbed SW radiation. This graph shows clearly the powerful effect of natural increased solar absorption (due to lower cloud cover) driving the warming.

increased simply due to rising temperatures. Further confirmation lies in the scale of the solar effect in Figure 2 (red line) rising by 3 watts or six times the rising carbon-dioxide effect of 0.48 watts as measured by surface instruments over the same time period.

This multiplying by a minus at the IPCC is subterfuge, of course. It is 'smoke-and-mirrors'. It also has nothing to do with the majority of specialist scientists who produce the data. Most likely they are unaware of how the data has been presented.

It reminds me of the last days of a UN inquiry in 1985 on the computer models of radioactive dispersal from its licensed dumping operations. The scientists concerned altered the trajectory of the pollution at the last minute, when Nordic countries began to express concern about radioactivity in their seawater. The altered trajectory—the path modelled for the ongoing release of the radioactive isotopes at the ocean floor—was such that the pollution would not surface until it reached Antarctica instead of the North Sea fisheries! Unbeknown to that team—from the UK's fisheries radiological laboratories in Lowestoft, who had devised the model—I had access to their first draft and presented that in comparison to the second (and doctored) report to the floor of the UN. Game over! [1,2]

That was 1985. The response of the UN International Maritime Organisation, realising they had been misled, was to bring me in as an independent consultant. Ultimately, the computer models were ditched in favour of 'clean production strategies' (i.e. not producing toxic wastes in the first place!). Much of that independent work was financed by Greenpeace International in the early days of its existence. Things are different now. Greenpeace have not so much as invited a single discussion after publication of my now 15-years-old critique of the UN climate models. And there are no interested mainstream media for this CERES story either. The reader must draw their own conclusions about this.

Computer models live on for now, but their days are numbered. The politicians and accumulated investment interests will not modify those models—despite the *good* news that carbon-dioxide mitigation is an expensive waste of effort. I think we are still dealing with matters of not wanting to lose *face* as well as vested (economic) interest. But as for science? That is an open question. Science has to relate to 'truth' via questioning or validation of models based upon real-world data and, so far, although most academies are keeping their heads down, the real-world data *does not* validate the models.

And of the future? This cannot be predicted. There are signs of a cooling to come—of expected La Niña, a decline in solar activity and the gradual descent into the next ice age based on previous cyclic timing. One thing is certain, what we experience now in the last few years: summer heatwaves, wildfires, heavy rainfall and flooding, regional drought, outbreaks of the polar vortex[3] bringing severe winters, hurricanes and cyclones, all of this will continue. Humanity is very vulnerable to climate change.

I am left with a more immediate pressing concern: that humanity is also very vulnerable to the corruption of science. The current technological elites, aided by the suppression of proper informed debate in the mainstream media, have, for a time, pulled science into their orbit, but that allegiance may no longer be guaranteed. There may yet be a *scientific* revolution where integrity reasserts itself and truth can prevail.

Notes

1. 'Dilute and disperse' is the practice applied to toxic as well as radioactive waste. This refers to the discharging of toxic chemicals or low-level liquid radioactive effluent to the environment in such a way that environmental conditions and processes ensure that the concentrations of the toxic substances are reduced to such levels that the impact (toxicological or radiological) of the released material is acceptable. In some circumstances the principle of 'delay

and decay' may be combined with that of 'dilute and disperse'. See: https://www-pub.iaea.org/mtcd/publications/pdf/te-1714_web.pdf

2. Not a lot of this work was published in readily accessible sources: for example: Taylor P. (1985a) *The disposal of nuclear waste to the deep ocean* PERG RR-15, Political Ecology Research Group, Oxford is on deposit at the British Library—as with all of PERG's research reports. Other sources are: Taylor P. (1991) *Environmental Capacity and the Limits of Predictive Science: the precautionary principle in the control of hazardous substances* in Proc. Symp: Joint International Symposium on Hazardous Waste Management, Swedish Environmental Protection Agency & CEC, Stockholm; Taylor P. (1993) *The State of the Marine Environment: A critique of the work and the role of the Joint Group of Experts on Scientific Aspects of Marine Pollution (GESAMP).* Marine Pollution Bulletin 26, 3: 120-127; Taylor P. & Jackson T., (1991) *The Precautionary Principle and the Prevention of Ocean Pollution* Paper to 1st International Ocean Pollution Symposium, Puerto Rico; see also: Taylor P., Jackson T. & Dethlefsen V., (1993) *The Precautionary Principle* in Clean Production Strategies. ed. Jackson, Stockholm Environment Institute; and: Stairs K. and P. Taylor, (1992) *Non-governmental organisations and the legal protection of the oceans* in International Politics and the Environment ed. Hurrell & Kingsbury, Clarendon, Oxford; and Jackson T. and P. Taylor (1992) *The Precautionary Principle and the Prevention of Marine Pollution.* Chemistry & Ecology 7: (1-4), pp.123-134.

3. The Polar Vortex is a natural pattern of spiralling winds creating low pressure areas over the Arctic Ocean, but it can suddenly shift in a southward 'break-out' loop of wind that draws down freezing Arctic air into Europe or North America.

4.3 Science and Activism in the 21ˢᵗ Century

This article appeared in New View, Spring 2024.

'Science leaders should ditch the activism. Why should we respect scientists when their role in the Covid lab leak debate revealed a worrying attachment to China?'

This was a headline 'comment' article in the UK newspaper *The Times*, 8 February, 2024, accompanied by a photo of the woman dubbed 'bat woman' by the Western media, of Dr Zhengli—a Chinese virologist—shown in her full Wuhan space-suit, subtitled—'Rumours that Covid originated from a lab in Wuhan have never gone away'.

On the face of it, it would seem that the journalists are waking up—in this case, a regular *Times* columnist Juliet Samuel—but, alas, the opposite may be the case. Journalists generally do not write the titles and captions—they are done by subeditors with agendas. A *rumour* that never goes away? So no establishing the *truth*?

Yet Samuel shows clearly that scientists *knew* the virus could have come from a lab, but colluded in a published scientific paper to say it was *not possible*—and later admitted they did so for two reasons: to protect commercial interests in China, as well as the 'reputation' of science itself. We know this, not thanks to journalism, or even scientists becoming honest, but because of US Congressional Hearings, subpoenas and an email trail left by the scientists who wrote the paper. We also know from US investigations that the virus was a *chimera*—an artificial lab manipulation of an original wild bat coronavirus—and we know the work was part funded by the US Department of Defense via a third party—the EcoHealth Alliance.[1]

It is also obvious that the UK intelligence services knew all of this at the beginning of the Covid Saga. What advice these services gave the Prime Minister at the time seems of no interest to the British establishment, nor the media, political parties, or environmental campaign groups. In my long time of working on environmental policy I have witnessed the steady decline of genuine investigative journalism. When occasionally something gets out—like the now proven collusion of a large group of scientists with a vested interest in pharmaceuticals, the system works to edit and downplay and sow doubt in the public mind.

There is a fundamental misapprehension that needs to be made clear—there was never a time when science 'leaders' were *not* activists.

I have personally known several top professors of outstanding integrity and involvement in public policy.

However, science, as we know it now—divested of Alchemy and its 'magic'—has been a long process of scientists seeking to control the political world and seemingly unaware of their own self-interest. In the 17th and 18th century they absorbed the whole of medicine and by the 19th, had significant influence upon the educational curriculum. By the 20th century they had birthed and controlled 'information technology' and developed computer-dependent defence and warfare systems, bio-weapons, mass vaccines and networks of gene-manipulation labs.

Standing above all of these however, is 'Climate Change', where almost every government worldwide 'follows the science'—the threat is supposedly so great that the only solution is massive investment in more technology, which scientists control, and a complete 'reset' of society toward Net Zero 'carbon neutrality'. The threat is first *defined* by science and the scientists' solutions are embedded in the nature of that defined threat; but where 'sceptics' so often see 'conspiracy', which, as we have seen, *does* exist, there is also an astounding lack of self-awareness among scientists regarding the interests of science itself, as an institution dependent upon government and industrial funding. The self-image of science is one of objective analysis and humanitarian control. I know of no published works on the collective shadow side of science, nor for that matter on the extensive series of errors made in its name, especially in environmental policy.

The Covid Saga taught us that when science 'leads', huge amounts of money are thrown in its direction. It was already the case with Climate Change and Net Zero, but it took Covid to wake some journalists up to the level of collusion, incompetence of government and vast sums of money being dished out. Did nobody tell those who parrot 'follow the science' (for example Greta Thunberg) that scientists are far from infallible and that, for example, prior to the 1990s, scientists had approved the use of chloroflourocarbons (CFCs) as being 'the least toxic substance known to man'.[2] I presume that journalists now have been taught that we nearly lost the ozone layer because of the widespread use of CFCs (for example in aerosol cans) and with it the ability of all sentient beings to be able to *see* the world —but I would not bet on it—the otherwise extensive Wiki reference (https://en.wikipedia.org/wiki/Chlorofluorocarbon) does not mention that the resultant increase in UV radiation due to the loss of ozone would have *blinded* almost all land vertebrates!

They will for sure have been taught that 'science' *saved* them (from this error)—just in time (the suspected impact was discovered in 1974 and the Montreal Protocol banning the use of CFCs was enacted in 1985), but not about the actual structures of science and industry that created and released the chemical in the first place. The same is now the case with Covid—Big Science 'saves' us with the so-called 'Vaccine' and the fact that it was Big (and corrupt) Science that created the viral monster in the first place—and patented it—has taken three years to be revealed in the mainstream media!

A few weeks ago, there was a press headline concerning PFAs. These are the latest in a series of man-made harmful chemicals—CFC, PCB or DDT—that never occur naturally in Nature and are released in large quantities.[3] PFAs are fluoridated organic compounds and 'forever' chemicals that never break down and should never have been released into the environment. Certainly not after the lessons of so many earlier errors, but it was deemed essential for the plastics industry and there was no obvious evidence of harm at the outset, so it is with us now—in drinking water, well over the World Health Organisation (WHO) supposedly 'safe-limit' for a suspected carcinogen, immuno-suppressant and endocrine disruptor (i.e. 'gender bender'). Science is kept very busy with billions of pounds dedicated to cancer research, not so much given for looking for its causes, but rather focused on alleviating, if not actually 'curing', its many diseases. When I was a student of science policy in the 1970s I met with Professor Sir Richard Doll, a British physician and epidemiologist, to discuss environmental issues that were then quite new and it was his opinion then that 75% of all cancers were due to environmental causes. When will the modern media circus look and point in this direction as cancer incidence rises for the general population in the West from one in three in a lifetime, to one in two? The standard explanation is that populations are living longer and the disease is due to internal breakdowns of the DNA rather than accumulated environmental effects.[4]

I have seen 'Science' from the inside. Most professionals are not academics—the biologists work for industries such as biosciences and medicine, nuclear power, agro-chemicals, brewing and food industries; the physicists are tied up in defence and aerospace programmes; and the chemists in the oil, gas, and chemicals industries. All of these research communities merge with those of the relevant technologies. The consequence is that most scientists are trapped in corporate power systems and subject to strict protocols of what they can and can't say in public. Meanwhile their 'leaders' sit on government advisory committees and 'captured' regulatory agencies—as revealed so clearly in the Covid Saga. The same process will eventually become clear in the Climate Saga, all the way up to the UN special committee.

Academics used to have great freedom, but that has been deeply eroded. Whilst there have been several brave and effective activist professors challenging government, industry and vested interests—some of whom were my friends, people of courage and integrity—the majority just kept their heads down. Several times, walking the corridors of government-funded institutes, scientists have approached me and said, 'We are glad you are here, you can say things we cannot.' Well, I am independent and, therefore, certainly underfunded!

Whilst the obvious forms of repression—fear of superiors, for one's upward career, a loss of income and how that impacts a mortgage, school fees and so on—are present, they are now complemented by darker forces. A US court case in February 2024 saw a well-known, former *GB News* journalist and long-time sceptic of global warming, Mark Steyn, lose a defamation lawsuit. The world-famous author of the 'Hockey Stick' interpretation of long-term global warming, Michael Mann, felt defamed when accused of fraudulent manipulation of past climate data. The sceptics were hopeful the case would be thrown out under 'fair comment' and freedom of opinion, but the judge awarded Mann damages of $1m. After the verdict, the harsh reality began to sink in: if the alarmists feel threatened, they can sue for eye-watering amounts. This begs the question of 'whither the legal system'?

'Fraud' is a powerful term in science; it is the worst of crimes to be accused of. Essentially, it is manufacturing and manipulating data to suit one's hypothesis. Mann's work was part of the infamous leak of emails in 2009 known as 'Climategate', which revealed some of the worst of behaviours in science, such as seeking to prevent other scientists publishing antagonistic analyses by conspiring to pressure journal editors. There is also a paper trail in respected science journals that shows Mann manipulated paleo-climate data drawn from tree-ring analysis to his advantage and refused for several years to release the algorithms (a specific set of instructions, e.g. like those placed in an internet search engine) used in the analysis of records going back a thousand years. Critics, such as Ross McKittrick and Stephen McIntyre, eventually received the data under Freedom of Information requests and demonstrated in a scientific paper that the algorithm used would generate a 'Hockey Stick' from even random data.[5]

In my opinion, Mann's original paper published in the *Nature* journal showing the 'Hockey Stick' was indeed a suspicious manipulation of data. (See the outline of the 'Hockey Stick story', 3.4, Fig. 1, p. 113-114.)

When the 'raw' tree-ring data actually showed a tailing *downward* in the final decades, in contradiction to the global instrumental records from land stations, Mann cut out the inconvenient final decades of the tree-rings data and simply spliced in the instrumental data to produce the graph in Fig.1.

In other words, tree-rings raw data, using the aforementioned algorithms showed a *decrease* in temperature in the 20th century whereas readings from scientific instruments showed an increase. Rather inconvenient. Therefore, he did not draw attention to the fact that the discrepancy with the instrument data cast doubt upon the reliability of the tree-ring data *as a temperature guide*. It is well known by scientists in the field that tree-ring growth is affected *not only by temperature*, but also winds and water availability and it cannot readily be compared to instrumental temperature records—certainly not to be able to say *with confidence* that recent 21st-century temperatures actually exceed those of the 12th or 13th century.

In the ensuing email controversy, the 'Hockey Team', as the international group under Mann became known, appeared to congratulate themselves on 'hiding the decline' (in the recent tree-ring proxy data) and using 'Mike's trick' of splicing in the instrumental data.

That should have been Mann's death knell as an honest credible scientist, but the UN's Intergovernmental Panel on Climate Change (IPCC) could not publicly back down; they had too much to lose as they had been awarded a Nobel Peace Prize (shared with Al Gore, the former US Vice President, in 2007) and Mann had been appointed lead author of a key section (paleo-climate) of its reports. Mann then went on to extrapolate the straight shaft of the graph back for 2,000 years purporting to show that not much fluctuated until the uptick (of the 'Hockey Stick') in 1900—thus making humans the obvious suspect for increasing CO_2 with its claimed effect. The alternative hypothesis, explored in my book, *Chill: A Reassessment of Global Warming Theory*, concerns long-term, repeating cycles of the same magnitude as 'global warming' peaking in the 20th century and with exactly the right timing that could explain 50-100% of the warming. My own estimate was about 75%.

The IPCC quietly dropped the 'Hockey Stick' graphs and interpretation for the next report and busied itself in the background finding others who would somehow corroborate Mann, while at the same time not showing any interest in an alternative hypothesis. Thus, in 2022, in their 6th report, the IPCC felt emboldened to resurrect the Hockey Stick under new authorship—a coalition of the willing, known as the PAGES (Past Global Changes) consortium. This is a large group of carefully recruited scientists, set up under the aegis of the European Space Agency's Copernicus Programme and according to their PAGES website, 'to support the policy' of the European Union on climate change adaptation and mitigation.[6]

In Figure 1 (p.102) we can see how they have extended the shaft of the Hockey Stick by another one thousand years (a), and the IPCC add how the instrumental data is matched by models—brown shading (b); and how models simulate what would have been the case without carbon-dioxide emissions. This biased approach to data erases all trace of the roughly 1,000-year cycle with its troughs (Little Ice Ages) and peaks (Minoan, Roman and Medieval Warm Periods) that would interfere with the narratives of 'hottest ever' current temperatures caused by human emissions and their extrapolations into the future.

The resurrection of Mann through the 'findings' in this 6th IPCC report proved too much for the community of tree-ring specialists, who published a critique, finding the IPCC 'biased' in their choice of experts and analyses.[7]

The scientific controversy is complex. Most tree-ring studies are at high latitudes and in the northern hemisphere, where the long cycle of recurring 'little ice ages'—roughly every 1,000 years—registers a 1-3°C fluctuation, with greater amplitude the further north the location of the trees (see Fig. 1, Section 3.2, p.93 and discussion p.96). The bias present within science (acted out by its leaders and their close relationship to policy makers) leads to a 'consensus' (that few dare to challenge), which appears to nullify—or at least obscure—the problematic 'little-ice-age' cycle of 1,000 years.[8]

For the lay reader, the different coloured lines represent different ways of treating much the same data by different research groups—the central green line represents a bias toward the tropics where there is limited fluctuation, and the red lines are from higher latitudes, mostly in the northern hemisphere. The 'Hockey Stick' approach relegates the latter as it does not represent the global average—the main index of the instrumental record. The reasoning is understandable, but it effectively downplays societally important recurrent cooling and warming periods in the industrial northern hemisphere.

There is also the issue of accuracy when comparing vast numbers of instrumental records to produce an average with large numbers of regionally based 'proxies' (e.g. tree-rings) of limited accuracy and then thinking one can state, with certainty, that the modern warm period is warmer than the previous 'Medieval Warm Period'—or, as has also been said by some scientists, warmer than any period in the last 100,000 years! This all has great relevance for industrial society and the global economy reliant upon the USA, Europe, China and Japan—most of which is located in the northern hemisphere. What is really happening with the climate? On a regional level it is not simply a matter of temperature fluctuations but major shifts in wind direction, rainfall and drought that impact on food production and the way people live.

The significance of all this is that this unscientific bias nullifies a recognition and understanding of the 'recurrent' warming and cooling that is shown clearly in both Greenland and Antarctic ice cores—whereby northern hemisphere warming over the last 100 years is the *expected* consequence of such a cycle (the southern hemisphere oceans have warmed to a much lesser extent and Antarctica not at all, indeed, it has cooled in the last 20 years). One has to look to centennial and *millennial* trends to get the full picture because over a single century like the last one, the northern hemisphere can warm faster than the southern. Over a millennium, however, the southern hemisphere and northern hemisphere synchronise. We may now be at the peak of warming, and the natural cycle will turn downward, perhaps first in the Antarctic and trend to the next Little Ice Age in about 300 years' time. Close to the more stable tropics the fluctuation over these timescales may be only 0.4°C, due to the large buffering expanse of ocean. Some tropical waters of the Pacific can fluctuate by an increase of 3°C and influence regional seas by 1-2° C during strong El Niño events, but these are short-term and the algorithms will iron out these regular fluctuations, as well as the stronger 1,000-year fluctuation in higher latitudes to produce the 'not much happening' line seen in Fig. 1a in Section 3.3.

Algorithms are now at the centre of virtually all interpretations of climate data. Even what one might expect as 'raw' weather station data first gets adjusted by an algorithm based upon what is expected—for example, an 'expected' uptick in temperature in the last decades of the 20th century; and then when all the data from all the global land stations is pooled, an algorithm weights them according to whether they 'look right'. I call this a 'hunting algorithm' (looking for what you expect to be there) and I rather think that is what Mann used and for so long refused to divulge. Thus, briefly, if the variations of past cycles are weighted by latitude, the ups and downs of Arctic and Antarctic long-cycles disappear as do, in particular, the Medieval Warm Period and the Little Ice Age. The Medieval Warm Period (MWP) saw the expansion of civilisations and the colonisation of Greenland—with white storks, a warmth-loving bird, nesting on Edinburgh Cathedral. The previous warm period in the cycle saw the expansion of the Roman Empire and the growing of vines as far north as Northumberland. Both warm periods ended with cool periods that saw famine, disease and the collapse of empires worldwide. These biased analyses are the 'tricks' of the trade that provide policy makers with the results they need to support their programmes. They are made possible because the IPCC does not cater for minority opinion (preferring a consensus of government-appointed experts), as likewise the courts do not.

Global temperatures are in fact at an all-time high in the 'instrumental' record of the last 150 years—with claims that they are now 1.5° Celsius above the Little Ice Age, pre-industrial level. I have to say that I am bemused. In 2000, the consensus across all data-sets was for 0.8° (plus or minus 0.1°) above the level in 1900 (effectively the same as in 1850) and most of the Little Ice Age (1400-1800). From 2000-2015 there was no increasing surface temperature—known as 'the pause'. Only since the *back-to-back* series of El Niños of 2016, 2019 and 2023 has there been an increase, but a big one of 0.7° Celsius.

What is happening is that the oceans have been releasing lots of stored heat. As noted, large El Niños typically have a global effect, from start to eventual La Niña, of increasing average global temperatures by about 0.7° Celsius.

We shall see how far down the temperature falls in the next three years. Of course, the 'follow the science' media will extol the power of a natural La Niña to explain the cooling, quietly forgetting the natural, rising power of El Niño that created the 'record' highs in 2023 in the first place. Meanwhile, Nature's natural cycles seem to have entered a chaotic phase typical of the end of the very long 10,000-year, 'interglacial' period in which we are now in the final few hundred years. No one who talks up the power of CO_2 to heat the planet talks about its concomitant power—if indeed CO_2 really is the driver of global warming—to stave off a descent into the next real ice age!

One thing is for sure—'science' is now so mired with government, media and campaign-induced vested interests that it has lost touch with the nature of scientific 'truth'. That truth is dependent upon open debate and respect for minority opinion. One recent example has been the trumpeting by mainstream media of 'tipping points', such as the impending failure of the Gulf Stream, a standing joke among sceptics as paper after paper models its collapse—as in the Hollywood film *'Day After Tomorrow'*,[10]—though usually only after several hundred years of computerised extrapolation of current small and questionable trends.[11]

There is, however, some light on the horizon within the science journals and conference circuits, where anger at the UN's bias is now evident.[9,12] I get weekly requests to publish papers and attend science conferences, all rather expensive undertakings for someone without a funded academic base. The alarmists can at present effectively ignore criticism, but when the natural cycles do turn downward, one way or another, the truth will out.

Notes

1. EcoHealth Alliance is an ostensibly independent organisation led by British zoologist Peter Daszak; its Wikipedia entry—https://en.wikipedia.org/wiki/Peter_Daszak—has not been updated to include the US Congressional Hearings and the controversy surrounding the multi-authored paper of which he was one signatory. Wikipedia still implies that the lab-leak is conspiracy theory, demonstrating the nature of its inherent bias. What is not so obvious in any of the coverage is that bio-defence (and warfare) programmes run parallel to what Daszak believes are concerns for wildlife conservation, and people, and take up their interests whenever a dangerous virus is discovered—as in the case of bat coronavirus and the Wuhan Institute work.

2. See: https://en.wikipedia.org/wiki/Chlorofluorocarbon for an unusually accurate account of the chemistry and history of CFCs and their regulation.

3. PFAS—Perfluoroalkyl and polyfluoroalkyl substances are a group of chemicals used to make fluoropolymer coatings and products that resist heat, oil, stains, grease, and water. They are now present almost everywhere: in the air, water, soil, food, clothing.

CFCs —Chlorofluorocarbons are non-toxic, non-flammable chemicals containing atoms of carbon, chlorine, and fluorine. CFCs react with sunlight in the Earth's stratosphere and break down the protective ozone layer, a layer of gas that shields the Earth's surface from damaging UV rays.

PCBs—Polychlorinated biphenyls are a group of highly carcinogenic manmade chemical compounds, formerly used in industrial and consumer products.

DDT—Dichloro-diphenyl-trichloroethane—a powerful insecticide that is also poisonous to humans and animals.

All of the above are man-made highly toxic chemicals called 'forever chemicals'—or POPs (Persistent Organic Pollutants) because they are virtually indestructible and do not break down in the environment.

4. https://news.cancerresearchuk.org/2015/02/04/why-are-cancer-rates-increasing/

5. http://news.bbc.co.uk/1/hi/sci/tech/4349133.stm; https://climateaudit.org/2023/11/24/mbh98-new-light-on-the-real-data/

6. https://pastglobalchanges.org/science/wg/2k-network/intro

7. https://wattsupwiththat.com/2024/02/11/tipping-is-optional/

8. I covered this issue in *New View* Summer 2023 but I consider it so important that I repeat it here. (See article 'Climate Watch: Clouding the Mind' in *New View*, Summer 2023.)

9. Büntgen,U.; Arseneault, D.; Boucher, E. et al., Recognising bias in Common Era 953 temperature reconstructions, *Dendrochronologia,* 2022 74 125982. 954 https://doi.org/10.1016/j.dendro.2022.125982

10. ttps://en.wikipedia.org/wiki/The_Day_After_Tomorrow

11. Op. cit., endnote 7.

12. Connolly, R.; Soon, W.; Connnolly, M.; Baliunas, S et al., 'How much has the Sun influenced Northern Hemisphere temperature trends? An ongoing debate', *Astronomy and Astrophysics*, April 2021 (accessed 14.7.23) https://arxiv.org/abs/2105.12126https://www.sciencedirect.com/science/article/pii/S1674987123001172?via%3Dihub. See also: Scafetta, N.; Bianchini, A, 'Overview of the Spectral Coherence between Planetary Resonances and Solar and Climate Oscillations', *Climate*, 2023, 11, 77. https://doi.org/10.3390/cli11040077. https://www.mdpi.com/2225-1154/11/4/77

{2024 Commentary: The original article in *New View* contained a box explaining the nature of the Hockey Stick for laypeople, together with references to Figure 1~3 in the article. These figures are repeated in other articles and to save space are Cross Referenced here.

Michael Mann's famous (or infamous, depending on your opinion!) chart showing a steep rise in global mean temperature from about 1900 onwards, after a more or less constant level for the previous 1,000 years. He attributed this rise to human activity (this is the moment the question of the action of CO_2 was brought into sharper focus). If the analysis had included oceanic records—70% of the planet's surface, going back another 1,000 years, the current uptick was not unusual, but part of a cyclic pattern (see Section 3.2, Fig.1, p.93). Some commented that this graph with its 'uptick' at the end was reminiscent of the shape of a hockey stick and the name stuck. However, Mann's graph caused controversy, as it did not take adequate account of oceanic and ice-core data showing regular cyclic rises of temperature and was therefore considered by many scientists to be falsely attributing an anthropogenic cause for the rise in global temperature.}

The original *New View* article had three figures, which are featured in other articles and not repeated here:

Figure 1. The original 'Hockey Stick' graph, showing gradual decline of temperature over the past one thousand years and the sudden 'uptick' at the end, simply viewed looking like a hockey stick lying on the ground with its end pointing upwards. [Cross Reference: Fig.1a in 3.3, page 102 and 3.4, Fig.1, page 114]

Figure 2. Left: reconstructed temperatures and observed instrumental data. Right: 1850-2020 observed and modelled. (https://www.ipcc.ch/report/ar6/wg1/chapter/summary-for-policymakers/) [Cross Reference: 3.4, Fig.1b, page 114]

Figure 3. The unbiased review of paleo-data from 22 professionals (Buntgen et al. [This is endnote 9 above]): note the little blue lines (at the top of the graph under the years going horizontally under the 'Common Era' heading denoting two 'little ice ages' separated by the 'Medieval Warm Period' (years 5-600 and around 1800) looking very similar in the bottom graph for both events. Also note that the lower graph is set out on a different timescale (see the horizontal years at the bottom) covering the two little ice ages. [Cross Reference: 3.2, Fig.1, page 93] Note: coloured figure available in electronic version only.

4.4 Plutonium Man

This article was published in New View, No 109, Autumn 2023.

Myths, as the storyteller and poet Robert Graves told, are psychological teaching devices central to the development of culture and they morph through times of conquest and change. Pluto appears in Ancient Greek myth as the Lord of the Underworld and in Renaissance paintings we see him by his alternate name of Hades abducting Persephone into his subterranean realm. Thereafter, the next we hear of him outside of esoteric circles, is as a metal fashioned into nuclear warheads capable of Mutually Assured Destruction (MAD)—a doctrine of defence with the main protagonists having about ten thousand each. Exploding just two hundred would generate a nuclear winter in which most, if not all, humans, animals and the more advanced plants would go extinct.

My attention was drawn to a press article (*The Sunday Telegraph*, 3 September 2023) on how modern 20-something climate activist 'influencers' (people who through the internet attempt to influence people's ideas and understanding on various issues) in Germany and Sweden were berating Greenpeace for (from their perspective) its outdated and unscientific anti-nuclear stance. This generation apparently believes that in order to save the oceans from boiling over (as the head of the United Nations recently put it), whatever the future risks of nuclear power—as one of the influencers argued concerning the problem of nuclear waste: 'my generation can figure out how to manage that at a later date…' —such risks for them pale compared to the so-called ongoing climate crisis. Reactor meltdowns, terrorist attacks, solar flares (see below) and weapons proliferation do not figure in their approach.

Sensing its change of fortune, the nuclear industry is now dusting off its long-abandoned plans for 'fast breeder' and 'modular' reactors using the 'everlasting' plutonium stocks as fuel. As for the Campaign for Nuclear Disarmament (CND)—they have a remarkably low profile considering the war in Ukraine and with Putin announcing he had refurbished the Russian nuclear submarine fleet with hypersonic missiles.

This apparent lack of concern contrasts starkly with the 1970s and 80s, when I was motivated to leave academia and join a growing anti-nuclear movement that did not separate nuclear issues into civil and military. The civil nuclear programme provided the weapons material and both contributed to the stockpile of nuclear waste. I became involved with Greenpeace—as detailed in my autobiographical account *Shiva's Rainbow*. The book ends with the sinking of the *Rainbow Warrior* when about to sail into the French nuclear test site at Mururoa in 1985. The Greenpeace flagship was sunk by French commandos in Auckland harbour, killing the photographer, Fernando Pereira.

My involvement with Greenpeace began with concerns over radioactive discharges from nuclear facilities and later the disposal of toxic and radioactive wastes. At the same time, having formed a small group of dissident scientists recruited from British universities, we extended our research to the potential consequences of aerial discharges and land contamination as a result of 'loss of containment' accidents. The latter are caused by failures in cooling systems—referred to as 'loss-of-coolant' incidents—amply illustrated in the Fukushima meltdowns in Japan of the reactor cores in 2011 and the subsequent loss of containment.

Molten fuel generates hydrogen explosions that destroy pressure-vessel containment and lead to aerial emissions of volatile radioactive elements. In detail: when uranium oxide fuel—which can at first be easily handled in the form of pellets contained in metal cylinders or rods that are lowered into a kind of honeycomb structure, often graphite, are brought into a close geometric relationship, the uranium starts to 'fission' in a controlled 'chain reaction' creating heat and a series of 'fission products' that are normally contained within the metal rods. The heat is used to generate steam in a turbine that then generates electricity. However, over time these fission products give off much stronger radiation than uranium itself. These rays require metres of concrete to stop them and hence protect the workforce. However, this concrete then traps the heat and so elaborate cooling channels are required. Coolants in the inner reactor circuits vary from gas—such as carbon dioxide used by the early fleet of British reactors, through water in American designs, to molten salt for modern breeder designs that use plutonium. If the cooling circuits fail for any reason (like loss of electrical power), the fuel will melt and the more volatile of the fission products will increase pressure until the concrete containment is breached and they spew out. At this point, the reactor building must be evacuated as well as the station site. The heat and radiation cause any water to produce hydrogen and that has massive explosive power, further shattering the containment and spreading radioactive gas, dust and debris far and wide—as happened at Fukushima and Chernobyl, but was narrowly avoided at Three Mile Island in Pennsylvania, USA.

Supporters of nuclear-generated electricity cite the absence of radiation casualties at Fukushima and the limited (30km) evacuation zones due to contaminated land. However, 80% of the radioactivity was blown out to sea. A less favourable wind would have extended the necessary evacuation zone by 100km and threatened major cities.

There are several potential causes of loss-of-coolant and subsequent meltdown with loss of containment. In 1979, the US plant at Three Mile Island suffered a loss-of-coolant and resultant hydrogen explosions came within 90% of the secondary containment's pressure limit. Major centres of population would have faced evacuation had the containment failed. At Chernobyl in 1986, the reactor had no secondary containment and the meltdown led to large areas to the north-west of the reactor being seriously contaminated. About 30 firefighters died from contact with highly radioactive reactor debris that they were not told to expect. For 100km to the north-west the land was largely uninhabited swamp forest. Had the wind been less favourable, Kiev would have faced evacuation.

However, there is a far deadlier loss-of-coolant that would potentially release hundreds of times more radioactivity and that is the storage of hot liquid high-level nuclear waste, of which there are stores in Normandy, France, and at Cumbria, England (and doubtless also in the USA and Russia). This liquid waste is generated only when the 'spent' fuel is 'reprocessed' to extract plutonium. The fuel rods are chopped up by robots and dissolved in concentrated nitric acid. The resultant devil's brew is highly corrosive, generates heat such that 24/7 cooling is required, otherwise it will melt the stainless steel and concrete containment with similar but more severe consequences to that of a reactor meltdown.

The storage tanks of this high-level waste require 24/7 management for several decades until cool enough for the waste to be solidified. Plans exist to bury the resultant solid (in the form of borosilicate glass) deep underground, but thus far, after 70 years of nuclear power, only low-level and intermediate wastes have been buried. Spent fuel that is not reprocessed remains intact, but still requires cooling—usually in large swimming-pool size open tanks.

By the late 1970s, my group had advised several public inquiries in Britain, Sweden and Germany. This was a time when governments actively sought dissenting scientists to counter the bias of industry experts and 'captured' regulators. My group—led by our engineer, Gordon Thompson, was commissioned to advise the regional government of Niedersachsen in Germany on an application for a 'reprocessing plant' that would extract plutonium from spent nuclear fuel, ready for the proposed Plutonium Economy. We provided detailed engineering analysis and computer simulations of a loss of coolant for the proposed high-level liquid waste tanks. The-then German Minister for the Environment, in turning down the plant, explained that 'had they such a plant at the end of the Second World War, Germany would be largely uninhabitable today'.

Any breakdown of social order—and such can happen in the aftermath of a solar 'mega-flare' (see later), will lead to nuclear disaster because cooling of reactors and nuclear waste tanks requires an intact electrical grid. Reactors can be shut down, but they still require electricity for cooling, and emergency diesel generators last only a few days. Britain has ten such station sites and one huge store of liquid waste as well as several hundred tonnes of stored plutonium oxide.

In those days, Greenpeace supported our research and activism—as did International Physicians for the Prevention of Nuclear War. Even the UK government commissioned research from us on dumping radioactive waste at sea (a practice then led by Britain) as well as land-storage options. In the years from 1976 to 1993, a small but worldwide group of dissident scientists, coupled with imaginative public action and legal interventions, succeeded in curtailing the worst of nuclear ambitions. The atmospheric testing of weapons was halted in 1963 by international treaty, but underground and underwater testing continued. The latter was the objective of Greenpeace's campaign against sea-dumping in 1985 and action against Britain's secret use of US underground test sites in Nevada, concluding with the climbing of London's Big Ben in 1984 to unfurl a banner 'Stop Nuclear Testing' by my brother Ronald Taylor, who also led an occupation of the Nevada test site.

The Comprehensive Test Ban Treaty came into force in 1996—banning all testing. Further work involved the Non-Proliferation Treaty and agreements to reduce the number of warheads (down now from 60,000 to about 20,000)—and thus far, only Israel, Pakistan, China and India have not signed, and gone ahead developing their own programmes—with over 100 warheads suspected in each country. North Korea has persisted with underground tests. Little known now is the complete halting of the Plutonium Economy, which required the reprocessing of spent uranium fuel. Plutonium is not only a weapon, it is also fuel for so-called 'breeder' reactors. As the initial plutonium fuel load is used up, its flux of neutrons breeds more fuel from a blanket of depleted uranium waste from conventional reactors and the non-fissile uranium isotope 238, which constitutes 78% of the natural ore.

This highly-dangerous fuel cycle was the industry's answer to the world's limited uranium resource. The initial weapons programmes over-produced plutonium and the weapons reduction treaties also liberated many tonnes. Industry specialists thus designed power reactors that could use plutonium as fuel and also use the waste uranium to 'breed' more plutonium fuel. This was sold to parliaments as an 'everlasting' source of power. The Plutonium Economy required vast investment, would stretch engineering to the limit, and of course create a lot of jobs in science and engineering—not to mention the special police forces, for such plants need high security.

In addition to action to halt the Plutonium Economy (which my German colleagues at the time dubbed 'Electrofascism'), in 1985, following what I can only describe as heroic action at sea by Greenpeace, coupled with strike action by the National Union of Seamen, the UK government appointed me to a commission of inquiry into the sea-dumping of nuclear waste. By the end of that year, the dumping was banned in Britain and later worldwide.

The awareness of youth now comes almost entirely from the media circus, the power of which we now know from the experience of the Covid years, feeding them only with what benefits the corporate sponsors. The media does not tell them that one microgram of plutonium is a lethal dose, and one kilogram enough to build an atomic bomb. Nor does it guide them to the links between technology and social control—the Plutonium Economy would require a police state to deal with the risks of terrorism and proliferation of nuclear weapons.

Do any of today's environmental activists know that a solar 'tsunami'—an enormous 'solar flare' pulse of magnetised plasma emanating from the Sun—would lay waste to the world's electrical grid, and could cause all of European, US, Chinese and Russian reactors to melt down as at Fukushima? If they do—they don't say. The silence is perhaps because of a Net Zero climate-change ideology that sees carbon-free 'green' nuclear as essential to maintaining power supplies.

At present, worldwide nuclear power currently accounts for less than 4% of energy supplies and about 10% of electricity generation. Relying upon nuclear stations is not a good idea for many reasons—waste storage, accidents, policing….but that one single natural event, a solar flare capable of paralysing the electrical grid, would lead to massive contamination. The natural event would be bad enough—no water in the taps, no food in the supermarkets, no fuel, no news, no phones, no papers, and all coupled to immediate martial law. But then, maybe a week later, because the grid would be beyond repair, each nuclear power station would blow its top, just like Fukushima, leading to millions of acres of un-remedial contamination.

I look with some foreboding upon these current times. The film *Oppenheimer* was released this summer, a biopic of the life and trials of J. Robert Oppenheimer, known as the 'father' of the Atomic Bomb. I recommend this extraordinary and moving movie. Poignant for me as I have participated in the annual ritual at Hiroshima where they float lanterns upon the river, one for every victim of that bombing. I made the pilgrimage when working as a scientist against the proliferation of nuclear technology—both civil and military. I was then regarded as an expert on radiation risks and I lectured widely in Japanese universities where there was at that time a strong anti-nuclear movement. We were successful only with regard to weapons and not the civilian use of uranium. Japan subsequently built a 'breeder' reactor and a reprocessing plant to isolate plutonium from spent fuel, but has given up on the idea of a Plutonium Economy of their own, probably because of the expense.

It is worth mentioning here that on 6 and 9 August 1945, the United States detonated two atomic bombs over the Japanese cities of Hiroshima and Nagasaki respectively. The bombings killed between 129,000 and 226,000 people, most of whom were civilians, and remain the only use of nuclear weapons in an armed conflict, to date.

It is also little known that the civilian nuclear energy programmes of the major atomic weapons powers were started as a cover for plutonium production. This element, unlike uranium, is not found in Nature. In the Periodic Table of elemental powers, uranium marks the boundary of what is natural—it is the heaviest element with an atomic weight with various isotopes from 233~238. Naturally occurring uranium ores consist of non-fissile uranium 238 (78%) and traces of fissile uranium 235, which then has to be 'enriched' to reactor grade or further to 'weapons grade' in arrays of centrifuges. The 238 isotope is 'fertile' in that it will produce plutonium 239 when bombarded by the neutrons from a 'breeder' reactor—hence the attraction of extending the use of otherwise unusable uranium.

The heavier man-made elements such as plutonium 239 are known as 'transuranics' and they require artificial bombardment with neutrons to produce them. In a nuclear reactor, the refined and concentrated uranium 235 is brought into a fissile condition (by altering the geometry of massed fuel pellets) such that fission occurs and new elements are produced—uranium in these conditions *decays* to *daughter* products, the first of which was named neptunium 237, followed then by plutonium 239. Plutonium was preferred to uranium for bombs because ten times more power is released per kilogram, but as noted its production requires *reprocessing* of spent nuclear fuel to extract the plutonium.

This process was undertaken under great secrecy in the post-war and cold-war years. It required huge expenditure and this was hidden under the guise of a nuclear reactor programme. For the first decade or more the fuel and reactor geometry were optimised for plutonium production, and heat was a useful by-product, being siphoned off to generate steam, drive a turbine and produce electrical power. The accident risks of this process, from fuel fabrication, years of reactor time and eventual waste disposal, were kept secret.

It was 1975 before the Nuclear Regulatory Commission in the USA broke the secrecy and published a report under Professor Norman Rasmussen on the potential for nuclear reactors to 'melt down'. The report's conclusions were extended by a review from the American Physical Society, which added more detail to the consequences of such failures.[1]

The British and French establishment, thus exposed, immediately argued *their* designs would not melt—but this was gainsaid by the British Royal Commission on Environment in its 1976 report under Professor Brian Flowers. These reports, coupled to gathering concern over discharges of nuclear waste to the environment, fuelled my own radicalisation. I left the Oxford academic environment and formed the aforementioned dissident scientific group replete with engineering expertise (The Political Ecology Research Group) and we placed ourselves at the service of a growing anti-nuclear movement. We were the first science group to make public the real consequences of a nuclear accident, in particular from the back-end of the fuel cycle, which stored the extremely radioactive hot liquid (acid) wastes containing plutonium.

In collaboration with European scientists and lawyers, our work culminated with the mothballing of the 'fast breeder' reactor at Kalkar in Germany, and at Dounreay in Scotland; we severely constrained reprocessing technology (abandoned in Germany and Sweden); stopped the dumping of nuclear waste at sea and discharges of plutonium to the marine environment around Windscale (now called Sellafield) in England. The nascent Plutonium Economy had been stopped in its tracks.

Plutonium is not only a weapon of mass destruction, as noted, it is one of the most poisonous substances gram-for-gram known to humankind. When ingested, it concentrates in bone tissue. The atmospheric atomic weapons tests of the 1950s and early 1960s spread a cocktail of radioactive elements including plutonium dust throughout the globe and penetrating down to the deepest ocean sediments. Future sedimentary geologists may well use this as the marker for the whole era of human domination. All humans now contain trace quantities of the element.

My reputation as a scientist was impugned—following which my good standing in the environmental-green world disappeared overnight—when George Monbiot of *The Guardian* newspaper read (parts of) my book *Shiva's Rainbow*, where I mused upon the succussion of a toxic element such as plutonium occurring when 'stirred and shaken' in the reactor; its subsequent homeopathic dilution in the world's atmosphere and oceans thus dosing the whole human population. I mused as to what *remedy* might be implicated? Unfortunately, even a musing along such lines drives the scientific world to distraction and Monbiot well knew this and wrote a piece in *The Guardian*, intent—I suspect since he was an advocate of climate-emergency—on denigrating my standing in the world of climate science.

He added another snippet, in that I partook of *astrological* lore in seeking an answer to the question on remedy, looking to Pluto, being not only the Ancient Lord of the Underworld, but a newly discovered planet beyond Uranus and Neptune. In astrological convention, Pluto rules the unconscious power-realms of the collective Psyche and when activated, his message is clear—*wake up or die (or die to the old ways to wake up to the new!)* He is the Lord of Rebirth. And the incarnate individual has then to wake up to and understand the essential *unity* of all of humanity.

With our weapons of mass destruction, tipped with Plutonian forces, we are far from unity. And so it goes on, if we consider Putin and his hypersonic missiles and the Western allies prodding and poking the Plutonian (Russian) Bear as if under some compulsive, enchanted, death wish. Meanwhile, where now is the Campaign for Nuclear Disarmament? Or Greenpeace? Gone are the days of protest. Nobody on the streets. No modern equivalent of my brother Ronald penetrating the Nevada nuclear test site, or unfurling a banner over the face of Big Ben. And zero opposition to a fleet of 'modular' (small scale, localised in cities) plutonium reactors as the nuclear industry dusts off its old plans! All eyes seem simply focused upon Net Zero and the Carbon demon.

If nuclear power is to be given serious consideration, then small-scale reactors that burn cleaner fuels (less waste) such as thorium, and using designs that cannot 'melt down' under failure conditions, should be the focus. Such reactors were long advocated by US scientists at the outset of the nuclear programme, but as the weapons programme was the main priority the uranium-plutonium option was preferred (thorium is abundant in the Earth's crust but it cannot be weaponised). There is now much talk of 'modular' designs for small reactors, but numerous enough to power many provincial towns. Britain, like other atomic-powered submarine builders, has the requisite expertise to build such reactors but currently the hitherto militarily subsidised uranium reactors have the economic edge, due to the extensive vested interests in the world of engineering.

Taking a deeper historical perspective for a moment: is it not surprising that a culture that has been science-led for the past 300 years, with all the advanced technology and megacities of today, does not *see* what it has created? The whole edifice of modern civilisation is vulnerable to a somewhat prosaic natural event, a solar storm, which according to recent estimates occurs every 60-600 years, the last of which was in 1859 (the so-called 'Carrington Event', named after one of the amateur astronomers who observed it) when the aurora spread around the whole planet and a few stenographers got their fingers burned, for in those days there was no electrical grid that today we are all so totally dependent upon. Today, if such an event occurred, such a large magnetised wave would create ground currents, supercharging long-distance high voltage power lines causing them and their transformers to melt. Repairs would not be possible because no power would be available in the grid and in the case of large transformers, there are anyway waiting lists of several years for replacement production.

It appears that the Greta Thunberg generation have no idea about these things. After 14 intensive years trying to get through to people about the real nature of climate change, I have decided to look into the psychology of it all—and it necessarily goes back to the beginning of this civilisation, tracing its roots, as it does, in Ancient Greece. What follows is but a glimpse.

I started at a lesser historical distance with the takeover perpetrated by scientists in the 17th century, completed in the 18th, which saw science institutions dominating first the medical field, followed by the educational, the agricultural, ecological and finally the psychological. To facilitate this takeover they first had to eliminate the competition—in this case, the Alchemists. It took a mere 50 years from the founding of the Royal Society in 1655, which contained prominent Alchemists and Astrologers, to get to a point where Isaac Newton, though resolutely defending Astrology, had to hide his Alchemical works in order to become its President. The resultant materialists found ready sponsors in the corporate expansion of the British Empire, its commodification not just of Earth's resources, but even its enslaved indigenous peoples.

In Ancient Greek, wisdom is called *Sophia*. Those men estranged from the feminine in 17th-century Britain, both within themselves as well as socially, called their new knowledge a *philosophy, (philo-sophia; love of wisdom)* but they were only *lovers* of 'natural knowledge', equating it only with the physical world, not the psyche.

In the book *In The Dark Places of Wisdom* by the highly respected Classical scholar Peter Kingsley, he relates Strabo (64BC-24AD), the Romano-Greek geographer, who tells of an extant practice in Ancient Caria in the now Turkish mountainous hinterland opposite Samos, where there still existed a cave, known in Greek as a 'lair', a working shrine to the 'god' Pluto. It was a ritually used cave called a *plutonium*, where seekers came to be 'healed' or made whole and it was attended by healer-priests experienced in the kind of journey that would unfold for the seeker involving a process of 'incubation'—lying still and breathing into a trance state that would induce a healing dream. Pluto, as the Lord of Death, then presided over a 'rebirthing' process that would heal the psyche. The process could take three days.

So, what had happened to the myth of Pluto? In its earliest versions, the Underworld Lord is Hades and *married* to Persephone who is honoured as 'Queen of the Underworld'. The later versions tell not only of her abduction, but her reluctance to partake of Hades/Pluto's gifts. But she errs and when the Lord of Death has his back turned, she picks a pomegranate seed from his table thus condemning herself to remaining in his realm.

Persephone is the daughter of Demeter (later Ceres) the Goddess of Abundance, and when she disappears, the Upperworld becomes as barren as winter. Zeus (Jupiter) intervenes and orders a compromise whereby she spends some time in the Underworld and sometime above. This teaching myth thus alerts us to our wish for ever fruitful summers and desire to avoid life's essential times of death and decay.

Yet earlier still, in Sumerian times, we learn that the Underworld journey is undertaken by the solar Queen of the Upperworld, Inanna, who descends to visit her sister Ereshkegal, the Dark Queen of the Underworld—a dangerous journey also with consequences.

If we are to understand the Plutonian nature of modern man, then Inanna's descent contains a central lesson: she makes the journey *voluntarily* and knowing what to expect. Since those matriarchal times, mankind underwent the most fundamental of all conquests—that of men over women and this has given rise to shifts of mythic emphasis. Firstly, by Greek times the Queen is replaced by Hades/Pluto and the wisdom to embark voluntarily upon such a journey is then gradually lost. By the time of Ancient Greece the feminine remains as one of the few Upperworldly powers—in this case as *Demeter*, later Romanised as *Ceres*, in the rather important realm of cereal abundance. However, she is not minded to spend time in the dark realms, which are lorded over, in any case, by Hades/Pluto, Lord of Death.

Pluto and the *forced* descent into the Underworld has become a central myth. Graves pointed out that as cultural conquests proceed through time, myth as initiatory story—often theatricalised—shifts according to the dominant power. By the end of the 17th century modern science has come to replace kingly or queenly powers entirely by the philosophers and their econometric ideologic attempts at wisdom. The dominating political power in the developing modern era, which geologists are now debating may deserve its own title, *The Anthropocene* (wherein the human species comes to dominate the ecology of Nature itself) and is now woven into the mythic realm, for in the evolving Western culture, with its roots in Ancient Greek and Roman logic and their panoply of Gods and Goddesses, scientists curiously name the elements and powers, even the technologies, after those ancient deities.

The first nuclear-weapons test in 1945 was called Trinity. The first research reactor in the UK was called Dido. The second decay daughter of Uranium (named after Uranus, the Greek God of the Heavens), was named Neptunium. Atomic submarines have been named Trident and Poseidon. I have some vague memory of an end-times prophecy that forewarned against taking the name of the Gods in vain.

Pluto remains very present as a power in the land—a nuclear power, now involved in a stand-off, long-running ideological war between West and East, wherefrom has arisen the technological ability to annihilate the works of Nature. Plutonium tipped weapons are pointed in their thousands at bitter ideological rivals, as sands shift and alliances change, and even a computer glitch in the Artificial Intelligence (AI) systems controller could reduce the Earth to the most barren of places. And the issues surrounding the containment of nuclear waste will be with us into the far distant future.

If we look to the paleo-climate cycles for guidance, then we are just beyond the apex of our current civilisation and it is downhill toward the next Dark Age. No oil left, no coal, no gas, with volatile and 'vandalising' masses migrating from the East, as of old, to challenge whatever is left of the new World Order. The respected geophysicist Kenneth Hsu, authored a 1998 paper on these cycles. It was published in a Chinese journal of Earth Sciences as *Sun, Climate, Hunger and Mass Migration*, concluding—'Perhaps the most important task at the present is not so much computer-modelling of a greenhouse effect on global climate, but water-management and agricultural researches to insure food-supply for an ever-increasing world population.'

In the paper he maps out the down-periods in the 1,000-year climate cycle, noting how they coincide with variations in solar magnetic activity, and then how changes in wind direction and drops in temperature lead to crop failures—some areas becoming too wet, and others too dry, and thus driving mass migrations. Historically, the 'dark ages' as they are called even by paleo-climatologists, coincide with the collapse of major empires—those with over-extended supply lines. In terms of timing—we are at a peak, and the next trough, assuming the pattern is repeated, is 300 years away.

However, the crop failures and famine are accompanied by what could also be termed a loss of consciousness. In the classic example of the decline of Rome, Vandals moved in on the remains of the empire and it was Christian monks who burnt down the library at Alexandria and brutally murdered the librarian, Hypatia, one of the most respected scholars of her time.

In the most recent Dark Age in terms of the effects of temperature and solar activity—roughly 1450-1850—the Viking colonies on Greenland and elsewhere collapsed, the Normans faded and their castles fell into ruins. As the Sun entered its recovery phase—roughly from 1700 onwards—the 'Enlightenment' began with the birth of science and its triumphant technologies. So followed the flowering of another 'empire'— economic and military and underpinned by scientific technologies, but with banking temples (Greek style) at the centre of rational 'worship'. US military bases now encircle their Eastern competitors, with a budget that equals the rest of the world's combined military expenditure. Western politicians profess to be leading the world in this All-American dream of democratic freedoms and material aspiration, their voices now hollowing as the tinkle of a cracked bell. Nobody looks at the shadow. In my mind, this marks the onset of mental and spiritual decline, and doubtless climate change will finish the job. Perhaps the most difficult thing for 'enlightened' minds to come to terms with is their own demise and annihilation of their material works—thus, the darkness they cannot face inside of themselves has to be projected and demonised onto an enemy, be it Russians, the Taliban, Isis or more mildly but disconcerting nevertheless, climate *heretics*.

Is there a positive ending? Of course—just as all empires fail and crumble to rubble and dust (note how concrete is not as immune to time as once thought), something always persists in the heart and spirit of humankind. I am not sure we grow *wiser* as the centuries pass—that will perhaps depend upon the future liberation of the feminine mind, both within women, its natural home as the wisdom-keepers, and within men as in a former alchemical balance. It is a matter of time and faith in the thread that connects us all to the ancestors who have struggled to manifest love, balance, and caring for all peoples and the Earth itself. That thread cannot be destroyed but I do believe that as *love* it has to be tested for it to grow strong and have real cosmic significance. Men and women must relearn that journey into the depth of their psyche wherein lie the gifts of Pluto. The shadows must be embraced before this seemingly endless projection onto 'enemies' ends all of us.

Notes

1. https://sgs.princeton.edu/sites/default/files/2019-10/vonhippel-1977.pdf

4.5 Net Zero Soul

This article first appeared in the 'Climate Watch' *series in* New View *magazine, no. 107, Spring 2023, pp. 67–70.*

The UK Parliament has signed up to Net Zero by 2050, and so has the USA under President Joe Biden, and the European Union and pretty much the rest of the world, except China. Even the oil company Shell, along with most of the corporate world, will aim for that goal. I would guarantee that very few citizens, even if they know what 'net zero' means in terms of carbon-dioxide emissions, have little idea of how the world intends to get there—with virtually no petrol, diesel or gas for transport and heating, and heavy industrial users relying on 'green' hydrogen.

As readers of my work on climate will be aware, there are significant scientific grounds to doubt that carbon dioxide is the 'control knob' for global warming. I am personally convinced that whatever the world achieves in emission controls by 2050, it will have zero effect on what the climate does.

With regard to climate dynamics, we are entering what may be a short cooling period—known as a Dalton-type solar minimum[1]—that may last this current solar cycle,[2] or this one and the next, and there are already signs of cooling. Some sceptics of the IPCC models hold that we are approaching a 'grand solar minimum' on a par with the Little Ice Age (1450–1850), when Europe in particular suffered severe winter weather and poor summer harvests, and China suffered drought and famine. My own work suggests—one cannot be certain—that the next Little Ice Age is 300 years away, and what cooling signs there are now will be relatively minor in comparison.

Meteorologists look at the past 30 years to derive a climate 'trend', with the current global temperature now lying close to the average of the 30-year period 1991–2020. The 21st century would be devoid of a surface-warming signal, had it not been for El Niño Southern Oscillation (ENSO) peaks in 2016 and 2020. The oscillation occurs when, every 3–4 years, winds that normally blow from east to west across the Pacific Ocean die down. These winds drive an 'upwelling' of cold water off Peru that extends westward in La Niña years. When these winds die down, the cold water does not surface, and warm surface water extends eastwards from a 'pool' in the western Pacific. Given that the Pacific is almost 50 per cent of the planetary surface, this dynamic influences global temperature by about 0.2–3 degrees Celsius. However, there is an irregular 'super-Niño' with a roughly 12-year period, which raises peaks and troughs in global temperature by 0.6–0.7 degrees.

The last two super El Niños were 'back-to-back'—an unusual event; but temperatures have now returned to pre-event levels.

The planet has in fact cooled by half a degree over the past six years; and if the longer term record is scrutinised, the main warming period was 1975–2000, a time when several decadal ocean cycles—Atlantic Multi-decadal Oscillation, Pacific Decadal Oscillation, and Arctic Oscillation—all peaked together. Oddly, nobody has put together a global estimate of these oscillations acting in concert—but a 0.2°C 60-year cycle is evident in climate records, and this may be the result of cycles coinciding. If so, this is about half of the late 20th-century rise of 0.4°C.[3]

In my analysis in the book *Chill: A Reassessment of Global Warming Theory*, which I also presented and debated with the Intergovernmental Panel on Climate Change (IPCC) modellers at a major climate science conference in Prague in 2019, I argued that these cyclic events were 'driving' the warming, estimating that their amplitude could account for about 75 per cent of the centennial temperature rise. Underlying these decadal cycles was a 1,000-year long-cycle of 'warm periods' and 'little ice ages'. In short, natural forces are driving the warming, and CO_2 has much less 'power' than the IPCC modellers have built in to their virtual-reality system. All the alarm over wildfires, droughts, heatwaves, hurricanes and floods has taken place in the absence of warming over the last six years! I am far from alone in this assessment.

Does the scientific criticism matter? As we know, the BBC attitude is standard—'the science is settled'—and this month as I write, the poster-child for the climate emergency, Greta Thunberg, published a 400-page tome of opinions by leading scientists, *The Climate Book*, saying, 'Science does not lie… follow it'.

The problem is that the institutions (and governments) *don't* follow the science: they avoid critical commentary, and despite the failings of the models, they join the alarmist cry of a 'climate emergency'. And it is upon this claim of 'emergency'—one supported by all the national academies of science, all governments, all major corporations (including the banking sector), the mainstream media and all environmental campaign groups—that 'net zero' policies are based.

The ideal of net zero is that by 2050, the UK will have weaned itself off oil, coal and gas, and any remaining emissions will either be absorbed by 'carbon capture' where the gas is pumped into old oil or gas wells, or offset by forestry. However, the UK produces only about 2 per cent of global emissions—so the strategy must run parallel with a huge global effort.

Of course, all of this effort will have zero effect on the climate if CO_2 is not the main driver of the changes we have seen—and politically, no one is questioning the role of CO_2. The problem is that the political and the scientific world bows to UN authority; this obedience is built into legal systems. Thus, even though thousands of qualified scientists sign petitions and declarations that 'there is no emergency', they are ignored, and critics are simply excluded from key committees. I have witnessed this on ocean-pollution issues (though by 1992 we, the critics, had prevailed), and it is obvious now with Covid science;[4] but nobody in government or the science institutions, nor in the supine British Parliament, is prepared to admit that this building of false consensus goes on. And further, the mainstream media, in particular the BBC, support that false consensus by ignoring sceptics, or by branding them 'deniers' of the science.

Whenever large-scale technical solutions are rolled out, they will have societal impact. If we look at net-zero policies, we should be scared—much more so than of the climate. A huge technological transformation of society is underway. In 2022, $1.4 trillion was invested in 'renewable energy'—that is, 1 per cent of global GDP (where the latter refers to the monetary value of all the goods and services produced by all countries in a year). By 2050, that sum will amount to $40 trillion. And yet nobody—not a single critic, not the environmental groups, the World Wildlife Fund, the Wilderness Society or the protectors of indigenous peoples—has made an Environmental Impact Assessment of this global policy. Renewable energy is diffuse and has to be harvested from the 'landscape'—biofuels, hydro-dams, solar farms and wind turbines, and on a truly vast scale. Current programmes are already impacting wilderness, indigenous peoples, and biodiversity—from Arctic Lapland to the tropics. These programmes have to be scaled up tenfold to meet net-zero targets.

The only campaigners against this madness who are vocal and effective are somewhat difficult to categorise—I call them 'the free marketeers'. Their most vocal concern is not just the huge cost (which might not be sustainable) but the required intervention in the world economy—which would effectively become a 'command and control' economy bordering on a 'communist' takeover.

Institutes such as the UK's Global Warming Policy Foundation (initiated by Nigel Lawson, a former Conservative Chancellor of the Exchequer), and the Heartland Institute in the USA, have marshalled all the sceptical science, with an impressive array of scientists and Nobel Laureates. All with virtual zero effect. Or perhaps they have led to some foot-dragging.

It is this group of right-wing, pro-nuclear, pro-GMO (Genetically Modified Organisms), pro-real-science activists who highlight the social impact of net-zero programmes. They are the only caucus that seems to understand that if humans do not effectively control the technology, that technology will control human society. They point to Chinese-style social-credit control, digital programmable currencies and mass surveillance systems in what global architects now plan as new 'green cities'. At different times I have had an advisory role with government agencies on nuclear safety and energy policy. The problem is that I have no allies in this sector; and as I remain anti-nuclear and anti-GMO I get very few invitations to discussions. Nuclear power does have environmental risks, but seldom mentioned is the way in which an extensive programme necessarily conditions society towards more surveillance and control—from, for instance, the industry's armed 'nuclear police' {note: a separate unit the Civil Nuclear Constabulary in the UK} and paramilitaries such as the black-clad GMs (the Gendarmes Mobile) in France that protected their prototype plutonium reactor at Malville. GMOs have similar societal ramifications in terms of corporate control of agriculture and medicine as well as any environmental or health risks.

Added to that, the left-wing 'environmentalists' like George Monbiot—a sometime writer in *The Guardian* newspaper on the environment—advocate the abandonment of farming in favour of rewilding the landscape, with humans eating fabricated food grown in laboratories. Furthermore, the aforementioned right-wing critics are the only caucus to highlight the plight of the poor—both within the rich 'north' and in the global 'south'. In the former, the cost of energy seriously undermines the quality of life; and in the case of the latter, economic and social breakdown leads to mass migration. They argue for an expansion of fossil fuels, as well as of nuclear-power generation to stave off the decline of civilisation. I used to regard myself as relatively 'left', but these days, the terms left and right, though used liberally by the media, do not mean what they used to mean. I don't have new words, other than that there exists a polarised spectrum, and somewhere in the 'centre' must lie social concern, effective control of corporations, and respect for individual freedoms. Since China is poised to become the world's superpower, it is a case in point—its supposedly left-ish elites exert maximum control on individual freedom combined with right-ish lax regulation of international corporations. In our own Parliament, there was unanimity on the vote for net zero, with Labour now making the running for more command and control to fight the climate war.

Then there are those who see Klaus Schwab's World Economic Forum (WEF) as wanting to 'reset' the global economy to the continued benefit of the global elite of oligarchs, their bankers and investment managers. Some see 'climate change' as a suitable scam for enabling a global government far removed from public accountability. This notion may be somewhat outdated, since these 'conspirators' meet publicly at Davos, Switzerland, and Schwab has already written their manifesto—so they are at least out in the open, but effectively unaccountable. Perhaps the only safeguard, at least here in the UK, is parliamentary oversight; but some years ago, Schwab was smart enough to instigate a 'global leaders' programme whereby certain individuals embracing the WEF agendas would come to positions of prominence, ensuring some complicity with WEF aims. Trudeau, Macron, Sunak, Ardern amongst others, were all on this programme.

That this particular train is heading for a cliff seems to have been forgotten by all sides—the continued loss of forests, water resources, soil and wildlife amidst a still-expanding human population. The economic critics focus only upon resource costs—of lithium, copper, cobalt and rare-earths for the battery-powered future. The politically aware focus upon the fact that China controls the market in all renewables, from turbines to electric cars, because it controls the processing of the necessary minerals.[5] The bankers don't care because they have all invested heavily in China—a capitalist workhouse of cheap labour and lax environmental regulations. And by association, they support China's expanding interest in buying tropical land for agricultural production, complete with railroads and port facilities.

China has also expanded its programme of coal-fired power stations. China remembers; it suffers worst during climate cycles, and their scientists studied those cycles in depth before they were told to toe the global party line.

In 2011, a team of Chinese scientists working in Tibet were the first to analyse climate cycles over a 2,600-year period (using tree-rings) and then extrapolate using sign-waves for a 1,100-year, 200-year and 100-year periodicity. They showed that temperatures would peak in this decade and then decline to about 2060. No other science team had done this with any climate proxies—such as ice cores, sediments or tree-rings. It is a simple technique. My colleagues and I did something similar with Antarctic ice-core data where the extrapolation forecasts cooling ahead,[6] but very few teams worldwide are touching upon the power of these cycles to bring a cooler future—the funding simply isn't there.

Nobody, however, is concerned about soul. It does not feature. The word does not dare surface in any political dialogue. We have already seen how China deals with spiritual heretics (such as those who practise Falun Gong).[7] In the UK, Europe and the USA, there is no soul language in opposition—I know, because I have tried to conjure up some resistance to this soulless future among professional ecologists and nature conservationists. They don't like to embrace soul. The wilderness protectors are hurting, for sure—I know some of them well; but they do not dare show their hurt—love and soul are not in the conservationists' bureaucratic vocabulary. Lovers of the wild are caught now in a mindless, spellbound river of humanity heading toward a techno-fascism that brooks no debate, discussion or dissent—for now is the China of everywhere.

Notes

1. See https://tinyurl.com/2nefaawv.

2. A solar cycle describes an approximately 11-year cycle of solar activity driven by the Sun's magnetic field and indicated by the frequency and intensity of sunspots visible on the surface. See https://tinyurl.com/ms3x5wck.

3. See https://tinyurl.com/bddnxmbf.

4. See this examination by the US Senate: https://tinyurl.com/2z6ewc5k.

5. See this interview with a minerals specialist—Mark Mills: https://tinyurl.com/3h2tcan6.

6. See https://tinyurl.com/54cu25fh.

7. See https://tinyurl.com/4fcbffkm.

Appendix to 4.5

Net Zero Strategy

The UK government issued a Strategy document in 2018 at the behest of then Prime Minister Boris Johnson's office.[1] It is 368 pages long and quite technical, but I recommend it to show that someone is thinking sensibly about how to get to net zero by 2050. However, the report deals with the technical solutions to reducing carbon emissions, and there is no environmental and social impact assessment that should be part of strategic thinking. Assurances abound—the strategy will be beneficial, promote jobs and 'levelling up' (addressing the disparity in wealth between the north and south of England in particular), as well as making Britain a world leader on the climate stage. We will 'build back better'—with money for 'Nature' and environmentally friendly farming and cycle paths.

The claim for 'lots of jobs'—in renewable technologies such as solar power and wind turbines, insulation, carbon capture, biofuels, hydrogen generation and electric-vehicle production—is not supported with any analysis of current manufacture and production. Neither does it report that China controls all the key technologies.

In brief summary, net zero will rely upon electrifying transport: cars, buses and trains, perhaps also heavy lorries—though they may use hydrogen as a fuel; electrifying home heating: using air- and ground-sourced heat pumps, coupled with better insulation; finding sustainable aviation fuel, such as bio-sourced, or electric motors or hydrogen; decarbonising power supplies—phasing out gas, phasing in more wind and nuclear (solar is almost irrelevant); reducing agricultural emissions (of carbon, but also of nitrogen oxides, methane and other greenhouse gases); and where emissions are unavoidable (mostly some industrial processes), capturing and storing carbon dioxide underground.

In the report's Figure 6, reproduced below, the 'high electrification' path to 2050 is shown as the end-product, with generation on the left and end-use on the right.

Finance

The most forthright criticism levelled at net zero is its huge cost, both nationally and globally. It is important to realise that without globally parallel action, the UK net-zero strategy cannot achieve significant results. In a longer treatment—for which readers can email me (peter.j.taylor108@

protonmail.com), I show that somewhat surprisingly, industry can afford the costs in investment terms; but of course, there is no way to calculate the 'cost' to people financially, socially and environmentally. My own suspicion is that the Great Reset is a last-gasp attempt at keeping the global capitalist boat afloat—in the name of 'civilisation', of course, but where the banks, ably supported by their 'green' advisors, take control.

Notes

1. See https://tinyurl.com/mvwfk8es.

Note: i) the heavy reliance upon wind and nuclear in electricity generation (green on left top), and their substantial use to electrolyse water to produce hydrogen fuel (in purple); ii) the miniscule amount of solar; iii) substantial biomass power generation, including imports—some of which is used to generate hydrogen; iv) the loop of 'electrolysis' from electricity generation then used to generate more hydrogen for heavy transport and industrial use; and v) the still-significant use of oil in transport—about one-third.

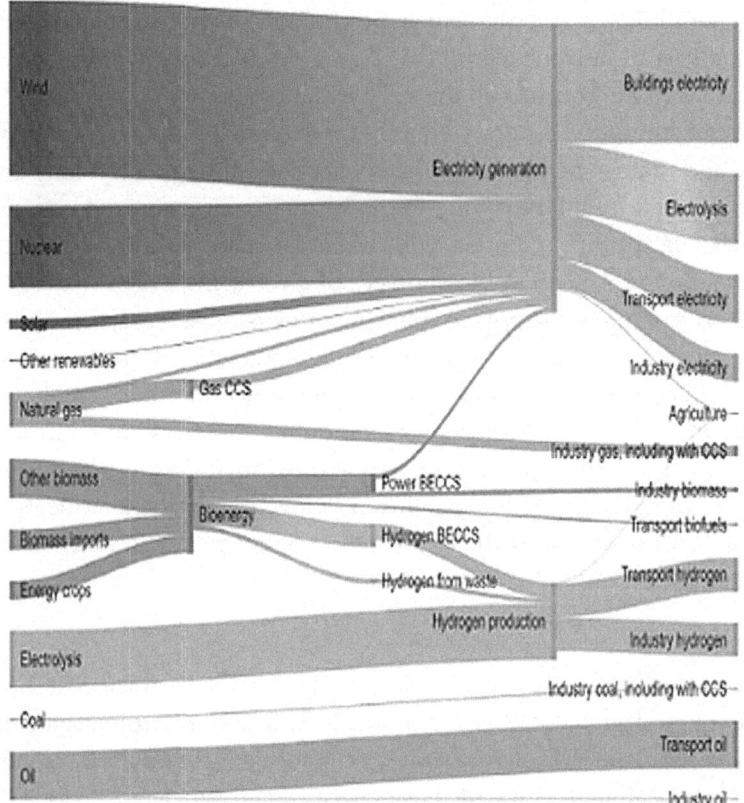

PART 5: COVID, CLIMATE AND CONSPIRACY

Preface

The Covid 'emergency' brought important lessons concerning the relationship of science to society. There is now no question that the virus was a creation of science—a laboratory construct. There remains a question of whether it was accidently or deliberately released. The latter is for many people unthinkable and derided by the mainstream media as 'conspiracy theory'. However, the former—the lab origin, was also initially branded conspiracy and is now beyond question.

The following essays were written as the saga unfolded and I have not had the time or resources to devote to a thorough investigation of its later stages. Here I can only add some signposts to the work of those people who have devoted such time.

I will not address the issue of whether the virus ever 'existed' or the issues of 'contagion', 'terrain theory' and transmission of disease. I do not doubt the existence of viruses or their power to cause disease, as some do, but that power, as we see with Covid and many other viral illnesses, does also depend on the immunity status of the exposed person—and reduced immunity is symptomatic of modern living.

I had Covid symptoms three times. The first time I came close to death from asphyxiation. I am asthmatic, somewhat old and at high risk, but not afraid of dying. My knowledge of breathing and of natural medications got me through—though 'Long Covid' gave me a terrible time.

There is much I know of how the virus works. As many virologists have pointed out, for a bat virus it is uniquely adapted to infect humans, and I have read much of their literature as to how that ability has been constructed. It can only have been done in a laboratory and despite attempts to suppress data and withdraw publications there is a clear trail in the literature as to how this was achieved at the Wuhan Institute of Virology in China. Some of the world's leading experts in virology and contagious disease have been outspoken on this issue.

There was, of course, a massive cover-up operation, firstly in China, but then with the collusion of the World Health Organisation and a complicit mainstream media, the cover-up was extended across all nations and the lab-origin 'theory' was labelled 'conspiracy'. In this Preface I will provide links to some of the ongoing battle to reveal not just the origins but the nature of the cover-up, which has, of course, huge implications for democratic oversight of science and the power of the media.

The whole sorry story has important lessons with regard to the still unfolding climate saga. Firstly, the two declared 'emergencies' have cadres of scientific experts at their centre of operations—both the nature of the threat (both have been massively overstated), the role of modern science and computer technology in particular, and the relation of science to investment houses hungry for their return on their investments.

The dark role of science and vested interests is hardly new. I encountered it during my years campaigning against the expansion of nuclear technology—in particular plans for a Plutonium Economy. We won that battle, though right now, those technological elites are dusting off their old plans, this time not to save us from a return to the Stone Age (as an ice age beckons) but from 'global warming' (itself a creation of another branch of science).

At one time, I was a student of science policy and even the philosophy of science. An essay I wrote (for *The Ecologist*) on nuclear power was a key text in the Open University course on 'control of technology', but like many scientists, I missed the contribution in the 1970s of Paul Feyerabend's *Tyranny of Science* and *Against Method*. I am indebted to Richard House for drawing my attention to this prophetic work.

However, I am far from 'anti-science'. I have had the great good fortune to know several academics who have risked their career by questioning the 'consensus' (behind which lay a great deal of 'vested interest').

The issue darkens when it comes to light that a Pandemic Response was planned in advance by a cadre of interests supported by the heavily invested Gates Foundation, pharmaceutical companies, virologists and the World Health Organisation. Their plans went against normally agreed scientific and policy responses and could only be implemented under a 'state of emergency' declaration by the WHO as an agency of the United Nations, itself heavily reliant upon funding by commercial interests. There is clear collusion between the UN agency, pharmaceutical companies and national governments. Such an 'emergency' allows the use of new and relatively untested techniques—such as mRNA 'vaccines' that act by genetically modifying cell activity.

There is clear evidence of attempts to control the narrative of the Pandemic Response by WHO, the mainstream media and national government agencies—such as censorship of alternative media outlets, de-platforming and labelling of critics (e.g. as anti-vaxxers or conspiracy theorists), pressure on science journal editors and psychological techniques to induce fear. There is also clear evidence that such techniques and the lessons learned will be used to further the 'climate change' narrative, in particular, with involvement of the World Economic Forum and the UN's Intergovernmental Panel on Climate Change (see:https://unherd.com/newsroom/wikipedia-and-uk-government-move-to-censor-climate-debate/).

It is quite bizarre, but very clear, that accusations of 'conspiracy theory' have been used by the very people who are actually conspiring—that is, meeting in secret, perverting the course of investigations and furthering a false narrative, both to protect the good name of 'science' and maintain highly lucrative funding streams—not least of which is the vast investments made by globalized capital (led by BlackRock and Vanguard) in China generally, and its pharmaceutical industry in particular.

I have not the resources to document all of this fully, and thus I recommend two trustworthy sources. First concerns the 'proximal origins' of the virus and relates to the initial narrative of a 'zoonotic' source (i.e. wild bats, with no laboratory interference). The strongest example comes from Dr Steven Carl who conducted a Bayesian analysis of the competing theories (this is an advanced technique to determine probability of a theory being true), and concluded from comparison of all the data available in January 2021 'beyond reasonable doubt that Sars-CoV-2 is not a natural zoonosis but instead is laboratory derived'. https://zenodo.org/records/4477081

In April 2020, as speculation mounted on the origins of the virus, a paper by leading experts was published in *Nature*, the foremost international science journal, dismissing the lab-theory.

Evidence has emerged from US Congressional Hearings that some of the chief advocates of a natural (zoonotic) origin did not believe their own narrative and deliberately colluded with both regulatory authorities in the US and a very senior executive within the pharmaceutical world in publishing this paper. US Congressional Hearings subpoenaed email traffic from the authors of the paper as well as key US officials and regulators in which are used the phrases—'stop the conspiracy theories' and protect 'science' as well as 'relations with China'. The best guide to this sorry saga is by Dr Roger Pielke, a science-policy analyst who also has extensive experience of climate policy in a testimony prepared for the House Select Subcommittee on the Coronavirus Pandemic, 16 April, 2024.

Statement of Roger Pielke Jr., prepared at the request of the House Select Subcommittee on the Coronavirus Pandemic, 16 April 2024:

The so-called Proximal Origins paper that dismissed the plausibility that COVID-19 may have resulted from a research-related incident sits among the most consequential failures of scientific integrity that I have seen in more than 30 years working on science and technology policy. My testimony documents these failures and argues that the production of Proximal Origins violated the Scientific Integrity policies of the Department of Health and Human Services and represented an improper mechanism of 'shadow' science advice led by government officials that compromised possibilities for a formal and institutionally-appropriate investigation of COVID-19 origins. Three key points:

1. The production, publication, and post-publication treatment of the so-called 'Proximal Origins' paper represents a major failure of scientific integrity by its authors, its unacknowledged ghost contributors (including U.S. government officials), and the academic journal that published it.
2. In their roles contributing to the coordination of Proximal Origins, U.S. government officials, specifically Dr Anthony Fauci and Dr Francis Collins, likely violated the Scientific Integrity Policies of the Department of Health and Human Services.
3. Proximal Origins was a form of 'shadow science advice' and, at least in the United States, effectively served as an alternative to the empanelling of a formal expert committee to investigate COVID-19 origins.

https://rogerpielkejr.substack.com/p/proximal-origins-scientific-integrity?utm_source=substack&utm_medium=email

The US Congressional Hearings are a beacon for democratic accountability:

https://oversight.house.gov/wp-content/uploads/2024/05/SSCP-Staff-Memo_Morens-5.22.pdf?utm_source=substack&utm_medium=email

https://oversight.house.gov/wp-content/uploads/2023/03/2023.03.05-SSCP-Memo-Re.-New-Evidence.Proximal-Origin.pdf

https://oversight.house.gov/release/hearing-wrap-up-ecohealth-alliance-should-be-criminally-investigated-formally-debarred/?utm_source=substack&utm_medium=email

https://oversight.house.gov/wp-content/uploads/2024/04/2024.05.01-SSCP-Report_FINAL.pdf

On the Pandemic Response itself—there is a UK Covid Inquiry underway, but I have no great faith in the UK system to effectively interrogate the officials concerned, largely because UK advisors are in more powerful positions and parliamentary oversight is much weaker than the US Congressional system of oversight

With regard to that response I recommend The Great Barrington Declaration, organised by senior virologists and health policy experts criticising the Pandemic Response. In December 2021, it had over 60,000 signatures by health professionals worldwide, and currently 940,000 (June, 2024). See: https://gbdeclaration.org/

And with regard to masks, lockdown policy, the impact on schools, health and education, as well as damage to the economy, I recommend this interview with Anders Tegnell, who supervised the Swedish policy of not locking down: https://unherd.com/tag/lockdown/

Robert F. Kennedy deals at length with all of these issues in *The Wuhan Cover-Up: and the terrifying bioweapons arms race.* (Skyhorse, 2023 and Kindle Edition). It is noteworthy that Sir Jeremy Farrar, who headed the Wellcome Foundation—one of the richest dispensers of research funding in pharmaceuticals, and who is implicated in the genesis of the *Nature* paper, was recently appointed chief science advisor at WHO; and Sir Patrick Vallance, who led the pandemic response in the UK, has been appointed chief scientific advisor to Sir Keir Starmer, Britain's new Prime Minister.

5.1 Covid, Climate and Conspiracy

This article first appeared in New View *Winter 2021-22 Issue 102.*

Covid, climate and conspiracy… these are the big issues of the day and since God will feature strongly in my analysis, for the sake of clarity I will start with my own take on divinity. I look at God through the eyes of a social anthropologist.

In my earlier studies of differing cultures, it had seemed to me at that time that God, or any form of divinity, was a projection of the human mind, entirely within the imagination, and that He, She or it took many forms. Naturally, as a scientist, I sought to find a commonality and that was not easy. What was regarded as divine, good or evil, or the ultimate cause, varied according to the ecology of the people, whether forest, savannah, desert, ice or ocean and then, the history of civilisations where peoples had created cities and their hinterlands. One thing was always featured: God as *creator*. No 'primitive' people, nor early civilisation, saw humans as self-created.

I first came across the concept of self-creation at Oxford (when at the School of Zoology 1967-70), as expounded by a fellow scientist who bagged the first class honours degree with an essay on 'self-assembly systems'—of which, he maintained, the Universe was one. I realised much later that physicists had taken over not just the Zoology syllabus and the whole of science, but the human mind on a much grander scale—they were everywhere as chief advisors to the city-states.

This success seemed to rankle the social anthropologists, who at one time had been angling for that position with some promise. As a student (1976~1980), I put this theoretical position to my superiors, that they were somehow imagining a 'Merlin' position (more on that later), for which they by rights ought to occupy. They were not impressed by this overture for self-reflection, and in any case, knew they had already lost out.

In the world of the physicist, there are only material forces, described as three nuclear plus gravity, with quantum mechanics and electromagnetism added on. They have a quest to reconcile all of these, which thus far, eludes them. If there is a God in their world, it is a private affair. For many physicists, God is an illusion—a creation or projection of the human imagination. For some, God is real, but interferes only in human affairs, and then rarely. In my observation, this God is usually a Father figure—almost entirely Abrahamic, loving and protective of His people, but often warlike and somewhat judgemental toward others; indeed, often enslaving them. For a small minority of physicists, God is in the detail of their Universe, in the Laws, in the symmetry and beauty of prediction. Curiously, that is close to how the greatest scientists saw things—like Newton, Galileo, Copernicus, and even Darwin in his early days.

I see an evolution, from many 'gods' among indigenous peoples—the 'animists'—toward a unified single God, usually solar, with a winding path through the early civilisations of theomorphs—half animal, half human; then a panoply of mythic super-humans, toward an eventual lone Father. At some time He may have been mythically divorced, as in the eventual loss of Gaia, wife of Uranus in Ancient Greece or Isis in Egypt and, of course, separated at birth from His Mother until, in modern times, God as Mother or Lover hardly exists at all outside of remnant indigenous tribal cultures.

So—am I left on the barren shores of the observational scientist? Not at all. Realisation came late that God could not or should not be apprehended by the altogether too tricky mind. Rather, God was reliably accessed only through the faculty of feeling. This went against all of my scientific training. Feelings were, after all, subjective—a personal experience, internal and hence not accessible to the lawmakers of physics. This is not true, of course. The feeling realm is accessible to study; feelings can be classified and related to causations and hence patterns. And the realm actually contains much of which all cultures would associate with God, such as love, compassion, caring and hence recognition, albeit often parental in nature, of the individual self.

The realisation of the import of feeling only came to me through yogic practice. The feeling nature evolves largely by a process of purification, an emotional cleansing that clears the body of its blocks and barriers to feeling the presence of the divinity that we might call God. This God had no gender as such, but would at times feel like a Father, and even speak like a Father, or a Mother, or a Lover. And my own evolution followed that order of experience. Nature at first felt empty and cold and only the Father's assurances were accessible; an imagined voice but nevertheless, it seemed much greater than my own; and then as my own feeling nature evolved, I began to sense the Mother's abiding presence, and in particular, how She nourished saint and sinner alike. Finally, came the Lover. Nature as Lover? Not an easy step for me, but oddly science itself showed me the connectivity. Everywhere in Nature, as Darwin was the first to emphasise, there is competition.

Nature always generates an abundance—genetically speaking—and this abundance is then subjected to the laws of Natural Selection, the Mother's laws where Death scythes away the unfitting. Only then can the Lover show herself, through the attraction of the fit to each other, according to laws that to this day, remain mostly hidden. Throughout Nature, it is largely the female, the lover but prospective mother, who chooses and this is true even at the cellular level of the ovum. Rape is very rare in Nature, and very largely confined to what may be an aberrant branch of our own human ancestry. Professor of Primatology at Harvard, Richard Wrangham, who was in the same Oxford Zoology cohort as myself in the 1960s, contrasted the 'demonic' dominating and controlling chimpanzee who could invade other territories, to terrorise, torture, rape and kill, with that of the bonobo, with virtually the same genetics, who was peaceful, loving, intensely sexual with a fundamental equality of power between male and female.

Well, you could not get to Oxford on the hippie trail in the 1960s, so neither of us had much contact with Flower Children and that decade of Love. Richard took a student expedition to East Africa and ended up a real zoologist studying chimps and bonobos in the field and I thoroughly recommend his book *The Demonic Male*. I explored the dark mountain forests to the north—the last before the Somali border and the desert. There I met my first magician—what anthropologists had labelled witchcraft—rather a difficult experience since he had been recruited as a tracker, was a very lazy man and instantly antagonised what was an otherwise superbly operating African support team. I quickly learned that the imagined powers had real consequences.

Partly for this reason, on returning to Oxford I eventually found myself studying witchcraft and magic among the ethnographies of various so-called primitive cultures, mostly African, but including, to the consternation of my supervisor, Carlos Castaneda[1] and even a delving into the recesses of the anthropological mind itself, including the propensity towards an advisory political power, imagined as that 'Merlin' position. Modern anthropology still talks in terms of 'speaking truth to power'.

Merlin is a derivation from the Celtic—Mervyn or Myrthin—and is, indeed a position, that of the magician or magus or shaman relative to the king. And is also the name of the small upland falcon *Falco columbarius*, an animal power. In the shamanic tradition, the merlin, falcon or hawk, is a messenger of the Gods; it travels between the worlds, of which there are only two: the physical or material, and the other world of the non-physical. We can trace this function back to Egypt and Horus, the falcon-headed 'god', later humanised as Hermes in Greek mythology (a combination of the ibis-headed Thoth with Horus-type powers, perhaps, but humanised, apart from the winged feet).

We shall have cause to return to the 'gods' of Egypt as they are still relevant in the modern world of hidden or esoteric practices—but to say here, that the Egyptians, with the exception of Akhenaton who made a big play for a single Solar Deity, did not have 'gods' as we know the term but rather *'neter'*, being a plurality of *powers*. Thus, as also in early Greece, modern civilisations at their outset had shades of a previous shamanic understanding.

Parallel to Thoth as the ibis-headed great teacher, the Greeks could still picture the hoopoe as 'king of the birds' (probably originating in Ancient Persia or Thrace) and the very first recorded political satire—*The Birds* by Aristophanes in 6th century BC—has two disgruntled politicians seeking a reclusive former politician of great influence who has become a hermit in the forest. They find him transformed into a hoopoe and attended by 22 helpers, all various birds—and hilariously recognisable as then extant politicians. The two miscreants are eager to reinstate certain privileges—among which was an acceptable access to young boys and enlist the help of the 'birds'. The avian allies create a walled-city in the sky called Cloud Cuckoo Land, the function of which is to intercept the voice of the Gods of heaven, and redefine the message to Earth for the benefit of the miscreants.

Aristophanes risked his life to get this play performed at a time when 'religion' was beginning to take over from individual conscience. He could see how the developing priesthood sought to mould consciousness to its own advantage—and always in the name of the Gods.

Cuckoos are a decidedly shamanic entity—they are parasitic. One only has to think about a small bird, usually a warbler, frantically feeding a giant juvenile, oblivious to its real nature, as if the slow growth from parasitic egg to adulthood makes the parasite imperceptible. Interestingly, the female cuckoo is brown and barred and sneaky, whereas the male is coloured like a hawk and draws the angry attention of the nesting birds away from the waiting female.

From this now ancient political wisdom-story I leave you with the concept of the Cloud Cuckoo—a parasitic life-form that is all-pervasive, exploitative yet imperceptibly dressed as divine authority. And return to the Merlin position and the nature of God.

I would dearly like to abandon the God term since it has overly masculine overtones, but will keep it for the present, as we focus upon the shamanic nature of the falcon and its ability to move between the worlds. In our own largely disavowed mythology, the Merlin is magician to the king—truth is speaking to power. Recently, a modern political episode went largely unnoticed: a banker by the name of Mervyn King pulled off an amazing trick; in 2008 he created money out of thin air. Hitherto, money had to be real—or close to reality, at least. Suddenly, as the Western economies faced bankruptcy and perhaps social disorder, he magically created a lot of money—cleverly disguised as 'quantitative easing'. Hundreds of billions were created in the British economy and the trick was immediately copied throughout the world.

Following the 2008 financial crisis, bankers were the only significant section of the power base that showed interest in my own work on climate cycles (*Chill: A Reassessment of Global Warming Theory* was published in 2009). They wanted to know whether the 'carbon bubble' could burst (that is buying and selling of carbon credits under the Kyoto Protocol to reduce emissions). I thought then it could, but wouldn't, unless the climate actually cooled, which it didn't. In fact, temperatures remained at a standstill from 2001 through to 2015, rose due to super El Niño and may yet cool.

I asked them what was happening to the money. It was not easy to explain, they said, but essentially the money has been given to the banks to buy stock, mostly government bonds. Did that mean, I asked, that governments then owed the banks interest? That is, the banks they were rescuing from oblivion. Essentially, the answer was yes.

That is quite a trick, no? And then, I had to look at the synchronicity of names. The Merlin had become 'King'—via the banking system! In fact, in 2011, while Mervyn King was still governor of the Bank of England, George Osborne, the-then Chancellor, instigated the 'Merlin Programme', aimed to rescue small businesses gutted by previous policies.

The advisor had become the power. And that caused me to look back in time to what had happened to the last real King, Charles 1, who in the 17th century had lost his 'head' as a powerful monarch and been replaced by the new power, relegating the monarchy to mere 'figurehead' status. What then was the nature of the new power?

I think it is an important question, but one thing I learned is that God, of whatever powers, has a sense of humour. I particularly remembered my first lesson in this aspect of divinity when challenging British

Nuclear Fuels on their propensity to discharge, safely—they claimed—the highly toxic plutonium oxide into the Irish Sea off Sellafield, then called Windscale. Their Press Officer was named: Con Allday! Perhaps the Gods do not want us to take it all so seriously?

After some 20 years fighting designs for a 'plutonium economy', I had grown alert to all the many currents at work and now spent some time looking at the nature of the transition that occurred in the 17th century and later, when royalty in the Western world at least, was divested of its power.

The Church—hitherto in cahoots with both royalty and its military—was already a waning power, no longer free to burn to death any challengers. Giodarno Bruno, for example, was not burned (in 1600) so much for his beliefs in a solar-centric system, rather his tendency to stir up the masses in the name of an alchemical freedom where love and real brotherhood reigned supreme. His contemporary, Galileo, was never a revolutionary, muttering the truth only under his breath and was spared that fate. Some writers say that over the preceding centuries *millions* rather than thousands of wise women were tortured and ritually executed, thereby eradicating the remnant colleges of feminine wisdom.

So extensive was the repression of feminine knowledge that even today the concept is almost non-existent. At the time of the transition, albeit a faded power, the death of feminine wisdom was lamented, none more so—but for particular reasons—than by the alchemist, Elias Ashmole who, in the biography (*The Magus of Freemasonry*) by the Masonic historian Tobias Churton, clearly experienced some difficulty with his women and marriage, it being, I would suppose, very difficult by then (early 1600s) to find a woman of equal power, as required for the attainment of an alchemical marriage in that esoteric tradition.

Ashmole was a powerful magus—an astrologer and chief advisor to King Charles 1 and even backed the royalists during the Civil War (1642-51) which they lost to the new powers, ostensibly Parliament but actually the landowners and their backers. Ashmole miraculously maintained favour. He was made a discrete offer by the new powers to come over to a nascent magical Order who did not include or indeed, need, women, in order to fulfil their inner destinies. Moreover, Ashmole, a nascent 'scientist', brought with him a good few worn-out alchemists and together with the new power's magical practitioners, created in 1660 a new 'royalty', The Royal Society of London (for Improving Natural Knowledge).

It was, however, still expedient to keep the esoteric side secret. Though the power of the Church had faded in the corridors of Westminster (England's seat of Parliament in London), it was still to be reckoned with within the popular mind where God was still decidedly Abrahamic. King James 1 (ruler until 1625) had not helped matters by fusing the New Testament, which had, after all, come to replace the Old, with the Old mythic Judaic, as if to legitimise the New. It worked, as indeed had all of the preceding translations and choices of inclusion or exclusion that had marginalised the God of Love and the Lover herself.

So—who were these new powers? Rather obviously, they were the rising bankers and investors. The bankers had made a lot of money lending to former royalty, particularly for their propensity to make war, for which they needed much financing. The House of Rothschild specialised in such deals. These were, of course, 'Jewish' bankers, skilled in networking across national boundaries, but also to become skilled in investment banking—not simply storing money, but lending it out to make more.

Much later, these traditional kabbalists were to incorporate the magical treatises of Egypt, once translated under Napoleon and central to the Oriental Lodge of Freemasonry based in Paris. And at some point, according to one defector disclosing at supposedly considerable personal risk, they incorporated rites and ritual usually reserved for the Babylonian deity of Baal—a horned God with goat's feet. Thus a fusion emerged, or may have emerged, of Jahweh, the Ancient Judaic, Baal the Babylonian and Osiris, the Egyptian, with no obvious female presence. Esoterics suggest that the alchemists brought some kind of inner feminine to the table, one accessible by the imagination rather than the flesh.

If all of this is so then small wonder the New World Order kept itself secret. The populace would never have understood, or tolerated. And in any case, the populace was hardly motivated to enquire, considering the forces unleashed by the New Order; everywhere in Europe, corporate empires were arising with those of Portugal, Spain, France, Holland and of course, Britain, spreading across the globe, ably supported by the old Church and financed by the new banks. Corporations rose to the status of colonial powers, backed by military might, and maybe it was at this point that the 'chimpanzee genes' began to run riot with invasion, genocide of the indigenous and the political suppression of women becoming a global rather than a Mediterranean (or Chinese) aberration.

It is rather obvious with whom sided the 'scientists'. Newton himself, a closet alchemist anxious to keep his lodgings in a still ecclesiastical Cambridge, became president of the Royal Society, which was then in the process of alchemical disinvestment. Soon to be gone were the astrologers, with the physicists rapidly gaining ascendency. Technology was moving at a pace and out-distancing both popular comprehension as well as parliamentarians and the scientists were quick to exploit their position of greater understanding. Their first great prize was medicine and, following that, the general education of the masses.

Hitherto, the alchemists had occupied the 'Merlin position' as advisors and educators to royalty. By 1600, they had served Elizabeth 1 and found favour with the Holy Roman Emperor in Prague. However, as fate would have it, James 1st was reportedly averse to 'magic' and hence was distanced from his daughter, Elizabeth, who was raised by the alchemists and married at 16 to the German aristocrat and noted alchemist Frederick of Palatine.

The alchemical couple initially lived in Germany, until Czech protestants in rebellion against the Catholic Empire, offered the couple to be their King and Queen of Bohemia, which they accepted. History focuses on the Protestant rebellion, from which King James was anxious to keep his distance, fatefully, at the time of his daughter's greatest need. The dark side of the Church, as was its habit, launched a crusade against the Bohemian heretics of Peace, Love, the Arts and, above all, the political equality of man and woman, a crusade led by Spanish mercenaries and ably reported by the embedded journalist of his time, René Descartes. Frederick was no soldier and his raggle-taggle pitchfork army was routed at the Battle of White Mountain, outside of Prague, in 1620, thus ending the real Renaissance and presaging the Thirty Years War. Twenty-seven Czech 'farmer lords' who backed Frederick were beheaded.

History doesn't have much to say about the inner philosophies, since it is written by the victors, who are still with us. For historians, it was a battle of reformist Protestants against the old Church Order, and alchemy was airbrushed out of the picture.

Al-chem, means 'out of Egypt', chem being a multi-layered word for 'black' but also soil, fertility and the nation nourished by the dark soil of the Nile's floodplain. The inner work of the alchemists involved transforming the 'base matter' of the soul into the crown of gold, a journey that parallels the raising of the serpent power of kundalini in yogic training from its base at the bottom of the spine moving through the 'chakras' or energy centres to the top of the head. Each centre—the second, sexual, relating to attraction and desire; the third, in the belly, relating to power; the fourth in the heart and all matters of the heart; the fifth the voice and the realisation (and speaking) of truth; the sixth, the inner vision; and the seventh, the liberation brought by surrender of the individual egoic self to the higher power.

This was a profoundly physical work best undertaken in sexual partnership—and as such, it had to be hidden from the Church for centuries and was thus heavily disguised in symbolism and by the alchemists' claim to be working on the transformation of base-lead into gold—something kings and emperors could more readily be seduced into supporting—as with the Emperor Rudolf in Prague in the years before the brief Bohemian kingdom.

Once purified by the inner work, the individual could thus reach oneness with the divine power and perforce be guided by the heart toward a mind balanced equally on a sexual level between male and female sources of wisdom—Logos and Sophia.

Apparently, the first Queen Elizabeth of Bohemia had herself a daughter who later (the family were exiled to Holland) wrote to Descartes in an attempt to understand the evolving separation of mind and body—the masculine from the feminine—but Descartes had already touched his destiny with the dictum 'there is no ghost in the machine' (now the divine becomes entirely human and Nature simply a mechanism). Henceforward, Nature would be seen as empty of soul, spirit, magic and what the Egyptians had called Ka.

This was not a difficult transition as the patriarchal militaristic, and soon-to-be corporate body politic, readily adopted Nature as part of the mechanism by which it could grow rich. Timber, minerals, slaves, whales... (and, much later in our time, coal, oil, uranium and consumers for the market), would become the objects of expansion and resulting competition for 'resources'. No mother, no lover tolerated in the machine—with women becoming either a willingly supporting underclass of mothers to the empire, or sexually exploited, largely in secret. The modern equivalent of the latter, being the Italian Silvio Berlusconi a one-time exposed member of the illegal Masonic Lodge—Propaganda Due or P2—where the Vatican's banker, Roberto Calvi, sat down with the Mafia, the Military, the Secret Police and the table-head, the Masonic Magus—Licio Gelli.

One of those P2 scions, either the Masons or the Mafia, assassinated Calvi after he made a run for it, perhaps with the intention of blowing a whistle on the financial deals made with nefarious regimes in

South America. Berlusconi, then at the table to represent the burgeoning power of the media, remarkably went on to become Prime Minister of Italy. Whether it demonstrates political naivety, or the opposite, the British Prime Minister, Tony Blair, went on a post-election holiday break to Berlusconi's famous party villa in Tuscany. The Italian was accused of sexually exploiting beautiful women long before the modern era (it is said that Kubrick's film *'Eyes Wide Shut'* reflects such exploitation). One model, Karima el Mahroug, known as Ruby the Heartbreaker, decided to write a book exposing the corruption (see https://time.com/archive/6595217/why-does-italy-put-up-with-berlusconi/), and the book *Karima* was recently published in Italian.

All of this is political and historical fact and not conspiracy. There exists a modern Masonic Order, still secret and global in extent (in Britain alone, its membership is held to run to around 600,000)—mostly lawyers, accountants, the judiciary, businessmen and police, and whose self-image is a benign society carrying out charitable deeds. The members of this Order founded the United States of America. It was the Paris-based Oriental Order that deciphered and incorporated the Egyptian rites. In 1982, on breaking open the P2 lodge, the Italian magistrates warned that all European capitals had lodges of this kind. But one cannot now discuss these political facts without being labelled a conspiracist.

But let us, for the present, dispense with labels. What we are dealing with is the ruling power of a warped imbalanced monstrous male mind. And it no longer feels the need to hide. It has a bible—The Great Reset, by Dr Klaus Schwab, convenor of the Davos gatherings of the World Economic Forum—of which he is its chairman—where billionaires, corporate leaders, Heads of State, old royals, entrepreneurs, film stars and other celebrities, vie for podium space. It talks now openly of the New World Order, something attempted many years ago by the American branch under Dick Cheney and George Bush Senior. Only now, it has the backing of the taxpayer, albeit not with their conscious will, this is forced by government dictat. In its future dream, it will have the backing of the global taxpayer.

Most State coffers, with the exception of China, are bankrupt and in desperate need of new money. Thus, they embrace the hitherto environmentalists, a new power of great influence among the populace, who have now themselves embraced modern world-saving technologies in The Green New Deal, itself embraced by the reformed bankers now under Mark Carney (a previous head of the Bank of England) as paymaster-general and the American politician and 'environmentalist' Al Gore as chief prophet of doom. Behind the scenes a new and largely invisible power, part corporate, part entrepreneurial, part banker—the investment houses—are busy gathering the money and deciding who gets a loan. Three such houses control trillions of other people's investments (pension funds, insurances, State players, other banks) chief of which are BlackRock, Vanguard and State Street, with the former guided by Larry Fink, the 'trillion-dollar' man, largely unknown to the general populace he believes himself to be serving. The aforementioned Dr Klaus Schwab believes fervently in this environmentally driven 'humanitarian' mission.

These powerful people do not seek election, of course. Their sole purpose appears to be to serve the investor—but actually, they and their advisors decide what gets built and where, even by State governments. And if one needed a reason why the 'independent' banks pay close-to-zero interest on the peoples' humble savings, it is to direct as much money as possible into the shares held by the investment houses.

In the 1970s, when I first became an environmentalist (old school, not New Green), the Open University adopted some of my writing for a course led by sociologists called 'The Control of Technology'. We were becoming rapidly aware that the kind of technology developed by scientists and their financiers had deep implications for the evolving body-politic. Parliaments the world-over were virtually devoid of scientists, as were their supporting civil services and hence not well placed to decide what risks to take on behalf of the people. And as the technologies advanced in complexity and deployment—for example, nuclear fission and fusion, pesticides and pharmaceuticals—they came to rely on scientific advisors to make the decisions.

One such example was the deployment of nuclear reactors to generate electricity. The scientists told the elected houses that reactors could not 'melt down' and posed negligible risk to the public. Some may have genuinely believed this fiction, but the institutions certainly knew, most especially The Royal Society, along with the engineering and chemical fraternity. Their cover was blown by the American Physical Society in 1975, later supported by the UK Royal Commission on Environmental Pollution, under Lord Flowers in 1976, but it was too late; the reactors had been built and more importantly, licensed.

As environmentalists then and since, we have watched the licensing of CFCs (and the subsequent damage to the ozone layer), PCBs[2] and the compromising of immune systems for all marine mammals, the X-raying of pregnant women and the dumping of radioactive waste at sea, acid rain, mercury discharged to coastal waters... all licensed by scientific committees but eventually, through the work of dissident scientists and environmental campaigners, banned under international law.

Science does not publicise these massive errors. And, it is my personal observation, that environmentalists have been neutered, their attention grabbed by climate change to such an extent that all other areas of concern are marginalised. The coalition of groups shows no hint of a former political awareness that would question the models, the mitigation technology, the impact of that technology, or where the new money trail would lead.

Thus it is that a former banned genetic technology—Gain of Function, where viral genomes are manipulated to become more transmissible and/or lethal—is relicensed, along with technology that manipulates the human genome. And largely happening without the general populace knowing that they paid for all this and will continue to do so. Nor were they appraised of the risks they might be subjected to, with, as it appears, the full extent of the risks not being known.

The Wuhan Institute of Virology was built in China with the help of specialist French architects, by Winterthur, with their plans reportedly modified according to the wishes of the Chinese military to include an office for the bioweapon developers, who already had their own laboratory just down the road. Apparently, and I have yet to confirm this, BlackRock and Vanguard, along with Axa Insurance, were major investors, which would be unsurprising since pharmaceuticals provide the number one investment opportunity in the world today.

So—let us recap: the warped imbalanced monstrous male mind, of which the political world, most particularly the mainstream media, is in denial thereof, has created first a deadly virus (regarded by Western intelligence services as a chimera and hence must be sourced from the military laboratory near the Wuhan Institute), and secondly, it has furthered a massive expansion of industrial production such that, so it believes, carbon-dioxide emissions threaten to destabilise the atmosphere and presage a major extinction event. We should note here that under the 1996 Kyoto Protocol (to limit emissions), China was granted permission to expand energy-intensive industries that were limited in the West, thus enabling a massive relocation of industry to not only less regulated factories but also much cheaper labour.

All of this is paralleled by continued development of atomic bombs, such as new submarine weapons of incredibly destructive power, such that even if ecological disaster is avoided, mankind still has the technology to lay the planet to waste.

What's not to like? Okay, I apologise for the flippancy. The situation is dire. Not, I have argued, on account of the climate; the analysis of that is flawed and in such a way as to benefit enormously the New World Order of carbon accountants, carbon banks, carbon currencies and green advisory committees—all requiring organs of global governance through which to spend their money (meaning our money). However, as an ecologist and scientist, I am convinced there is an ecological emergency of degraded forests, water resources, soil loss, reduced biodiversity and abundance of Nature, as well as a psychological emergency caused, in my view, by the suppression of feminine wisdom, lack of acceptance of natural cycles in the environment, denial of death and scarcity but also the primacy of love—both of self, society and Nature.

One look at a horizon dominated by mega-cities should be enough to puncture any sense that this system can be reformed or sustainably maintained by solar panels, wind turbines, biomass and nuclear power stations. I suspect the 'elite' are only too conscious of the mirage and hence are busy paying themselves massive salaries, building gated communities in such places as the Caribbean, (but not the Arctic as once advised by James Lovelock), or even planning to colonise Mars on the back of profits from electric autonomous cars![3]

And we haven't yet talked about the Bat from Hell![4] The Covid Saga is still running. The New World Order has eagerly embraced the political technology of Mass Vaccination and Lockdown—ably supported by a populace in fear of Death, most of whom are confined to cell-block living in the metropolis and plagued by massively compromised personal immune systems. The virus could not have been designed better for it takes down the weight of an ageing unproductive part of the population. The 'pandemic', whether by accident followed by opportunism—or designed at the outset—furthers vaccination, a transfer of personal empowerment via one's own immune system to that of the technological magician. The Pandemic response (most certainly planned in advance) socially isolates the heretics and legitimises force against any rebellion; and then transfers trillions more to the accounts of the billionaires (whose stock at the top of the pyramid is reported to have increased by 36% during 'the time of covid'), who then hand it all over to the investment houses for financing the Green New Deal and an Old World Order renewed.

It would be a simple matter to end here, with a conspiracy that is not exactly a conspiracy theory since thus far we have only spoken of Western magicians. The oldest magicians must surely be the Chinese—and they are not at all obvious. Maybe Mao and the Cultural Revolution did for them. And maybe not. If they were smart—and my sense is they would be—they would not have hidden in the banking system, better the military. They would have witnessed the transfer of power, from Maoist to the men at the Hong Kong Banking Corporation, the rise of Wuhan and mega-city cell-blocks, the surveillance State and the pervasive loss of soul. Maybe they care about that, enough to take action.

In shamanic lore, in order to create something that is not 'legal' or acceptable to the ruling power, you have to dream it happening by accident. Of course, in the world of magic—things are rather far from Harry Potter and the wielding of wands—everything comes down to dreaming. All that we have thus far described as the work of a burgeoning New World Order, has been dreamt. The American Dream of freedom is still the most powerful motivating force in this new world and it is built on an illusion that everyone could be free. There is a telling BBC documentary on Wuhan, where a struggling entrepreneur states that he wants to be rich because in China, that is the only way to be free. Now is the China of everywhere!

Just maybe, there are Chinese magicians of the old school, who, having seen where the new world was heading, have 'dreamt' a jumping of the gun—the release of the viral plague before it could be perfected, to awaken, via the prospect of death, to an essential rebirth of consciousness. Who knows?

And our work then would be to better understand what we might see as the works of evil, or Ahriman, or the Devil incarnate, because that is all unfolding under the auspices of a greater God—the God of a Universal Love that demands all are tested for their development towards free, loving, beings. We can but hope not to be given the choice of 'joining the Empire or face a pit full of hungry lions'. At present, we certainly face a philosophical challenge of acceptance and wisdom to challenge what constitutes appropriate loving action. I am, personally, in the midst of that process.

Notes

1. I personally liked what Castaneda brought to the table—the first look into 'non-consensual reality'. Even though I realised from the linguistic constructions that his work was largely fictional, I approved of the use of fiction, in this case, to communicate deep aspects of reality to a wide audience. I also feel that Castaneda must have had some kind of teacher, though not his fictional

character of Don Juan Matus. Castaneda's works are often dismissed as unforgiveable deception without any discussion of the actual content and meaning of 'other realities', which actually cannot be accessed by the objective stand-off nature of most anthropology.

2. Many environmental poisons are known by their initials—like DDT—which refer to their complex organic chemistry. These artificial compounds are persistent and were initially regarded as harmless based on simplistic laboratory tests for toxicity. Later, they were shown to have long-term eco-toxicity.

3. The Tesla car company, headed by Elon Musk, now the largest car maker in terms of capitalisation, attracted vast investment long before it was profitable and is built entirely on a future dream of 'connected' cities using Artificial Intelligence. As a multi-billionaire, Musk is now free to indulge his space fantasies.

4. Though now widely recognised as a lab-based genetic manipulation, the Covid virus is built upon the 'backbone' of a wild bat virus that had been cultivated in the Wuhan Institute over a number of years.

5.2 Masks—What They Show and What They Conceal

This article was originally published in New View *Autumn 2020 issue 97.*

My local cafe, here in Somerset, England, is a small family business with a funky art gallery and the best coffee in town. The owner's son, and his Gothic girlfriend, often serve and he is a mover in the local community—once to my great delight putting on a Flamenco fusion with Senegalese drums and original performers from Spain and Africa. They had to close for the whole of the lockdown, but thankfully survived. Many cafes have not. Indeed, the whole hospitality sector of the economy has been irreparably damaged. Additionally, yoga classes, dance classes, therapists and a host of creative self-employed and generally low-earning people have lost their livelihood.

In the cafe, food is served, and therefore there is no requirement to wear a mask. But people come in off the streets of hot sun and UV radiation (which inactivates viruses within seconds) wearing thick black masks. He gently tells them they don't need to, and always they take them off. He looks at me with a wry smile and does the open-hands-out-to-side-gesture. He is alarmed at what is happening out there and hates it with a vengeance, but has compassion. Outside, however, a palpable fear stalks the streets and a mask is its calling card.

Fear and confusion
In my High Street some hurry along, weaving avoidance, and exuding an air of medical safety when wearing the light-blue surgical type mask that is now so prevalent, signalling the medical emergency that Covid apparently presents—and their eyes show fear. There are others with cowboy bandanas and eyes of mischief. I wear a yellow Buddha scarf of infinite compassion. The fine ladies and some gentlemen have found funky designs. None of these masks can make much difference and everyone knows the policy is a shambles—but each reacts on a spectrum of fear and amusement. Some people are really annoyed. They see another 'they' at work—the bureaucrats and controlling authorities who stoke up the fear. Billions of people the world over are now being urged or compelled to wear masks. And I have seen recent disturbing videos of heavy-handed police responses to people not wearing masks—worse in France and Australia than in Britain, but many people are concerned that if protest grows, police action will intensify.

Masks have been used in ritual for thousands of years. They conceal individual identity and signal into the collective consciousness. Unlike any other aspect of the Covid experience, the mask visibly enters the public arena—it is the 'face' of the virus. Its meaning is held, however, not in what it covers—the lips, for example, are sealed from view; hence the voice is somehow 'muzzled', nothing can be said—because right now, in front of you, on the streets and on the buses and in the trains and planes, there is an *emergency*! It is the eyes that tell the story. They are almost always fearful. A very few laugh behind the masquerade, pretending to be bandits, lone rangers, gunslingers entering the Last Chance Saloon or some other fantasy intention like robbing the banks—but for most people the face-mask of the virus is one of *fear*.

This is where science ought to really help, because it definitely does not help to listen to the politicians. In Britain, right at the outset, when the public saw that all the doctors were wearing masks, they naturally asked—should we not also? No, said the government—it doesn't help. In fact, during the crisis, a number of doctors and health care workers were infected and died despite masks and in Intensive Care Units (ICUs)—and virology labs,—full breathing apparatus is required for effective protection, not masks.

These surgical masks are flimsy things; they won't protect you, though they will stop you spreading it if you have it—or so the UK government *claimed* was the advice it had received from scientists. The average person in the street was left to wonder—if masks stop people spreading it and everyone wears one, then the virus will diminish and we are all protected—so how come they were not mandatory at the outset?

Government had other issues to deal with—like 'How many masks can we deliver?' It was a matter of logistics. They did not have enough masks for everyone—not even the frontline health workers. Doctors, yes. Care workers, no. Moreover, in an advanced industrialised nation such as Britain, they could not source more masks quickly enough. There was a global demand and actually, nobody in Britain currently *made* them. They would have to be imported from China.

Gradually, with social distancing and the lockdown *apparently* the cause, infections have dropped and few people are dying. And at which point, the UK government suddenly changed the rule: masks would now have to be worn on public transport and in shops, (but not restaurants). This was important, they said, in order that the virus would not 'come back'. The public is rightly confused. If the masks did not contribute to the demise of the virus, how now can they keep it at bay? Ivor Cummins has made a recent summary of data that shows even where various mitigations were enforced they did not in any way affect the trajectory—the statistical trend—of hospital admissions and deaths.[1]

What the science has to say about the effectiveness of masking
As a preface, there are two realms of science—the natural and the social: a division of physiology and sociology. Perhaps more relevant in the latter case is the sociological subdivision of social anthropology with its grasp of the symbolic and the role of theatre.

Natural science relies upon data. I will paraphrase from the hydrologist, Demetris Katsoyiannis, that if the dark side is *fear*, the bright side is *data*. He was actually talking not about Covid but climate change. There are clear parallels.

To assess whether masks have any effect, the scientific method starts with a 'null' hypothesis that they have no effect and then martials the evidence to see if the hypothesis is supported or rejected. My summary of recent science papers shows that there is *no evidence to reject the hypothesis*. A recent paper from the Royal Society in London states that masks *ought to be effective*—it gives detailed laboratory assessments of the different mask constructions and their effectiveness at reducing expelled droplets, but can report no studies that isolate the effectiveness of masks as a mitigation strategy in the public arena. Even in surgical use, surveys have not demonstrated advantages. The only properly controlled studies were in surgical settings and surprisingly found no significant difference in infection rates, when masks were worn, or not. Data on community policy in comparison is confounded by a multiplex of other factors such as 'social distancing', reduced travel and commuting, staying at home, 'shielding' (isolating), etc., which means that any studies on the effect of masks cannot be isolated. Thus, this form of science cannot help. This was borne out by the World Health Organisation (WHO) guidelines, issued early on in the Covid 'pandemic', suggesting masks made little difference and in the UK, mask wearing did not become mandatory until after the 'first wave' had subsided. One might well ask why.

Theoretically, well-fitted masks of the right material will reduce droplet or aerosol dispersion and contain the spread, but do little to prevent entry of the virus through the mask.

There is no evidence that masks will significantly reduce the risk—but that does not mean they have no effect, merely that it cannot be disentangled from other mitigating measures. There is only one reasonable comparison: that of Sweden, which did not impose lockdown nor authoritarian restrictions—relying on its citizens to be sensible with regard to the risks, especially with regard to social distancing and working from home. Their rate of infection and death during the Covid period do not differ substantially from other European nations, though are higher than for either Norway or Finland, both of which did lockdown.

With regard to broader mitigation strategies, there is good data from the example of Sweden, where less stringent measures were taken: no lockdown, no mandatory masks on public transport, normal but sensible gatherings in restaurants, bars and cafes and no fines or heavy police actions. The rates of infection, hospital cases and deaths in Sweden follow the same curve as most other affected countries—thus providing some evidence that mitigation strategies in those countries had little effect on the trajectory of the viral epidemic. Sweden's neighbours, Finland and Norway did lockdown and fared better (in death rates)—but they also fared much better than other lockdown countries, suggesting other factors were present, as has shown to be the case. In Cummins's recent study, he noted that Finland and Norway differed from Sweden in having relatively normal flu deaths in the months prior to the Covid peak, whereas Sweden, in common with most European states, had below average.[1] There is a phenomenon known to epidemiologists as the 'dry tinder' effect—a build-up of the numbers of frail and vulnerable (mostly old) people who would normally succumb to flu and this then fuelled the Covid spike. This factor was at work in Sweden and affected their death rates for Covid (as was the case with other European countries) in relation to Finland and Norway.

It should be noted that this Covid virus is behaving in a 'classic' way, known as the Gompertz Curve: a steep rise as it moves through the most susceptible in a population, a peak and then a long tail-off. 'Second waves' are not typical, since resistance has built up in the population and there is solid evidence to support this.[2]

As noted, Sweden avoided lockdown and had a relaxed attitude to social distancing but failed to shield care-homes, yet the cases and deaths in them were not significantly different to countries with strong lockdown measures but high prevalence of infection to the virus. In all of this, there is no evidence at all for community benefits relating to mask-wearing. It must be said that the benefits are likely to be very low in absolute terms.

A case can doubtless be made that there has been an overreaction to the risk:

(i) The risk does not justify a *fear-based* reaction.
(ii) Provided care-homes and pensioners were shielded, the death rate would be much lower and in any case is comparable to many accepted lifestyle risks.
(iii) Provided the Health Services were adequately provisioned—for example, to cope with 10 times the number of ICU cases, as in a bad flu year, there would be no need to shutdown the rest of the National Health Service (NHS) (to treat anything other than Covid) with as yet untold health consequences.
(iv) As was demonstrated in Sweden, there was no need to shutdown transport systems, industrial production, office-work, the hospitality sector, tourism and holidays, with as yet untold consequences for the 'creative' sector.

It is clear, policy was partly driven as much by other factors than risk: for example, the run-down of the NHS in terms of beds and ICU capacity and the under-supply of personal protective equipment within the NHS. This might explain the 10 times lower death rates in Germany, for example, which has a more robust national health system.

The lockdown and emptying of UK hospitals in readiness for a wave that did not manifest has as yet unquantified knock-on effects—though one, at least, can be quantified: the dispersal of elderly patients from hospital to care-homes (without testing due to the inadequate supply of testing kits), which accounted for about 50% of Covid-related fatalities.

The combination of the overestimating of deaths by computer modelling in the face of uncertainty and the unpreparedness of the health services, as well as a lack of mass testing regimes, thus gave politicians the world-over reasons to impose strict lockdowns.

My local experience. What are the risks?
In Somerset, the English county where I live, at the height of the pandemic there were 500 'cases' in a population of 500,000—one of the lowest rates of infection in Britain. During this 'first wave' (and noting that such a description already contains a bias, with no one talking about the Gompertz Curve) a 'case' was then defined as admission to hospital coupled with a positive test for Covid—an important point for later discussion, as hospital admissions were heavily triaged[3] out of fear of overloading the NHS, which had limited capacity in terms of beds and ICUs. Only those with serious breathing difficulties were admitted to hospital.

During the three worst months of the epidemic a denizen of Somerset had a 1in a1,000 chance of hospital admission. Of those cases, 20% died, and at least half were seriously debilitated. That seems a high death rate (1in 5,000), but even so, at that time there were no masks on the streets or mandated on public transport. There were then no reliable estimates for the *prevalence* of the virus in the population at large, but estimates can be made based on a London survey—of the order of ten times the reported 'cases'. Hence, there was perhaps a 1 in a 100 chance of *encountering* the virus on the streets or in shops.

It was known from Chinese data at the outset, that as many as 90% of infections were likely to be asymptomatic (showing no symptoms) or create very mild flu-like symptoms; however, for the remainder, especially the elderly and those with underlying health issues, the infection could be debilitating with prolonged effects and one in five did not make it out of the hospital in Somerset. With less stringent triage, more widely defined 'cases' would lead to a lower death rate—globally, 3-4% is the norm. Comparisons from country to country are complicated by the definition of 'cases'—those with a low Case Fatality Rate (CFR) may be including all positive test results in the wider community, even those who are without symptoms, and there is no accepted protocol.

This rate of death was communicated to the population as a deadly 'pandemic' creating widespread fear and almost unanimous support for strong measures. I did not see any mainstream media compare the disease with influenza or, objectively, with other risks in daily life.

The national picture and European averages
For comparative purposes, risk is usually presented as a rate per 100,000 of a 'standard' population with typical age structure over one year. Some of these risks can be surprising—for example, for men, the risk of dying in any one year of a heart attack is 160 per 100,000 (about 1 in 600); or from an accident: 40 per 100,000.

We have a measure of background risks in the overall death rate (for preventable diseases, suicides and accidents, for example), where the European average is of the order of 230 in 100,000. This can also be expressed as about a 1 in 400 risk of dying in a year, with the male death rate from heart disease dominating the figure. However, this is the average. For the elderly *subgroup* the age-related annual risk of dying is much greater, depending on their state of health. For example, for a 66-year-old man with a pulmonary disorder, the normal annual death rate would be 6% (6 in every 100, which is the same as 24 in 400 to compare with the overall death ratio of 1 in 400 mentioned above) and about 25,000 in this category die each year in the UK.

However, these are risks from what are termed 'avoidable' diseases or accidents, and the main comparison needs to be with a very bad flu, which is also highly contagious, can be very virulent and stress the health services and has a greater impact on the elderly and those with underlying health conditions. Flu can also reach pandemic proportions, yet has not engendered great fear nor lockdown with damage to cultural life and the economy.

Given the controversy over what counts as a Covid-related death (the system of recording allows for considerable discretion), rather than measuring 'cases' it is better to look at the 'excess' deaths—those deaths over and above what is normal for any one month. Since Covid is a flu-like illness, we can look at excess deaths in a bad flu year to get some idea of how serious Covid is.

Deaths and how to measure them

According to the Public Health England (PHE) website, in an *average year* the whole of England sees about 3,000 hospital admissions for flu, with about 300 deaths—a 10% 'case fatality rate' (CFR) where 'case' is defined as a hospital admission. This, note, is quite close to the CFR for Covid in Somerset. In the rest of Britain, there were just over 40,000 claimed Covid 'case' fatalities out of a total of about 260,000 admissions producing a CFR of about 15%.

The standard quoted CFR for flu is 0.1%, so it would be easy to think Covid was 150 times worse, and indeed, this was how the media and government presented the 'emergency'. However, this is where the definition of a 'case' becomes crucial. If we restrict the definition to 'hospital admissions', then the CFR for Covid is comparable to the PHE figure of 10% mortality for flu (i.e. 300 deaths from 3000 hospital admissions).

However, there have been bad and very bad flu years where the numbers can be much higher than the recent PHE example. In the really bad years of 1999/2000 and 2014/2015 there were just over 40,000 flu-related deaths and even if we do not have so readily to hand the hospital admission data, this total number is comparable to the claimed 40,000 Covid fatalities.

Another similarity is that most deaths occur in people with comorbidities or the very elderly, though flu also affects infants. Of note is that I had to really search for the data for really bad flu years—one PHE readily accessible graphic started in 2015/2016 through to the present, thus obscuring the reality of a bad flu epidemic, the last of which was the year before. The Office for National Statistics (ONS) is a better source. (Again one might reasonably ask why 'bad flu' data is not easily available on the PHE website.)[4]

There are complications that relate to the definition of a 'case' and the cut-off point for 'fatality' from cases can include a lot of people who were already dying (known as comorbidity factors—e.g. heart disease). However, a look at the 'excess' deaths for each week, or month, of the year (the figure over and above the average number of deaths for that period in an average year), gives a good indicator.

Thus, in the so-called 'first wave' of Covid in Spring and early Summer this year, there have been some 60,000 'excess' deaths from all causes. Of these, about 40,000 had Covid written on the death certificates. Thus, it could be argued that the lockdown response to Covid, especially the suspension of normal medical services, has led to 20,000 excess deaths. Eventually, we will see a breakdown of these numbers and their nature.

One would think that at this stage, all this information would have been widely broadcast to an increasingly informed public in order to make comparisons—but that is not the case. It looks like Covid is equivalent to a relatively recent very bad flu year or, if we go back a few decades, is equivalent to the *average* deaths from flu in, for example the period 1966-1982, which was also around 40,000 (ONS data).

We can also look again at the objective risk level: the Covid risk for the 66 million population of UK would be 66 million divided by 40,000—which comes to a 1 in 1,650 chance of death. This comes way below the annual average risk from preventable illness and accident at about 1 in 300.

We can go back to winter of 1999/2000 to find a comparable excess mortality of 40,000 due mainly to flu. Such figures were calculated as the *average* during the decades from 1966-1982. In terms of individual risk of death: for a mild-flu year—1 in 200,000 and a very bad-flu year 1 in 1,500, with the latter figure directly comparable to the Covid epidemic figure of 1 in 1,600.

So far, therefore, there is no statistical evidence to justify a fearful and draconian response that appears to have caused about 20,000 excess deaths as 'collateral damage'.

Some people argue that the Covid peak would have been much worse without those measures—and indeed, modelling exercises performed in February and March indicated the death toll could have been as high as 500,000, mostly in the 'at risk' group of the elderly coupled with comorbidities. These are, however, risk assessments, statistical exercises that can point out worst-case scenarios. Whilst it is prudent to 'hope for the best and plan for the worst', policy makers have to look at the bigger picture in such risk assessments and adjust things over time when more information becomes available. Large numbers of people appear either immune to Covid infection and large numbers have only mild symptoms—the percentages are not yet known, but figures of 80-90% appear likely. In the general population, 13% are over 70 years old and about the same percentage have life-threatening 'morbidities' such as heart disease, kidney malfunction and diabetes. There were Covid related fatalities in all age-groups but generally, death was *very rare* in young people and children without comorbidities.

Policy, however, focused upon the possible death toll in the 'at risk' group and there were key calculations as to the likely severity under different levels of infection—and it was one such study, producing a figure of 500,000 excess deaths (primarily amongst the elderly), 'if nothing were done' that led to 'lockdown' and 'social distancing' as the main strategy because clearly such a death toll would overwhelm the NHS, which had about 6,000 Intensive Care Units (ICUs).

The lockdown policy in the UK derived from an assessment of the risk to an accurately identified vulnerable sub-population (mostly the elderly over 70 and those with already compromised immune systems). The data were published in May 2020 in the *Lancet*, the prestigious and well-respected medical journal. Risk factors for age-groups and comorbidities could be drawn from Chinese studies but were imperfectly known. It was also not known how much infection might spread to vulnerable subgroups. The computer model had as its *extreme scenario* a high-risk factor coupled to 80% spread within the population.

The study identified 8.4 million people as extremely vulnerable—a combination of age (over 70) and underlying conditions such as heart disease. This was based upon data from 3 million sampled individuals and extrapolated to the 66 million general population.

The sample provided a *baseline* where the numbers in each category of the high-risk group were known, as well as their normal risk of death in that year. The next step in the model was to multiply the number at risk in each age-group and comorbidity with the *relative risk* (RR)—i.e. the increased risk of dying due to infection with Covid. However, this was not known with much accuracy and for the purposes of modelling, several RR factors were modelled—ranging from 1.2 through 1.5, 2 and

3 times the normal risk (recall that a 66-year-old with heart disease has a normal risk of dying in any year of about 1 in 15).

The *relative risk* then multiplies the numbers that usually die in each category together with some idea of the infection rate. As with the RR numbers, the infection rate—a measure of how many of the at-risk group would be exposed to the virus, was not known. With neither of these factors certain, tables were drawn up combining different RR values (using factors of 1.2, 1.5, 2 and 3) with different levels of infection—from a few percent to 80% of the population in order to model different 'mitigation' scenarios.

In a 'do nothing' case, with maximum exposure of the 8.4 million at-risk group combined with an RR of 3, then 500,000 more people would die than in a normal year and over a few months. In such a case, the NHS would be totally overwhelmed.

This would have been about 8 times the eventual observed excess deaths during lockdown and hence the government could claim that lockdown was 'effective' in saving 440,000 lives.

But here we are rather 'playing' with figures because we cannot say for sure that the drop in infections, hospitalisation or deaths is due to the mitigation measures because the virus has its own inherent dynamic depending upon the spread of infections and, as already mentioned, epidemics follow the Gombertz Curve pattern where the virus fades away, and Covid looks like all of those previous cases—so far.

'First' and 'Second Waves'

Now that the 'first wave' of Covid has petered out, hospital admissions and deaths are in single figures and the NHS is not now overloaded. However, since the triage criteria were not quantified and we do not know how far the triage criteria have been relaxed, current hospital 'cases' do not offer reliable comparisons with the peak period.

The situation has been further complicated by extension of testing to the general public—'cases' are now synonymous with a positive test result and do not necessarily imply serious symptoms, or that everyone with symptoms will get a test. And 'cases' do not imply hospitalisation or death. The latter are barely happening at all at this time (September). But 'cases' are the new 'fear' factor.

Thus, so-called 'first wave' and 'second wave' data are not readily comparable—at least not without knowing the hospital admission figures and any changes in triage. In fact, the BBC, which has published figures for each region on a weekly basis, now confirms that its figures for 'cases' include those from the wider testing programme, thus making its own figures not comparable. This is important, because a 'second wave' may be appearing simply as a result of wider testing and of large numbers of people who, anyway, will not get sick. This would be an important element in the justification (or not) of another lockdown and prolonging existing measures.

The fact that hospital admissions have fallen to very low levels and deaths to single figures, whilst at the same time the virus is spreading, ought to be good news (compared to the previous months). It could mean that natural immunity is strong and may be strengthening.

Effectiveness of mitigation
At present we are considering masks—but in the context of social distancing and limited gatherings. Very soon we will have to consider vaccines. If we wish to assess the *effectiveness* of any mitigation strategy—whether it be a vaccine or a mask, we need to understand how effectiveness is measured and communicated. For example, flu jabs are typically quoted by Public Health England (PHE) as 68% 'effective'.

This means, in simple terms, that 2 out of 3 people who might normally get flu, do not, and this could be described as very effective. But let us look more closely as to what this statistic really means. A typical rate of illness for flu in a seasonal episode is only 5% of the UK population and a reduction using vaccines might bring this down to 2%, thus affecting a 3% reduction in case load. Three percent does not sound quite so 'effective' and so this measure of risk is not given much publicity by a government keen to vaccinate and hence reduce the possible economic impact of infection. Furthermore, a three-percentage point change is not likely to be visible as a reduction of total flu cases in yearly statistics due to natural variability and the error margins in calculations.

Numbers for the 'second-wave' risk will depend crucially upon how the 'case' figures are calculated. At present, the increased number of 'cases' has not strongly impacted on 'excess' death figures, nor in hospital admissions—and these are the figures we need.

As I write this (mid-September), the UK government has shifted toward a stronger policy with heavy fines for non-compliance with a limit of six people for public gathering—and pointing to the rise in 'cases' mostly among asymptomatic young people. These draconian measures are said to be justified because young people are thought to be spreading infections that will ultimately reach their vulnerable grandparents. This is ironic considering it was government policy that exposed so many elderly people in care-homes to the virus and led to their deaths. Not once does any government spokesperson talk about boosting immunity as a protection.

And then there is another interest group sitting alongside or standing slightly behind the politicians, and these are the people of the future, waiting to step in and alleviate the fear—with a vaccine.

Many of the 'annoyed' section of the population are aware that the single largest company in Britain and the most profitable is a pharmaceutical one working on a vaccine, heavily subsidised by the taxpayer (billions of dollars have been invested worldwide). And some of them know that the virus very likely escaped from a lab that was working on defences against viruses should they go pandemic; and that this work involved *making* new viruses to test the defences—even 'bad-ass' viruses the like of which Nature had never created. Indeed, the latest non-official expert assessments point to a chimera with elements of HIV and designed for wider ranging vascular effects than usual respiratory viruses. The term 'chimera' refers to a virus that has a combination of genetic material from two or more unrelated viruses and is an indication of a laboratory manipulation—in this case, manipulation of the natural bat coronavirus. We may not yet have seen the full implications. Only the government of Australia has called for an investigation as to the *origins* of the virus—in doing so they received threats of economic retaliation from China. [In relation to this there has been an important development. The reader is encouraged to read endnote 5 for details of this.—Ed][5]

Thus it is, that a simple surgical mask carries a whole agenda with it—so many players in the field, so many interests at stake, truth and deception in equal proportion for sure in a somewhat fogged-over past and an uncertain future.

The Gates of Heaven and the road paved with good intentions...
The stage is set and many of the players wear masks. Enter, then the Messiah. The one foretold. The Saviour who will save, not by grace, not by healing, not by spiritual awakening—but by technology.

In Britain, as noted, about *half* of all so-called Covid-related deaths were in care-homes—and that means they died without intensive care, even when the intensive care units were heavily undersubscribed, including all of the rapidly built (and never used) 'Nightingale' hospitals. The NHS actually emptied out the 'dry tinder' (the sick old folk), buying beds in care-homes and sending them there with no testing and inadequate supplies of Personal Protective Equipment for the care-workers. As one medical professor remarked—'It is as if world governments designed a policy of cutting down the numbers of the elderly and infirm.'

Any scientific unit worth its analytical salt would have foreseen this. Indeed, there were several 'pandemic' exercises in previous years to test resources and response strategies, but these 'plandemic' simulations were heavily focused upon civil response, medication and the preparedness of vaccines—there was little attention given to immune support, such as vitamin-D and C, or protocols for the protection of care-homes and shielding of the elderly. It is well known that vitamin D deficiency is common in the elderly and a key factor in lowering immunity.

Scientific policy is about making sacrifices. Scientists think along humanitarian lines, much as a major or general would in wartime, and measure deaths, resources and consequences against the broader strategy and available choices. Deaths to an econometric mind become 'working-days' lost. The choice of action is always political, not scientific—but then the research direction and the funding and the future of science is also political. Most scientists acknowledge the need to sup with governments 'using a long spoon', but the self-image remains that of a 'humanitarian quest'.

Science thus sees itself as a noble cause, and there is a phrase current—which arose during the climate science debates (in the times when there *was* debate)—called 'noble cause corruption'. The carbon climate coalition leader, Al Gore, when challenged on his use of ice-age graphics—where he failed to state that CO_2 levels always rose *after* the temperature did, replied famously—'It doesn't matter whether the science is wrong, when it is the right thing to do.' Soon after, all media empires agreed and the science institutions have rapidly adapted by constantly feeding government and media with the scariest climate projections despite the very great uncertainties in their predictions—uncertainties that tend to be admitted only in scientific forums and when journalists are not present. As a consequence, several billion dollars are spent annually on climate science and *hundreds of billions* on industrial subsidies and carbon credits.

Intention and the devil
There is much thought about conspiracy—that behind this madness (which includes the engineering of lethal viruses in the first place) lies intention. Conspiracists point to an 'Illuminati', but the devil may be closer to home.

Humanistic psychologists have a concept of the shadow-self and its dreaming powers. It is unconscious dreaming that betrays conscious good intention. There is however, a matter of fuel. Simple mentality is not much of a fuel. That is why most dreams are idle.

In Depth Psychology, it is said that to know one's own hidden intentions, one must look at the things one did *not intend* as consequences of one's actions. The conscious mind is filled with good intentions, and the world is filled with things that people did not mean to cause to happen. On the therapeutic path the individual must learn to take responsibility for the unintended consequence and wisely look under the surface and ask—What part of me intended that unwanted thing?

This is how the 'otherworld' of psyche, not physic, works. It is personal, but also collective—as in an institution or a society. For example, mental racism has little power until it becomes *visceral*—hence fuelled by emotion, at which point it becomes extremely dangerous.

Deep-rooted and unvisited psychic fears have the power to rise from deep within and possess the physical body. The ancient Magii held that *djinn*—thought-forms that existed within the dark and invisible realm of the collective psyche—had the power to possess the individual and to emerge on the collective stage. Indeed, early in Ancient Greece, the law allowed for possession by 'gods' (invisible archetypal *powers*) and did not focus so strongly on personal intention and culpability.

No one person *intended* to herd old people like cattle into holding pens to await the viral reaper. But a *djinn* had been created by repetition of an economic mantra that saw old people as a future humanitarian disaster—where too many elderly and expensively infirm would bankrupt a State that lacked numbers of the young and firm of body. And the unconscious modes of architectural and corporate structure confirmed the old as surplus to daily working and family life—even to become seen as a burden for the remaining workers.

Thus, no one virologist, whether vaccine designer or bioweapon defender, may have *intended* to create a virus that targeted the old. What happened has, however, fulfilled a dream held barely conscious in the collective psyche of all so-called advanced economies.

And no one pharmaceutical professor welcomes this virus as a booster for student enrolment and grants to the institute—these are simply consequences. And the directors of private companies patenting the medicines? Well, they have a duty to shareholders and, after all, it is a 'noble humanitarian cause' backed by capitalist shareholders upholding 'freedom and democracy'.

All noble causes face corruption—that is the test of nobility, which cannot itself evolve without it. The signs are not good. Reports from the 'alternative' health community are rife of censorship on anything related to immune support—particularly on social media. The humanitarian Gates Foundation has funded all aspects of media as well as science research related to vaccines and the communication of their benefits with *billions* of dollars. The Foundation has a non-charitable investment wing heavily invested in pharmaceuticals. Bill Gates has personal connections with the chief US advisor on the Covid emergency, Anthony Fauci, as well as funding connections to scientists in the UK advisory group (SAGE).

The 'interest' of the pharmaceutical industry is obvious—with numerous vaccines in development and very large investments so far, with production poised to ramp up once the vaccines are proven 'safe'. In this case, safety protocols have been minimised—limited to the very short-term reaction to the jab, and the efficiency of protection still unproven where time-consuming case-controlled trials would be the gold standard. This September the UK government provided a consultation via their website, with only a brief time in which to respond, to allow the public to express any concerns on proposed changes in the law to allow rapid mass vaccination, including removal of indemnity for vaccine producers. It has also announced a widely derided so-called 'Moonshot' programme of mass testing—ramping up from a few hundred thousand tests per day (with all manner of difficulties already present) to *10 million* per day. The estimated cost is £100 billion, equivalent to the annual UK education budget. That is, by a long shot, a great deal (of work) for the pharmaceutical industry.

And of course, if the pandemic has truly petered out and the scary 'second wave' is a mirage created by wider testing and exposure of relatively immune sections of the population, with hardly any hospital 'cases' or deaths, (this will be known within a period of weeks), the vaccine industry may find it has far fewer customers. The danger is that the image of a 'second wave' can be created by 'false-positive' tests—apparently the 'PCR' tests used do not distinguish an active from an essentially inactive virus as they are often identifying only 'debris' of the virus within the wider, now immune, community.[6]

There is now an expectation of further government policies on the need for vaccine passports—in schools, on planes or even for employment. Small wonder, I think, that so many people feeling powerless and at risk, see a consortium of very rich elite 'humanitarians' planning a future that might not really include them.

Peter Taylor lives in Somerset, England. He is an environmental scientist and policy analyst currently working with the Environmental Studies Institute, Santa Cruz, California, the Wildland Research Institute at Leeds University and the Institute for Life-based Architecture, Furth am Wald, Bavaria, Germany. His current interests stretch across ecological policies for human communities and wildlife, the impacts of energy production and the preservation of indigenous knowledge. He is a member of the Royal Anthropological Institution and holds degrees from Oxford University in Natural Sciences and Social Anthropology.

Notes

1. For by far the best scientific treatment of comparative excess deaths throughout the world, (especially Sweden) and analysis of 'second wave' potentials, see Ivor Cummins: https://www.youtube.com/watch?v=8UvF-hIFzaac&feature=share and also an interview with Sweden's chief epidemiologist: https://www.youtube.com/watch?v=hStrML7vk5k

2. Cummins shows examples of the Gompertz Curve, where a slow beginning accelerates to a point where it slowly curves flat. This is the Gompertz 'sine function': (https://en.wikipedia.org/wiki/Gompertz function). The peak then falls slowly and tails off during typical epidemics. However, Cummins also identifies a broader humped curve that seems to represent the way the virus operates in 'southern' populations—thereby effecting the overall population figures, (not so pronounced but lasting longer in its effect) such as in the USA and possibly also applicable to France and Spain, where infections are now rising somewhat after the long tail. In France the worst hit is the city of Marseille in the far south of the country.

3. Triage is the term used by medics to prioritise treatment when resources are stressed, such as on a battlefield or during a severe epidemic. Hospital admission and ICU support are then limited according to agreed criteria of likelihood of recovery and also age and normal life expectancy.

4. The ONS is a better source of statistics than Public Health England, with data going back to the high influenza years of 2014/2015 and 1999/2000. The recent excess spike for the Spring of 2020 at 60,000 is comparable to 1960s and 1970s and about 20% higher than the bad-flu year of 2014/2015. See https://www.ons.gov.uk/peoplepopultionandcommunity/birthsdeathsandmarriages/deaths/articles/rofexcesswinter-deaths since19992000/2015-11-25

5. In late September, we learnt that a Chinese virologist, Dr Li-Meng Yan, had recently defected under threats at home, leaving her job at Hong Kong

University, claiming the virus came from the military wing of the Wuhan laboratories. In response, the scientific community are resorting to obfuscation—claiming the virus has a natural source, as if this were an adequate explanation. It does, of course, have a natural origin, but the evidence for lab manipulation is overwhelming. Unfortunately, Li-Meng uses the words 'not natural' and the critics home in on this. See https://www.youtube.com/watch?v=0mP7T-Dg4j4

6. The PCR test is very sensitive. It amplifies genetic material from the virus, but false negatives are common, leaving some (between 15-30%) contagious people unrecognised (https://www.thedailystar.net/opinion/news/how-accurate-rt-pcr-diagnosing-covid-19-1916709); and it cannot discriminate between 'A person shedding a large amount of active virus, and a person with leftover fragments from an infection that's already been cleared, who would receive the same—positive—test result.' This, according to Prof. Heneghen, a leading expert consulted by the BBC. See: https://www.bbc.co.uk/news/health-54000629)

Sources

- The Royal Society Study (in association with the British Academy), 26 June, 2020: *'Face masks and coverings for the general public: behavioural knowledge, effectiveness of cloth coverings and public messaging'* 'a rapid review of the science of effectiveness of different mask types' https://royalsociety.org/-/media/policy/projects/set-c/set-c-facemasks.pdf?la=en-GB&hash=A22A87CB28F7D6AD9BD93BBCBFC2BB24
- The Lancet Study: 'Estimating excess 1-year mortality associated with the COVID-19 pandemic according to underlying conditions and age: a population-based cohort study, *Lancet* 2020; 395: 1715–25. Published Online 12 May, 2020. https://doi.org/10.1016/S0140-6736(20)30854-0
- The BBC has provided daily and weekly summaries of Covid 'cases' and deaths by country (UK) and postcode.
- Eurostat provides an abundance of data, not always easily navigated but deaths from all causes are here: https://ec.europa.eu/eurostat/statistics-explained/images/3/35/Causes_of_death_%E2%80%94_standardised_death_rate%2C_EU-27%2C_2016_%28per_100_000_inhabitants%29_Health20.png
- The Office of the Mayor of London provides data for London hospitals: https://www.london.gov.uk/coronavirus/coronavirus-numbers-london

- For the comparability and effectiveness of flu jabs, I gained a great deal from the statistician: https://statisticsbyjim.com/jim_frost/ (However, his page on the flu is not now readily accessible; you would have to log in—free at: https://www.qualitydigest.com/read/content_by_author/27530?page=1).

5.3 Awakening the Dream

This article was originally published in New View Winter 2020-21 Issue 98.

I know little of the writings of Rudolf Steiner, but one phrase to which my attention has been drawn resonates strongly—that at some time in a dystopian future, mankind could be *inoculated* against spirit itself.

Inoculation is a word with layers of meaning—like something that gets under your skin, your layer of protection, unnoticed, part of a deliberate act that leaves you forever changed, an act behind which there is a perpetrator, but of course, 'it is for your own good'. The word is old, from Latin and is rooted in the idea of grafting a bud onto a fruit tree, an ancient practice that most certainly has contributed to the betterment of society.

Humanity is now on the verge of a mass inoculation the like of which has never been attempted. Within the course of 2021, governments around the world will attempt to inoculate 70% of their populations, at huge cost, with a novel vaccine that not only gets under the skin, but embeds itself at the heart of cellular genetic structure.

Currently, a jab costs between $10 and $40 depending on the vaccine type, so, to vaccinate, say, 5 billion people, the cost will lie between $50 and $100 billion for the injections alone. On top of this are the subsidies to the vaccine companies and contributions from private foundations such as Bill and Melinda Gates that enabled the vaccine development, plus the infrastructure to distribute the vaccine and immunise so many people.

Not that the cost alone should be simply judged. I did a short survey on international humanitarian and development aid about ten years ago, and found that aid stood at $200 billion (half private, half governmental) per annum—a somewhat similar amount. However, only about 5% would, in my eyes as an ecologist, really constitute humanitarian aid—for sustainable agriculture and forestry, clean water and sanitation. At that time, it was estimated that $20 billion was all it would take to provide water on-tap to those who did not have it in the world, another $20 billion for sanitation and $20 billion to prevent deforestation. Some $60 billion in all. Britain alone has already spent directly about $100 billion attempting to protect its elderly and infirm (but has that really happened with the tragedy of deaths in care-homes and the like?) from an admittedly nasty virus if it takes hold and indirectly spent much more in printing money to salve the economic damage of lockdown policies.

I have thought about what Steiner could have meant. I live in a town famous for spiritual things—teachings, artefacts, healing, where crystal shops vie for custom with witchy paraphernalia and all the great religions have their representatives in the marketplace. It causes amusement among my friends and some reflection with me upon what exactly is the real meaning of spirit and what is the mark of a spiritual person?

One mark, I feel, is that a spiritual person is not afraid of death. A person rooted in spirit is not attached to this physical body, the vessel in which the spirit breathes, lives and loves. That does not mean they automatically know what lies beyond death, such as an afterlife, or even a before-life like a past-life; for many here it is perfectly spiritual to simply reside in the present moment and dwell in the great mystery of it all.

However, living in a town with more than its fair share of spiritually minded people, brought a revelation when my father was hospitalised with terminal cancer many years ago at the age of 80. The nurses allowed me and my two brothers to stay by his bedside. We made sure one of us would be there around the clock after his heart began to falter and his lungs filled with fluid. The nurses told us he wasn't expected to last the night. Around 2am on that first night, he emerged briefly from the morphine and I knew he could hear me. A week or so before, he had been panicking at the prospect of death, feeling he had not been a good man. To help him I had taught him to breathe in what the yogis call a 'connected' breath—no pause between the inhale and the exhale, both at the 'top' of the inhale and the 'bottom'. Most of us hold our breath there. This is the place in the body, a space at both turning points, where fear is stored—fear of receiving all of what life has to offer and fear of letting go. In particular, the subtle movement of pushing on the exhale—pushing the life experience away, requires guidance to release. After five minutes of practice, a trance-like state unfolds and the breath itself establishes its own rhythm where no effort is required. In that space, the guide stays close, as memories long stored in the body and the mind come to the surface.

I whispered for my father to start the breathing and to ask humbly for someone on the other side to come and guide him over, to not be afraid, that there was no judgement awaiting, for his greatest fear—only half-joking—was he had heard of reincarnation whilst fighting the Japanese in Burma and that he would return as a worm!

Five days later he was still breathing in that rhythm—quite unheard of among breath-workers. He had had no food and no liquids, the nurses having been instructed not to let him drown in his own fluid. He looked like a mummified Egyptian, just skin and bone, but he glowed and with his last breath, he went smiling onward to whatever lies ahead. We sang his soul on its way.

It was during this time I met real angels, down here. They were the night shift at the hospital. Quite likely Christians all. What hearts they had! They shone brighter than any spiritual person in my famous town and I guarantee they did not see themselves as spiritual people.

This Covid emergency has been revelatory. The majority of my country and indeed, most other countries, live in such fear of death, perhaps less for themselves as for the old people at risk, that they surrender some of their most basic and cherished freedoms—the kind of freedoms their forebears fought and died for, hoping the emergency is temporary and the virus 'enemy' eventually will come under 'control'—or as Boris Johnson said in an unguarded slip of the moment, will be 'put back in the box'.

My father did not die in the last World War, but a part of him did—a part that he would otherwise have been more able to give to his children. He had lost so many friends he had become afraid of attachment, afraid to love fully, afraid of the pain of loss and separation that would surely come. He had no spiritual grounding, nothing to anchor him except perhaps during those last moments and after the requested help had surely come.

Meeting those nurses, I realised humility and a practical love are the qualities I associate with spirituality. Lacking both in any great quantity, I decided I would work to protect those who carried the torch. One thing I have concluded is that fear of any kind is incompatible with a spiritual life. Fear constricts. It is born of a lack of trust in the moment and in the power of life. And it is a subtle thing that resides in large part in the unconscious. Nobody wants to admit to living in fear.

And the observer in me sees how the fearful are easily manipulated—especially those who fear death or disease. Fear paralyses the rational faculty. It causes people to merge together and follow whoever promises security, something that is not at all the same as freedom from fear. Supposed leaders then harvest their allegiance and can quickly turn nation against nation, majority against minority, race against race, orthodox against the heretical.

As a part-time yogi, breath- and body-worker, I have seen where fear is lodged in the body-mind, and how social conditioning and constant programming maintain its presence. It starts at the very base and foundation of the human system—the sacrum. A fearless base is a rare thing: no fear of losing a 'job', of a receding economy, non-payment of mortgage, lack of communal support, of destitution or dependency and being a burden to those you love.

There is a yogic law that in the absence of fear at the base, the first basic level of consciousness, a natural energy starts to awaken and move upward in the spine. I would call it *ki*—like ki in Aikido, *Chi* in Tai Chi or *kundalini* in yoga. This energy is also becoming recognised by those working on the frontiers of Western science, those with knowledge of the quantum field, dark energies and dark matter. These scientists know that within the cosmos a great power that is not measurable and not visible is ever present and ever moving. Scientists are beginning to suspect that in this dark field lies the creative ground, the darkness from which all that is light emerges. Few yet suspect that *ki*, which they hardly know, is the same powerful force, and that it is not just physical but *psychic*.

Martial artists have perhaps the best grasp of its power. I have seen the laws of normal physics broken with ease by the monks of Shaolin and by my own Himalayan yogic master. And as a some-time anthropologist I am convinced such power is a human birthright quite common among indigenous peoples, all of whom dedicate a mediator role to the shaman-healer and ceremonialist.

When the *ki* is felt and honoured, cultivated and most importantly, invoked, it uncoils and reveals its hidden nature, a serpentine power that spirals, energises and *heals*. It is also highly sexual. When a deep level of security is manifest—a sense of being at one (first level in a journey of levels) and at peace with everything, the *ki* rises to a second level, or energy storage and distribution point, where, in keeping with the number two, a duality unfolds out of the unity. And if here it encounters no fear, a great joyous pulse begins and the games of duality, love and procreation begin.

Alas, there are few modern cultures that do not harbour fear in the sexual centre. It is a long work to dissipate the blocks and liberate the *ki* at this level and that is not the whole of the work. This energy needs to move upward at full power if the fullness of human potential is to be realised. In an over-sexualised culture, such as is so prevalent today, this power is distracted and dissipated.

I suspect, but cannot prove, that early human evolution was led by the females as they were more able to cultivate sexual energy and move it consciously to the next level, the third—which I would call the *power* centre. The female form looks to me as if it were designed to cultivate that energy and store it in the belly, where it becomes a powerful attractive force; whereas the archetypal male warrior must learn and practise to build this power in what martial artists would call the *hara* (centre of gravity) from which all action stems as it becomes an *extension of ki*. In this energetic space, the empowered self does not give away that personal power to false authority, and only recognises authority, such as that of a chief, if it is truly merited.

In my observation, modern Western culture—which now also predominates in the East—is built upon fear of authority, of what it can do to the person who errs. In my perception, there is little real choice—the political faces may change, but not the deal being offered. In exchange for free-will, the State and its corporations offer security and the chance to prosper and better the material life. A few of my friends live freely— they do what they want to do and follow their dream, which is a natural dream of love and a community to which they can contribute. But most people I see on the street live in fear, most especially of expressing their own creative power and its dream. Very few know the security of a real community.

It is not hard to see how the 'system' most of us live in inculcates fear and lack of that creative power. Hence the vast majority are robbed of their greatest birthright, the power available when the spiralling serpent ascends through the narrow channel from its well in the belly and into the heart—the fourth centre in the yogic system. However, seldom taught is how this channel enters the heart from *below* whereas many cultures fill the heart from above. The lower entrance leads to what I would call the basement of the heart. Masters have told how most of us live in the basement, hardly aware of the rooms above and the possibility of windows! It is an apt metaphor, but I prefer another. We live on the first floor of the heart, but are haunted by the invisible ghost of our unredeemed, unhealed and transformed self, locked in the basement and desperate to come up into the light. This ghost is the hurt-child, the abused, the resentful and the vengeful. It is the serpent's power to heal, which paradoxically generates fear of the healing, thus the channel, which the Druids call the Derwen (after the oak tree), is held tight and narrow. Their herbalists tell that the oak flower, yellow as the Sun, holds the remedial power to open the ailing human heart.

It is the healing of the fearful heart that is the greatest task of humanity. Few people will go there voluntarily. The unhealed heart is a saboteur of love and all good intention. It carries the shadow of generations, all the pain of past humiliation, occupation, domination and exploitation.

Without this healing, the heart has not the power to love unconditionally. It has been the undoing of all the Abrahamic religions that somehow, against the teachings of their masters, they married the God of Love to the God of War, hence serving both masters. They also demonised both the serpent and any woman who personified that power.

And though I have much admiration for the Buddha, I do not see that the path of renunciation and freedom from suffering works well in the West (and all the territories Western mentality has occupied). If sex and the feminine are not deified, an imbalance in the energy currents guarantees an imbalanced mind. To rebalance we might learn some basic Alchemical lore regarding balancing energies.

The West, in Druid and Native American lore is a *direction*—in much the same way that in physics there is a recognised rotational power which is directional—it is *spiral,* moving energy upward or downward; thus directionality is coupled to polarity of North and South (defined at right-angles to the rotation) and it is a universal coupling found everywhere astronomers look. Modern science apprehends only the physical reality—even though it understands that all atomic reality is ultimately wave-form, and it does not concern itself much with the ocean upon which all waves must move and have their being. And where it does, fleetingly—as in 'there must be a dark, invisible and immeasurable force' (because we can measure its gravitational effects) it does not concern itself with the *content* of this power realm. I would use the couplet 'physic-psychic' to describe this reality, where both are not separated and indeed, *should not* be separated.

Here we touch on the origins of Science itself, with its linguistic root in the Latin 'scire', meaning *to separate* (later in Old French it became to 'know', or 'knowledge'). Much of 'Enlightenment' thinking extols the virtues of demoting the psychic realm and the apparently undoubted benefits of rationality.

Druids understand that the physical world and the psychic world interpenetrate. There is a dance going on—a tango, if you like. In the East lies unity, the rising Sun, the source of nourishment and heart; in the West, lies the setting Sun and the night-sky, the place of duality, the play of life, drama, theatre and the game of love. Where modern physicists can at least talk of waves and fields, they miss the *content* and fields of meaning. Very few scientists study humanistic psychology and works such as those of Carl Jung on the nature of the shadow play, or Wilhelm Reich on bio-energetics and how the physical body stores emotional memory.

Where the heart may be energised by the rising Sun, it must not be extinguished by whatever content lies in the darkness that inevitably follows. This is the place of dreaming and all fear is a dream of that which we do not wish to happen. This is where the shadow and the monsters live, but also, the very spark of creativity and the birth of stars. It should be a place of indigenous joy in the song and dance of it all. I think it used to be. Nowadays, individual fears coalesce and build a collective shadow in the 'otherworld'—the underworld of the psyche, where such power may rise uninvited and possess the upper world.

It is easier to see now how gender imbalance, fear in the human system and a doctrine of separation that demotes the feminine powers of heart and feeling, have led to the current dystopia of a degraded Earth. Science, which in many ways got us into this mess, offers salvation, but then stokes the fears—of climate change, disease, extinction, energy scarcity or annihilation by a heavily armed enemy, and all to its own institutional benefit.

Men and women are now mired in the aftermath of patriarchal domination, where trust is still fragile. To emerge into fuller expression of who we are there must be power in the heart, and above all *balance* between the male and female expression *within*. Only when men are fully at one with their own feminine, the receptive, the feeling, the intuitive and where the God of Love is master, will they be free to love the feminine outside of themselves. And that is not an easy journey in an intensely competitive and unequal society.

However, when a balance *is* achieved, the *ki* moves with great force— in what Tibetan masters would call the marriage of the two dragons, red and green, to create the blue electric, the ultimate creative (and destructive) power. It is important then that the *ki* moves upward to the fifth level, each level being described by yogic science as a 'wheel' or chakra of spiralling energy, and at this point the journey needs both invocation and *pull*. The energy is pulled upward as the voice is engaged and this is augmented by invocation in mantra or song. Freedom of speech, of course, but also, the freedom to sing. Songs are dreams. When the heart is in the voice, it creates *tone*. Sometimes the heart must grieve for where love and romance have brought attachment that is then lost; in grieving fully it lets go of the past. Teachers of all paths have taught us that to know the heights of joy, we have to experience the depths of sorrow.

It is, however, in singing that the greatest freedom is born. In song, which I associate with the sixth centre of consciousness or 'sixth sense', the dream-centre infuses melody, orchestrates tonal quality, creating its dreams to radiate outward and communicate to other hearts. This interplay is a prerequisite on the yogic path—the vision centre must be prepared by purification of thought, before power is moved upward, because empowered dream quickly manifests in the outer world.

Sadly, few now feel free to express their truth in words or songs. Most minds have had visions implanted and people live a dream that is not their own, like the American Dream that has occupied so much of the planet, even though so many know the promised freedom is an illusion, a trick, where only some can prosper.

Thus, the saddened human now moves along shuttered streets, gathering food and distractions, individualised and afraid of the future. Covid is the last nail. Climate, Terrorism, Cancer, Drugs, Poverty—all have had their 'wars on…' exhortations, built on fear. The spell has been cast. The harvest of souls nears completion. The Pyramid men are inoculating the spiritual heart with the virus of fear. I need not dwell on for whom this bell tolls, nor who benefits. In the long run of geological time, all we see now will be dust. The Vikings are dust and the Romans, the Greeks, the Egyptians… you now have to dig to find their traces.

What to do about it? That is the question facing all who would align with the spirit of what it is to be human. Clearly, the work to free people from this spell of bondage is a big work! Community, sexuality without fear or guilt, personal empowerment, feeding the heart and the soul, freeing the voice and singing a vision of the future, for there is an ultimate level of consciousness—seventh *heaven*, so to speak, at the *crown* where the beauty and the true magic lies.

This level for the yogi, the shaman, the true Christian, Sufi and even, I would say, the real scientist, is about *surrender* of the individualised human spirit to Great Spirit or Great Mystery, where the fully empowered egoic self is given as a *gift* to the source, by whatever name, the one source of *ki*—the love, the power, the creativity, and the *weaver* of Fate, with the humble request to do love's will.

The Himalayan masters teach it simply—that *within* each of us lies all knowledge, all truth, we just have to realise it. Once realised, the real work begins.

This is the *royal* path, it underpins the origin of *real*. The gold of Alchemy emerges as an energy from the Crown, after all the centres have been cleansed and aligned, and it was this path that the Alchemists followed all the way from Egypt, but was rather lost here in Britain when around the 1650s they gave up the struggle for equality of man and woman, the balance of respect for the male and the female within, and allied with the emerging power of Science—itself allying with the corporate world and the State and calling itself then and now *The Royal Society*.

The esoteric path was kept hidden and distorted beyond recognition. It is no surprise to me that scientists most likely created this virus, whether deliberately released or that it escaped their controls, nor that it is scientists who now offer salvation. And that, with the collusion of the State and the fearful masses, they obfuscate the nature of the pandemic, sowing fear and obedience and reaping vast funds in the process. But I do suspect, that they, the institutions of science, are themselves being played.

What to do about it? Science has a vision for us, a future of the genetically manipulated trans-human, in a world forever controlled, in a Green New Deal of shining glass and concrete powered by solar panels and nuclear reactors, where, as the leader of the World Economic Forum would have it, we, the future people, would not need to *own* anything, without adding who would own everything! I doubt enough will reject the vision. The spiritual task is to keep ourselves free of fear. That is a work. And to be available to help as Chaos (whom the Ancient Greeks deified as Kaos) begins to reign—as She must, for a while. This is the *real* world. Ups and downs. What goes up, must come down. And for many of us, we need to dance and sing our future dream. Time now for a Ghost Dance, a conjuring of all the demons onto the dance floor, as when the Lakota faced their last battle and danced for a union of red-man and white-man hearts beyond the grave—but a tango this time, man and woman spiralling in union, one that opens the basement of the heart and weaves a new dream, a brave new song, a gift of human Gold to the Cosmos that emerges at the Crown.

As Jupiter and Saturn conjunct at the Winter Solstice on 21 December in the first degree of Aquarius, this apparently sorry saga will shift into new territory, a new cycle. The leaden energy of the New World Order needs to be balanced by our golden vision, one that the Old Order in a new Green guise do not yet appreciate, where man and woman, the feminine and masculine powers, are balanced in total respect for each other. In this endeavour, the Bat Virus with its protein Corona, has been a great awakener—who is to say it was not conjured by Ancient Chinese magicians grown impatient with the totalitarian elite that so recently occupied their own illustrious Land?

APPENDICES

1. Responses to Criticism
2. Reviews
3. Are there Gender issues in Climate Science?
4. Renewable Energy Strategies
5. Summary of collaborative work at ESI
6. Previous critique of UN structures and development of The Precautionary Principle.

1. Responses to Criticism

The letter of criticism linked below was published in *Caduceus* 91 (2015) and is followed by my response which was sent to Tony Wardle directly. See: OceanEarthSystems.net/climate

2. Reviews

2.1 In May 2019, pressure was put on the Editor of *Caduceus* after I wrote a review of 'The State of the Climate' a report by the Global Warming Policy Foundation, a think tank set up by the former Chancellor of the Exchequer Nigel Lawson. The report is a regular production by Professor Ole Humlum of Oslo University and contains reliable data on aspects of climate change. The GWPF is an avowedly anti-green, pro-nuclear champion of the free market and therefore not a natural ally of mine, nor do they use my work—but I am grateful for a lot of what they do in the distribution of sound science, such as Humlum's commissioned annual 'State of the Climate' reports.

My review in the books section caused a reaction. One of *Caduceus*' trustees resigned in disgust at giving a 'climate denier' (me, apparently) space in the magazine, and her partner Herbert Girardet, a respected professor of environmental policy, also complained to the Editor, who passed his comments on to me. I wrote to Girardet, someone I had known (and highly respected) from his past work in the early days of environmental campaigns (before the climate became a focus). See: OceanEarthSystems.net/climate

'State of the Climate' 2018 report allays fears of global warming.

> Peter Taylor, whose article in the last issue highlighted the natural cycles affecting climate change, assesses a new report from the Global Warming Policy Foundation:
>
> This new report by Professor Ole Humlum is a most useful one—if you can read graphs! It deals with the past 15 years of climate change in the context of several natural cycles; using official data to show that temperatures, sea-level, cyclones, hurricanes, wind speeds and snow cover have not risen, let alone 'accelerated' over the first decades of this millennium. The spike of 'records' in 2016, that appeared to end the scientifically attested lack of surface warming, was entirely due to the natural El Niño cycle.
>
> Humlum is Professor of Physical Geography at Oslo University and he keeps an updated record on key climate indicators, so this data is entirely trustworthy. It does show the decline in Arctic ice-cover to 2012, but a gradual recovery since then. It highlights a steady drop in North Atlantic, sea-surface temperatures since 2012, which I suspect will contribute to increasing sea ice and probably accounts for recent reports of the iconic, Jacobshaven glacier in Greenland reversing its centennial trend and beginning to advance again.
>
> The report outlines the key ocean oscillations: Pacific Decadal, Atlantic Multi-decadal and the Southern Oscillation, the warming phases of which contributed to the 'global warming' of the past three decades. All of these now appear headed for a downturn
>
> Sea-level rise, contrary to media reports, is not accelerating, at least not on tidal gauge analysis, only on much-adjusted satellite data. It continues its centennial path at about 2mm/year, or about 8 inches per century. The satellite data seems to show an increase to 3mm/year, or 12 inches per century, if maintained at the same rate. Alarmists are keen to see an acceleration because that can be extrapolated, i.e. constant acceleration, to arrive at several feet.

The Figure 1 graph in the report is among many myth-busters; here, for example, that storms are getting stronger. It can clearly be seen that cyclone energy is oscillatory and nothing unusual is shown to be happening over the past 50 years.

Similar graphs on snow cover and hurricane landings debunk media claims of disaster. Of great interest are several graphs mapping the increased heat absorption of the oceans, showing that it is mostly located down to 200m depth in the equatorial regions; that the circum-Arctic waters are cooling; and that circum-Antarctic waters are stable.

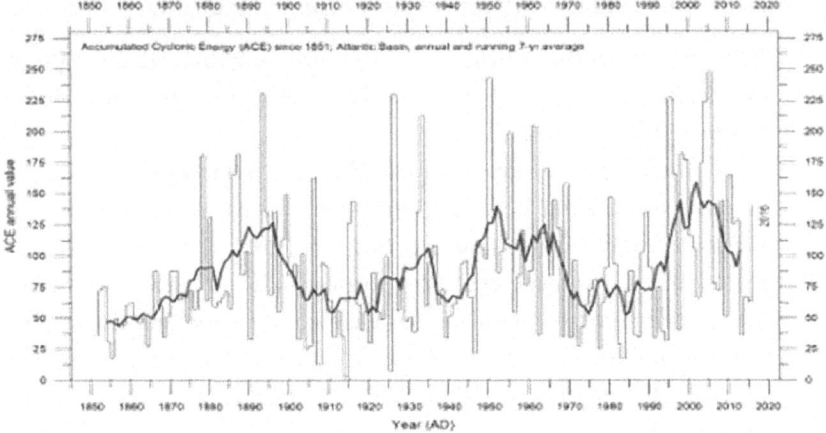

Figure 1. Accumulated Cyclonic Energy: a measure of the total power within cyclonic storms, for the Atlantic basin, 1850-2016.

The GWPF was founded by Nigel Lawson and set up to counter alarmist propaganda with critical scientific analysis. This report can be downloaded free on their site: www.thegwpf.org

2.2   *The Climate Book* created by Greta Thunberg—contributed by multiple authors, Allen Lane, London, 2022. Hb, 446pp, £25. ISBN 978 0241547472 A critique of the new 'bible' of the climate alarmists (see: OceanEarthSystems.net/reviews)

2.3   Healthy Planet—Global meltdown or global healing (review of Hargender in *Caduceus*, 107, 2022) See: OceanEarthSystems.net/reviews

3. Are there gender issues in climate science?

Seminar Paper to World Congress on Anthropology of Climate Change at the British Museum, (2016). See: OceanEarthSystems.net/climate

4. Renewable Energy Strategies

Landscape, climate and renewable energy: envisioning future options. In a project for the Countryside Agency, Ethos has been pioneering virtual reality models of landscape and future technology. These techniques of visualisation may provide a template for a more democratic and less conflict-ridden process of development for renewable energy in the countryside. Seminar to World Congress of Anthropology, 2016. (see; www.OceanEarthSystems.net/renewables)

5. Summary of collaborative work at the Environmental Studies Institute (ESI), Santa Cruz, California

Following publication of *Chill* in 2009, and in response to the negative reactions of environmentalists who refused to even review the book let alone invite discussion, I spent the next ten years working with my colleague Professor Jackson Davis at ESI, where I had collaborated as a Research Associate on ocean policy work. The Institute was a small private not-for-profit vehicle for policy work outside of the University of California, where Jackson Davis was professor of biological sciences. From 1982 to 1993, Professor Davis and I collaborated on marine policy issues such as ocean dumping of radioactive waste, incineration of toxic substances at sea, the nuclear test ban treaty and the introduction of the Precautionary Principle in maritime law.

Having read the draft of *Chill* Professor Davis endorsed the cover, stating that the questions I raised must be answered before current global warming theory could be accepted. In a nutshell, that theory holds that carbon-dioxide levels are the 'control knob' of climate. He had had a lead-role in setting up the UN's Framework Climate Convention, where through the auspices of ESI he represented a consortium of the Pacific Island States, and he was a participatory author of the UN's Kyoto Protocol for the reduction of carbon-dioxide emissions.

Having spent the best part of 20 years campaigning on climate issues at the UN, my thesis was a big challenge. In 2010, he accompanied me on visits to the University of Colorado and the US National Center for Atmospheric Research (NCAR) where he was able to see first-hand the response of UN advisors (modellers all) to the real-world data I presented them with. He became convinced and began his own self-funded research programme, the first paper of which, published in 2017 in the journal *Climate* examined the geo-biological history of carbon-dioxide levels and temperature. To his surprise, when looked at over 500 million years of evolutionary time, temperature and carbon-dioxide levels *are not correlated*. Only the last 2 million years shows a strong correlation—the time of ice ages, but temperature rises *before* carbon-dioxide, which is released from the warming oceans.

5.1 The Relationship between Atmospheric Carbon Dioxide Concentration and Global Temperature for the Last 425 Million Years

W. Jackson Davis

Published in *Climate* 2017, 5, 76; doi:10.3390/cli5040076 www.mdpi.com/journal/climate

> From the abstract: Spectral analysis, auto and cross-correlation show that proxies for T, atmospheric CO_2 concentration and $DRFCO_2$ oscillate across the Phanerozoic, and cycles of CO_2 and $DRFCO_2$ are antiphasic. A prominent 15 million-year CO_2 cycle coincides closely with identified mass extinctions of the past, suggesting a pressing need for research on the relationship between CO_2, biodiversity extinction, and related carbon policies. This study demonstrates that changes in atmospheric CO_2 concentration did not cause temperature change in the ancient climate.

I urged Professor Davis to study *cycles* of natural climate change—since I was convinced the current warming period was driven by the peaking of a 'low frequency' oscillation in the global system (about 1,000 years in period). Note however, that he discovered a correlation between CO_2 and 'mass extinction' events in ocean biodiversity on a multi-millennial scale of 15 million years periodicity, and this would become a great concern in later papers.

He decided to analyse the Antarctic ice-core record, which hitherto had been regarded by specialists as 'too noisy' to derive a signal over such a short period—meaning, very variable and chaotic over centennial timescales. However, applying 'old school' methods, he was able to isolate signals of that periodicity and show that there was a repeating pattern throughout the vast continent of Antarctica with its many drill sites.

5.2 The Antarctic Centennial Oscillation: A Natural Paleoclimate Cycle in the Southern Hemisphere That Influences Global Temperature

W. Jackson Davis, Peter J. Taylor and W. Barton Davis

Published in *Climate* 2018, 6, 3; doi:10.3390/cli6010003 www.mdpi.com/journal/climate

> From the abstract: We conclude that the ACO: encompasses at least the EAP; is the proximate source of D-O oscillations in the Northern Hemisphere; therefore affects global temperature; propagates with increased velocity as temperature increases; doubled in intensity over geologic time; is modulated by global temperature variations associated with planetary orbital cycles; and is the probable paleoclimate precursor of the contemporary Antarctic Oscillation (AAO). Properties of the ACO/AAO are capable of explaining the current global warming signal.

Note the final sentence of the Abstract—Professor Davis had become convinced *by the data* that cycles in global temperature were capable of explaining current global warming. The second paper explored the way in which Antarctic cycles were capable of driving all the ocean cycles, as if the dynamics of the circumpolar ocean currents were the engine of global temperature change.

5.3 The Origin and Propagation of the Antarctic Centennial Oscillation

W. Jackson Davis. Peter J. Taylor and W. Barton Davis

Published in *Climate* 2019, 7, 112; doi:10.3390/cli7090112   www.mdpi.com/journal/climate

> From the abstract: We postulate that the ACO/AAO is generated by relaxation oscillation of Westerly Wind velocity forced by the equator-to-pole temperature gradient and propagated regionally by identified air-sea-ice interactions.

Following a session at ESI in 2018, whilst examining the accumulated data, I noticed an extra-ordinary pattern in the data on dust deposition in the ice cores—this being a proxy for both wind strength and changes of direction. Similar proxies had been used for the Greenland ice-core record by Bond at the Lamont Docherty Laboratories in the USA where he deduced that major changes in wind direction in the North Atlantic were driving temperature and precipitation on the Greenland ice cap. We worked on a third paper together, but for various reasons I could not participate fully and it was published in 2020.

5.4 Antarctic Winds: Pacemaker of Global Warming, Global Cooling, and the Collapse of Civilizations

W. Jackson Davis and W. Barton Davis

Published in *Climate* 2020, 8, 130; doi:10.3390/cli8110130   www.mdpi.com/journal/climate

> From the abstract: The largest 20 human civilizations of the past four millennia collapsed during or near the Little Ice Age or its earlier recurrent homologs. The Eddy Cycle of sunspot activity oscillates in phase with the AIM temperature cycle and therefore may force the internal climate cycles documented here. Climate forecasts based on the historic ACWO wind pattern project imminent global cooling and in ~4 centuries a recurrent homolog of the Little Ice Age. Our study provides a theoretically-unified explanation of contemporary global warming and other climate milestones based on natural climate cycles driven by the Sun, confirms a dominant role for climate in shaping human history, invites reconsideration of climate policy, and offers a method to project future climate.

We would argue that this work provides the basis for cycles of wind-driven ocean currents and surfacing of warm/cold waters drives a variable millennial cycle. Furthermore, extrapolation of the wave-form shows that the cycles peak during this current 'warm period'. The question then remains as to how much of a contribution is made by the main anthropogenic greenhouse gas—carbon dioxide. The answer has major policy implications, of course.

In 2019, on the basis of the three then published papers, I took up an invitation to speak at a major global summit on climate science, held in Prague. I was invited as keynote speaker and to chair some sessions. Here is the abstract upon which the invitation was based:

5.5 Natural drivers of global warming: ocean cycles, anthropogenic greenhouse gases and the question of percentages.

Peter J. Taylor (www.OceanEarthSystems.net).

Journal of Environmental & Earth Sciences (2025). 7(2): 262-290. DOI: https://doi.org/10.30564/jees.v7i2.7683

> Abstract: At present, there is a widespread policy assumption that anthropogenic greenhouse gases are the main driver of the observed 1°C rise in global surface air temperatures since 'pre-industrial' times. This paper demonstrates that the onset of the current warming trend began in the mid-19th century and is consistent with the rising phase of a variable 800-1200 year global warming and cooling cycle evident in the Northern Hemisphere and a 750-year cycle in the Southern Hemisphere. The last trough of these cycles, known as the Little Ice Age, coincides with the baseline of pre-industrial times used to calculate the impact of Anthropogenic Global Warming. Yet, half of the observed 20th century temperature rise occurred before 1950 when carbon dioxide levels remained low, with the remaining half happening at a similar rate of warming despite the much higher concentrations of greenhouse gases in the atmosphere. This study shows that when the amplitudes and rates of change of the long-term global cycles are considered, the anthropogenic component of warming can be reduced to 38% (using factors derived from the latest IPCC Working Group reports) or as little as 25% (using observational flux data of dominant Short Wave Absorbed Surface Radiation). These long-term global cycles can be extrapolated into the future and the implications for policy of a large natural component to climate change are explored—in particular, the potential for mitigation strategies to have minimal impact and for the climate to cool as a consequence of a cyclic down-phase.

5.6 Mass Extinctions and Their Relationship With Atmospheric Carbon Dioxide Concentration: Implications for Earth's Future

W. Jackson Davis

Citation: Davis, W. J. (2023). Mass extinctions and their relationship with atmospheric carbon dioxide concentration : Implications for Earth's future. *Earth's Future, 11*, e2022EF003336. https://doi.org/10.1029/2022EF003336

> Abstract: Industrialization has raised the concentration of carbon dioxide (CO_2) in Earth's atmosphere by half since 1770, posing a risk from ocean acidification to global biodiversity, including phytoplankton that synthesize approximately (~) 50% of planetary oxygen. This risk is estimated here from the fossil record and implications for our energy and economic future are explored. Over the last 534 million years (Myr), 50 extinction events present as peaks of genus loss-and-recovery cycles, each spanning ~3–40 Myr. Atmospheric CO_2 concentration oscillates with percent genus loss, leading in phase by ~4 Myr and sharing harmonic periodicities at ~10, 26 and 63 Myr. Over the last 210 Myr, where data resolution is highest, biodiversity loss is correlated with atmospheric CO_2 concentration, but not with long-term global temperature nor with marginal radiative forcing of temperature by atmospheric CO_2. The end-Cretaceous extinction of the dinosaurs is anomalous, occurring during a 20-million year depression in atmospheric CO_2 concentration and rising global temperature. Today's atmospheric CO_2 concentration, ~421 parts per million by volume (ppmv), corresponds in the most recent marine fossil record to a biodiversity loss of 6.39%, implying that contemporary anthropogenic CO_2 emissions are killing ocean life now. The United Nations Intergovernmental Panel on Climate Change projects that unabated fossil fuel use could elevate atmospheric CO_2 concentration to 800 ppmv by 100, approaching the 870 ppmv mean concentration of the last 19 natural extinction events. Reversing this first global anthropogenic mass extinction requires reducing net anthropogenic CO_2 emissions to zero, optimally by 2% per year starting immediately.

My own position is under review. Initially, I was very sceptical of his final conclusion because there is a long time lag of three million years in the historical/geological record between rising carbon-dioxide levels—which are clearly cyclic with a period of 15 million years, and the onset of extinction events as measured in the decline of marine biodiversity. Also, there is no current data on any recent loss of diversity in terms of genera—but that does not mean there is no effect, perhaps more that nobody has been looking. There is, however, evidence of a marked decline in the *abundance* of plankton species. The Precautionary Principle would apply—but an essential caveat (see next section) relates to feasibility, costs and the environmental and social impact of alternative policies (i.e. mitigation strategies involving massive deployment of low-carbon energy technologies). This will be a key subject of future collaboration.

6. Previous critique of UN structures and development of the Precautionary Principle

6.1 The State of the Marine Environment: A Critique of the Work and Role of the Joint Group of Experts on Scientific Aspects of Marine Pollution (GESAMP) *Marine Pollution Bulletin,* Volume 26, No. 3, pp. 120-127, 1993. See: OceanEarthSystems.net/marine

6.2 The Precautionary Principle and the Prevention of Marine Pollution. *Chemistry and Ecology,* 1992.vol.7 pp123-134. See: OceanEarthSystems.net/marine

Books to challenge  *your perception of reality*

A message from Clairview

We are an independent publishing company with a focus on cutting-edge, non-fiction books. Our innovative list covers current affairs and politics, health, the arts, history, science and spirituality. But regardless of subject, our books have a common link: they all question conventional thinking, dogmas and received wisdom.

Despite being a small company, our list features some big names, such as Booker Prize winner Ben Okri, literary giant Gore Vidal, world leader Mikhail Gorbachev, modern artist Joseph Beuys and natural childbirth pioneer Michel Odent.

So, check out our full catalogue online at
www.clairviewbooks.com
and join our emailing list for news on new titles.

office@clairviewbooks.com